dr foster

Your Guide to Better Health

DR FOSTER
HEART DISEASE
GUIDE

1 3 5 7 9 10 8 6 4 2

First published 2003 by Vermilion,
an imprint of Ebury Press, Random House,
20 Vauxhall Bridge Road, London SW1V 2SA
www.randomhouse.co.uk

Random House Australia (Pty) Limited
20 Alfred Street, Milsons Point, Sydney,
New South Wales 2061, Australia
Random House New Zealand Limited
18 Poland Road, Glenfield, Auckland 10, New Zealand
Random House South Africa (Pty) Limited
Endulini, 5a Jubilee Road, Parktown 2193, South Africa

The Random House Group Limited Reg. No. 954009

Papers used by Vermilion are natural, recyclable products made from wood grown in sustainable forests.

Printed and bound in Great Britain by
Bookmarque Ltd, Croydon, Surrey

A CIP catalogue record for this book is available
from the British Library

ISBN 0091883806

dr foster

Your Guide to Better Health

DR FOSTER
HEART DISEASE
GUIDE

Researched and Compiled
by Dr Foster

Text by the Society of
Cardiothoracic Surgeons
and Jane Smith

Vermilion
LONDON

Who is Dr Foster?

Dr Foster provides authoritative information on health services of all kinds in the UK. Our aim is to empower patients with information to help them access the best possible care. We are supervised by an independent Ethics Committee that has legal powers to ensure that guides meet the highest standards and to investigate complaints.

The Ethics Committee currently comprises the following members:

Vanessa Bourne, chair, Patients Association

Dr Harry Burns, director of Public Health, Greater Glasgow NHS Trust

Trevor Campbell Davis, chief executive, Whittington Hospital

Dr Philip Davies, medical director, Pontypridd and Rhondda NHS Trust

Dr Michael Dixon, chair, NHS Alliance

Bridget Gill, head of communications, North and East Yorkshire & Northern Lincolnshire Strategic Health Authority

Dianne Hayter, board member, National Patient Safety Agency and the National Consumer Council

Sir Donald Irvine, past president, General Medical Council

Professor Alan Maynard, director, Health Policy Unit, York University and chair, York Health Services NHS Trust

Dr Jack Tinker, emeritus dean, Royal Society of Medicine and chair of the Ethics Committee

Douglas Webb, operations and development director, Friends of the Elderly

Professor Nairn Wilson, president, General Dental Council

To contact the Ethics Committee, email: ethics@drfoster.co.uk or write to the committee at:

Dr Foster Ltd
Sir John Lyon House
5 High Timber Street
London
EC4V 3NX

Dr Foster Help at Hand

Dr Foster collects data on local hospital, maternity and fertility services. It also has comprehensive information on hospital doctors and complementary therapists. Call the

Help at Hand Service on **0906 190 0212**

to find the right solution to your health needs.

Calls cost £1.50 per minute; costs from mobile phones and some other networks may be more. Callers must be aged 18 or over. Lines are open Monday to Friday 8.30am – 8pm, Sat 8.30am – 6pm.

You can also visit **www.drfoster.co.uk** for information.

Contents

4 YOUR LOCAL SERVICES AND SPECIALISTS

Acknowledgements

We would like to thank the following individuals for their hard work, help and advice:

Ben Bridgewater, South Manchester University Hospitals Trust

Elaine Griffiths, Cardiothoracic Centre Liverpool

Leslie Hamilton, Newcastle Hospitals (Freeman Hospital, Newcastle General Hospital, Royal Victoria Infirmary), Newcastle upon Tyne

Colin Hilton, Newcastle Hospitals (Freeman Hospital, Newcastle General Hospital, Royal Victoria Infirmary), Newcastle upon Tyne

Bruce Keogh, Queen Elizabeth Hospital, Birmingham

Eve Knight, British Cardiac Patients Association

Patrick Magee, London Chest Hospital

James Roxburgh, St Thomas' Hospital, London

We would also like to thank the committee members of the Society of Cardiothoracic surgeons.

Preface

Bruce Keogh is a busy cardiac surgeon in Birmingham and Secretary of the Society of Cardiothoracic Surgeons of Great Britain and Ireland. Bruce is quite unusual. He is one of the most vocal advocates of patient involvement and putting the consumer at the heart of healthcare. The NHS is in the throes of a radical change in which it becomes accessible and accountable to its users. Bruce and his colleagues at the Society of Cardiothoracic Surgeons have been among the pioneers in this area. They were among the first to publish information about their own surgical performance.

This book was Bruce's idea. He believes that patients, their relatives and the wider community should know much more about what heart disease is, how to prevent it, and – should you become its victim – how to ensure you find the best treatment. More than that, he felt that the best people to provide that kind of insight were the doctors themselves. This book is the result of a unique collaborative effort between the Society of Cardiothoracic Surgeons and Dr Foster and has quite literally been designed, written and edited by a collaborative team of practicing heart surgeons and Dr Foster.

Dr Foster, an organisation I helped to found in 2000, was created to provide independent information to help patients find out more about local health services and do so in the most accessible fashion possible. This is one of our proudest achievements – a definitive introduction to everything you ever wanted to know about heart disease and its treatment. It does everything it says on the box.

Tim Kelsey
CEO, Dr Foster

Foreword by Colin J Hilton

When a patient discovers that he or she has heart disease it can feel like a death sentence. Anyone in this situation has a multitude of questions – What is it that I have got? What are my chances? Am I going to die? What can be done for me? Who can I turn to? The anxiety and fear created make it difficult to remember what is told to them. There is a need for information in an easily understood form that the patients can study at their leisure.

This book is a collaboration between Dr Foster and the Society of Cardiothoracic Surgeons of Great Britain and Ireland. The aim is to provide a source of information for heart patients that they can consult at leisure. It will not answer all their questions but should act as a guide to what they should know and help them in their dealings with their doctors.

There is a section on the specialists and hospitals specialising in the treatment of heart disease to allow patients to compare them and perhaps make informed choices for themselves.

The Society has been in the forefront of attempts to inform patients of the results of treatment of heart disease. In the new National Health Service, patients will have choices to make, and we believe that this book will help provide the information upon which they can base their decisions.

Colin J Hilton
President, Society of Cardiothoracic Surgeons

Introduction

If you have recently been diagnosed with a form of heart disease or are recovering from a heart attack, you are likely to be quite frightened by what you hear about heart disease. Heart disease is undisputedly the biggest cause of death in the UK. The Government have focused on heart disease, creating extensive National Service Frameworks to deal with both its prevention and treatment. Such emphasis on the dangers of heart disease can fill a newly diagnosed heart patient with dread.

This is probably not helped by the fact that heart disease and its treatment are extremely complicated subjects to understand. How to interpret your diagnosis, let alone decide which consultant and treatment option would be the best for you? What questions should you be asking and how can you understand the answers?

The aim of this guide is to give you easy to understand information about your condition, the various treatment options open to you, who will treat you and also, perhaps most importantly, what you can do to help yourself. We also give a comprehensive guide to heart services throughout England, Wales, Scotland and Northern Ireland so that you can understand not only how the hospital system works but also how to get the best care in your local area.

How to use this guide

This guide is divided into four sections. The first explains the basic function of the heart and what can go wrong. It also outlines your path through the NHS or private sector from diagnosis, from referral through to surgery.

The second section outlines diagnostic processes and subsequent treatments, both drug based and surgical. This leads into the third section, which deals with rehabilitation, how you're likely to feel after surgery, and everything you need to know about getting back on your feet. The final section is a reference section with extensive information about NHS cardiac units and treatment and private hospitals providing cardiac surgery throughout the UK.

The Guide aims to be as comprehensive as possible in its listing of treatments and support available. Whatever your diagnosis and wherever you live, the *Dr Foster Heart Disease Guide* tells you everything you need to know to get the best treatment and support possible. For example:

What is ischaemic heart disease and am I at risk?

On p.6 we explain what different terms for heart disease mean and how they might affect you.

How will my GP monitor my care after I've been referred to a specialist?

On p.26 we explain how care for heart disease is co-ordinated outside the hospital and how you will be looked after post-surgery.

What are the NHS recommendations concerning cardiac rehabilitation?

The Government's recommendations for rehabilitation services and after-surgery care are explained on p.126.

How can I be sure my surgeon is good?

Surgeons' ongoing performance is monitored closely within each hospital – new procedures were introduced after the Bristol Inquiry.

Cardiac surgeons (through their Society of Cardiothoracic Surgeons: www.scts.org) have led the way in collecting data on performance and have recently published survival rates in each unit in the UK. On pages 160–180 we give you performance data for each unit in the UK alongside the SCTS figures.

Understanding
the basics

The heart and its function

The heart lies in the chest behind the sternum (breastbone) and sits upon the diaphragm. The diaphragm is a sheet-like muscle that plays a major role in breathing. It also separates the contents of the chest (heart, lungs and great vessels) from the contents of the abdomen (stomach, liver, intestines etc.). The lungs (left and right) are on either side of the heart. The ribs link the spine (backbone) and the sternum; thus these vital organs are protected by a strong bony cage, known as the thoracic cage. The thoracic cage is covered by different groups of muscles (intercostal and pectoral muscles). These muscles and the diaphragm do the work of breathing.

What is the heart and what does it do?

The heart is the engine that drives blood around the body through the blood vessels (arteries, veins and capillaries). Blood carries oxygen, energy and vital nutrients to all the cells in the body. Therefore, if cells are deprived of blood they die. At rest (while you are reading this book!) the heart pumps around 4.5 litres (1 gallon) of blood every minute. This amount will increase as you do more exercise or get stressed, as this increases the heart rate. The faster the heart works, the more blood it pumps. The heart continually re-circulates the blood and can easily pump over 6,500 litres a day. The heart, like an engine, is made up of several distinct components, and it is important to understand how they function as this is the key to understanding heart disease and the symptoms it produces.

THE HEART MUSCLE

This is known as the myocardium, and provides the power for the heart to pump blood around the body. The muscle forms the four cardiac chambers.

THE CARDIAC CHAMBERS

These are divided into the atria and the ventricles. The atria are the chambers in which blood collects ready to fill the ventricles; which are the main pumping chambers which push blood out to the body.

THE STRUCTURE OF THE HEART

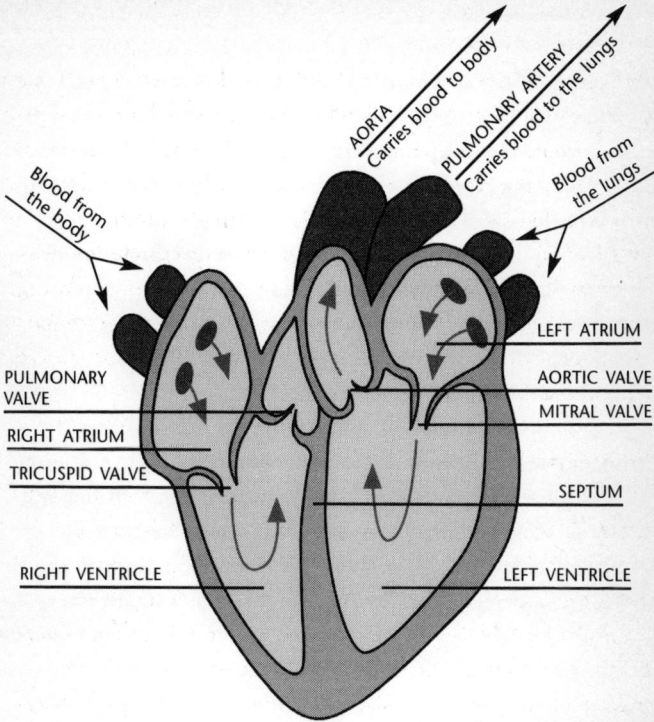

AORTA Carries blood to body

PULMONARY ARTERY Carries blood to the lungs

Blood from the lungs

Blood from the body

LEFT ATRIUM

AORTIC VALVE

MITRAL VALVE

PULMONARY VALVE

RIGHT ATRIUM

TRICUSPID VALVE

SEPTUM

RIGHT VENTRICLE

LEFT VENTRICLE

THE HEART VALVES

These valves ensure that blood only flows one way around the heart. The tricuspid and mitral valves sit between the atria and the ventricles while the pulmonary and aortic valves act as one-way valves for the pulmonary artery and the aorta which carry blood from the heart.

Blood low in oxygen flows back from different parts of the body and returns to the heart through the superior vena cava (the vein carrying blood from the head, arms and upper body) and the inferior vena cava (the vein carrying blood from the lower body and legs) and flows into the right atrium. The triscuspid valve opens and blood enters the right ventricle. The right ventricle contracts, and the pulmonary valve opens to allow blood to leave the heart; the blood is carried by the pulmonary artery to the lungs, where it receives oxygen. This is known as the right-sided circulation and is a low-pressure system.

The blood flows back to the heart through the pulmonary veins and enters the left atrium. The mitral valve opens allowing blood to flow into the left ventricle from the left atrium. The left ventricle contracts and blood is pumped through the aortic valve into the aorta, the major blood vessel, and from there to the rest of the body. This is the left-sided circulation and, since high pressures are required to maintain the blood pressure, the left ventricle is larger than the right ventricle (see diagram p.3).

THE CONDUCTING SYSTEM

This is the 'engine management' system for the heart. The myocardium (heart muscle) contracts in response to electrical currents, which are controlled by this conducting system and ensure that the muscle contracts in an efficient and co-ordinated manner. There are two collections of specialised cells in the heart known as pacemaker cells, which co-ordinate this contraction; they are known as the sino-atrial node and the atrio-ventricular (AV) node. The contraction of the heart is known as the heartbeat. This can be felt by placing the hand over the left side of the chest just below the nipple. The pulse is simply the force of the heartbeat being transmitted down the arteries where it is felt in an artery that is close to the skin. This is why the pulse is usually taken by feeling an artery at the wrist.

What exactly is the heartbeat?

The heartbeat is produced as the heart muscle contracts to force blood around the body. There are three stages of the heartbeat:

1. Diastole

The two atria contract simultaneously and expel blood into the two ventricles, which are relaxed and empty.

2. Systole

The two ventricles contract and expel blood into the pulmonary artery and the aorta, while the two atria relax and fill with blood from the vena cava and pulmonary veins.

3. A rest period

This lasts about 0.4 seconds in an adult.

The heart rate (the number of beats per minute) varies with muscular activity, age and gender (it tends to be higher in men than in women), but is approximately 140 beats per minute at birth, and about 72 beats per minute in an adult.

When the heart valves close a sound is produced and this is what is heard through a stethoscope.

THE CORONARY ARTERIES

The heart is like any other pump and cannot work without a continuous supply of energy. The arteries deliver blood (and therefore oxygen and energy) to the myocardium (heart muscle) and allow it to pump around 100,000 times a day. The coronary arteries are the first branches of the aorta and about five per cent of the blood that flows out of the heart flows down these two main arteries. The right coronary artery supplies the right side of the heart and the conducting system, whereas the left coronary artery provides the left ventricle (the main pumping chamber) with blood. The first part of the left coronary artery is short and is called the left main stem. This divides into two major branches, the circumflex and the left anterior descending. There are therefore three major coronary arteries that run on the surface of the heart and thus can be operated upon (see p.79).

What can go wrong

Heart disease can affect the heart muscle, the arteries or valves or any combination of these. However, before talking about these in detail it is important to understand the most common disease that affects arteries: atherosclerosis. Atherosclerosis can cause strokes, heart attacks, angina, heart failure, kidney failure and many other medical problems.

What is atherosclerosis?

Atherosclerosis is a 'furring' or hardening of the coronary arteries, and is the main cause of heart disease. It develops gradually over many years due to a build-up of cholesterol, calcium and abnormal cells, which form a fatty substance (called atheroma) in the artery walls. These patches of fatty deposits (known as plaques) can have three effects:

- They reduce the width of the blood vessels, making it more difficult for blood to flow through the arteries. This reduces the delivery of oxygen to the tissues downstream of the narrowing.
- The lining of the blood vessels becomes abnormal, and this increases the chances of blood clots forming. These blood clots can lead to sudden closure (occlusion) of an artery. The tissues downstream of this blockage will be deprived of oxygen and may die.
- Blood flow to the artery walls is also reduced, and the arteries lose their elasticity. The loss of elasticity in the artery walls causes an increase in resistance to blood flow and the blood pressure can rise. The most common effect of atherosclerosis is high blood pressure.

What is high blood pressure?

The blood that is being pumped into the arteries from the heart is pulsatile. This means its pressure rises with each heartbeat (systole) and then falls (diastole). Blood pressure measurements are given as two numbers, both of which are in millimetres of mercury (mmHg). The top number is the systolic pressure, the bottom the diastolic pressure. Normal blood pressure varies from person to person, but for adults it should be below 140/85 mmHg, although the acceptable limits increase with age.

The arteries have to adjust to the different amounts of blood that are pumped by the heart during different activities. High blood pressure occurs if the artery openings narrow and the walls lose their elasticity so that they can no longer make the necessary adjustments. High blood pressure causes tiny cracks in the artery walls, which can lead to leakage. It can also cause the formation of blood clots or complete blockage of a blood vessel in the body.

The other danger of high blood pressure lies in the extra strain it puts on the heart and arteries, as the heart has to pump much harder. High blood pressure increases the risk of heart attacks and strokes and, if it is not treated, can lead to kidney failure and even visual problems. The heart may also become abnormally large (left ventricular hypertrophy), which increases the risk of heart failure. Although many adults have high blood pressure (hypertension), most are not aware of it, as mild hypertension has no symptoms. The first symptom you may notice is shortness of breath when exercising.

DISEASES OF THE CORONARY ARTERIES

Atherosclerosis is the most common coronary artery disease. It is also the most common cause of other types of coronary artery disease. Atherosclerosis causes the coronary arteries to become narrowed, and sometimes completely blocked. The arteries then cannot supply the heart muscle with enough blood to meet its oxygen needs. Common symptoms of coronary artery disease include:

- Myocardial infarction (heart attack, see p.10). This is often the first time the symptoms of coronary artery disease occur and may well be fatal as it can lead to ventricular fibrillation (a life-threatening irregular rapid heart arrhythmia) or severe heart failure (cardiogenic shock)
- Angina. A pain or feeling of tightness or heaviness in the chest, arms, neck, jaw or stomach on exertion, which lasts about 15 minutes and stops when you rest (see p.10).
- Breathlessness
- Lethargy (tiredness).

Christopher Halstead

I've had hypertension for a long, long time. It first came to light in my early twenties when I was doing my training to be a chiropodist. We were practising taking each other's blood pressure and it was noticed that mine was rather high. Of course, being a chap I didn't do anything about it.

It was then picked up much later in life when I went to have the varicose veins in my legs done – I had them stripped and tied, as far as I remember. They kept me in overnight and monitored my blood pressure constantly. I think varicose veins are a family trait rather than something to do with my blood pressure; my father had thrombosis and his father died of a stroke so there are problems like that in the family.

I take lisinopril (Zestoretic). It's only a low dosage – 28mg I think, once a day. I've no symptoms that I'm aware of. I used to get very bad migraines, but it seems to run in the family, so I don't think it's got anything to do with the blood pressure. The tablets seem to work very effectively. I go for a check-up every six months and the doctor says my blood pressure is perfect, but when am I going to give up smoking? We gloss over that! The hypertension doesn't bother me at all though; I never think about it. Strictly speaking I haven't got high blood pressure now because the tablets work so well!

As a chiropodist, I'm trained to identify heart and circulation problems in my patients. There are things that you notice: for example, if they're on beta-blockers, which reduce the flow of blood to the extremities, their feet will probably be very cold and you have to be careful that they don't cut themselves because of the risk of infection etc. You can pick things up if you take the pulse in the feet. I had a patient recently whose right foot and lower leg were cyanosed – she had the classic blotches and swollen joints, one of which was pre-ulcerative. It used to be called incipient gangrene; it's not a term they use now, but it's the same thing. She works at the local nursing home, and she let slip that she often takes the bus the half-mile to it – she could only walk about 50 yards before stopping because of the pain. So I wrote her a letter and she was seen by her doctor within two days. He then referred her to a circulation specialist and the leg has been saved.

What is a heart attack?

A heart attack is more properly called a myocardial infarction (MI). This simply means death of part of the myocardium (heart muscle). It is caused by sudden blockage of the blood supply to the heart, usually because of a clot. The coronary arteries are particularly vulnerable to fatty deposits or atheroma, and one of these may burst open, leaving a rough surface on the artery wall, on which blood may collect, forming a clot. This causes a complete blockage of a coronary artery or one of its branches. During a heart attack, the area of heart muscle that isn't getting any blood and oxygen quickly becomes damaged, and if not rapidly treated may die, leaving a scar. If this area is small, the heart usually recovers and can continue to function. However, in more serious cases, the heart stops beating altogether (cardiac arrest) and, unless it starts again within a few minutes, the person will die. The consequences of a heart attack thus depend on which part, and how much, of the heart is damaged.

Sometimes, a heart attack is the first sign that there is anything wrong with the heart and its arteries. Some people are unaware that they have had a heart attack, but most experience severe chest pain (which may spread to the arms, neck, back, jaw or stomach), sweating, nausea, vomiting and breathlessness. Unlike angina, the symptoms of a heart attack do not get better of their own accord and do not improve with rest. Interestingly, the amount of discomfort felt does not relate to how serious the heart attack is. Even minor ones can cause a lot of discomfort while major ones can be virtually painless.

What is angina?

During exercise, after heavy meals, on exposure to cold winds, during sexual intercourse, anger or excitement the heart beats faster. Because it is working harder, it requires more blood. If the arteries are narrowed, not enough blood can be provided. The heart will continue to beat even if it is not receiving enough oxygen and will use its own supplies of energy. The by-products of this process cause a heaviness or cramping pain, usually in the chest, arms and sometimes the throat and jaw. This is called angina and is a warning signal. Stopping the activity that brought on the angina will allow the heart rate to fall, and so the amount of oxygen delivered to the heart muscle will meet its needs and the pain fades.

What can I do and am I at risk of coronary artery disease?

Choose your parents carefully! – a big part of your risk is related to your family history. Your GP will be able to calculate your risk by looking at your 'risk factors'. They will check for diabetes, and measure your blood pressure and cholesterol if they think you are at risk. From your point of view, you can eat sensibly, watch your weight, exercise regularly and, above all, do not smoke.

What is ischaemic heart disease and am I at risk?

Ischaemic heart disease is the name used to group together all the diseases of the heart that are due to atherosclerosis, ie heart attacks, angina and heart failure.

To some extent, everyone is at risk of developing heart disease as they get older, but some groups have an increased risk. Although you are more likely to develop atherosclerosis if you are a smoker, are overweight, have a history of heart disease in the family, have diabetes, a high cholesterol level or high blood pressure, are inactive and eat a poor diet or are under stress, some people develop it without having any of the recognised risk factors.

What about familial hypercholesterolaemia/hyperlipidaemia?

About one in 500 people in the UK have inherited a high blood cholesterol level due to a condition called 'familial hyperlipidaemia' (FH), sometimes also called 'familial hypercholesterolaemia'.

In people with FH, the way LDL cholesterol (see p.111) is removed from the blood circulation works only about half as effectively as normal. This means that their cholesterol level roughly doubles. FH is almost always inherited from a parent. If you have FH, it is important to tell other members of your family to inform their doctor and have their blood cholesterol level measured. Anyone with FH who has a child should find out as early as possible if their child has inherited FH.

What are the signs of FH?

Among adults, signs of FH may develop which in themselves carry no risk. These include hard lumps in the tendons at the back of the ankles and often also in the tendons which run near the knuckles on the back of the hands. A white ring may also develop close to the edge of the coloured part of the eye.

What are the effects of FH?

FH affects men and women equally. However, its effect on the risk of coronary heart disease is rather different. Without treatment, most men and half of women with FH will suffer angina or a heart attack before they are 60. Even at the age of 70 some women who do not have treatment are free of heart trouble.

What if I am thinking of having a child and I have FH?

There is an extremely rare cause of particularly high blood cholesterol in childhood called 'homozygous FH'. This can happen if both parents have FH. If you have FH and are thinking of having children, your partner should ask the doctor to check his or her blood cholesterol level. The risk is small, but if he or she does have FH, you will need special genetic counselling to advise you about the risk of your child being seriously affected. If your partner does not have FH, your children will have a 50/50 chance of inheriting your type of FH.

Are there any other inherited conditions that put me or family members at risk of heart disease?

Scientists at the University of Leicester have recently discovered a 'critical gene' in families with a history of the inherited condition partial lipodystrophy. The condition develops during puberty and prevents the body from storing fat under the skin. Sufferers also have raised blood fat levels and insulin resistance, both of which are major causes of heart disease and diabetes.

Am I overweight?

If you really want to know, calculate your Body Mass Index (BMI). To do this, multiply your height in metres by itself and divide your weight in kilograms by the result. The answer is your BMI – it should be less than 25. If it is 25 to 30 you are overweight.

If I don't have risk factors, does this mean I won't get heart disease?

The risk factors listed in this book do not explain all cases of coronary heart disease. Some people develop hardened arteries and heart disease without having these recognised risk factors. For more about reducing your risk factors, see p.110.

Can heart disease be caused by infection?

There is no conclusive proof that bacteria cause heart attacks. However, results of recent trials have shown an association. Pneumonia caused by the chlamydia organism and Helicobacter pylori (bacterium linked to stomach ulcers and gum disease) are thought to be related to heart attacks and strokes. It has been argued that these infections could cause high levels of inflammation in the blood vessels, which could be reduced by antibiotics. Long-standing infections might also trigger the process of atherosclerosis.

DISEASES OF THE HEART VALVES

The four valves of the heart are:

- **tricuspid valve** between the right atrium and right ventricle
- **mitral valve** between the left atrium and left ventricle
- **pulmonary valve** between the right ventricle and pulmonary artery
- **aortic valve** between the left ventricle and aorta.

As blood passes through the valves, the flaps (or cusps) in them open and close to make sure it flows in the right direction. Valvular heart disease is quite common and is caused by damage to the valve mechanism interfering with the flow of blood through the heart. Valvular heart disease can be caused by infection such as rheumatic fever. Rheumatic fever is now rare, but because its effects often only come to light after 20–30 years, it is still a cause of valve disease today. Other infections can lead to an acute deterioration in valve function (bacterial endocarditis). A heart valve that hasn't developed properly before birth (congenital defect) can lead to problems in later life. Deterioration in the tissues of the valve or its supporting mechanism is a common cause of valve disease. However, in many cases it is simply due to the effects of ageing.

What can go wrong with the valves of the heart?

A valve may be stiff and narrow and unable to open properly (valve stenosis), which puts a strain on the heart as it has to pump harder than normal to force blood through it. Alternatively, the valve may be unable to close properly, allowing blood to leak back through it (valve incompetence or regurgitation) so that the heart has to work hard to pump enough blood around the body. In fact, damaged valves are often both leaky and narrow. An increase in pressure (called 'back pressure') can develop in the blood behind the valve, leading to a build-up of fluid in the lungs or lower body.

Disease can damage any of the heart valves, but the mitral and aortic valves are usually affected. Defects in the pulmonary and tricuspid valves are rare in adults.

Mitral valve

- **Mitral stenosis** – this is narrowing of the mitral valve, which causes an obstruction to the flow of blood coming back from the lungs. It occurs most commonly as a side-effect of rheumatic fever. Because of the obstruction, the left atrium becomes enlarged and this can cause the heart to lose its normal regular rhythm. The blood pressure in the lungs becomes elevated and this can cause damage to the lungs themselves.

- **Mitral regurgitation** – this is leaking of the mitral valve, so that every time the left ventricle contracts, instead of pumping blood forwards around the body, it pumps some of it back into the left atrium and back towards the lungs. This causes the left atrium to increase in size and then the left ventricle starts to stretch, and pump less strongly.

Aortic valve

- **Aortic stenosis** – this is a narrowing of the aortic valve, which causes an obstruction to the flow of blood out of the left ventricle. Initially the left ventricle compensates for the narrowing by increasing the thickness of its muscular wall and pumping more strongly. However, with time the left ventricle starts to become stretched and its pumping action fails. The aortic valve usually has three cusps, but occasionally it only has two. When it has two cusps it is more likely to develop aortic stenosis, but a normal valve can sometimes become calcified, thickened and narrowed.

- **Aortic regurgitation** – this is when the valve between the left ventricle and the aorta becomes leaky. This can be due to abnormalities of the valve itself, or due to increasing size of the aorta, which thereby causes the valve to leak. Mild aortic regurgitation causes few problems but more severe regurgitation leads to an increase in the size of the left ventricle and a gradual decrease in its pumping activity.

What problems does valve disease cause?

This depends on the valve(s) affected.

- In mitral valve stenosis, blood collects in the left atrium of the heart and fluid builds up in the lungs, which become congested, causing shortness of breath.
- In aortic valve stenosis, the walls of the left ventricle thicken (known as left ventricular hypertrophy), eventually causing shortness of breath, pain in the chest (angina) or dizziness.
- Mitral or aortic valve incompetence can also cause thickening of the walls of the left ventricle and problems in the lungs, which may lead to damage to the right ventricle and collection of fluid in the legs and abdomen.

DISEASES OF THE HEART MUSCLE

The most common form of heart disease is heart failure. This simply means that the heart is not pumping blood to the muscles and organs as effectively as it should. Normally, every beat of the heart pumps about 70 per cent of the blood that is in the ventricles into the major blood vessels. In heart failure, the heart muscle has become damaged and less efficient at ejecting blood out of the ventricles. In severe cases the heart may only pump 20 per cent of the blood out with each beat. As the heart muscle fails, the heart becomes enlarged. If the left ventricle is damaged, this causes left heart failure (left ventricular failure) and fluid will begin to collect in the lungs, which is why shortness of breath is a major symptom of this type of heart failure. If the right side of the heart is involved, fluid can start to build up in the lower body, and this is why you may get swollen feet, ankles, legs and possibly a swollen stomach (congestive heart failure).

What causes heart failure?

Although in some cases the causes of heart failure are unknown, there are a number of possibilities such as:

- a heart attack
- high blood pressure
- faulty heart valves
- a viral heart infection
- drinking too much alcohol.

A heart attack and/or high blood pressure are the most common causes of heart failure in the Western world, and both are due to atherosclerosis. A heart attack occurs when atherosclerosis leads to the blockage of a coronary artery and some or all of the heart muscle supplied with blood by that artery dies. This affects the pumping efficiency of the heart, and may lead to heart failure. In many cases, symptoms only occur when the heart is made to pump faster when doing exercise, such as walking up a hill. However, if a large area of heart muscle is damaged, then even mild exertion may lead to symptoms. In patients with long-standing high blood pressure, the heart begins to fail as it can simply no longer cope with the increasing amount of work that is required to pump against stiff, 'furred-up' arteries. In the majority of cases, patients with heart failure will also have 'furred-up' heart arteries as well as other major arteries.

What are the symptoms of heart failure?
- Difficulty breathing, especially on exertion; for example, when you are exercising or doing housework.
- Difficulty breathing when lying down.
- Waking up breathless at night.
- A frequent dry 'hacking' cough, especially when lying down.
- Tiredness and weakness, especially when you are exercising.
- Swollen feet, ankles, legs and perhaps a swollen stomach.

What is cardiomyopathy?
Cardiomyopathy is abnormality of the heart muscle that prevents the heart working properly. It often causes congestive heart failure and sometimes arrhythmias. You can have either primary cardiomyopathy (the cause of which isn't known) or secondary cardiomyopathy (which is often associated with disease affecting other organs). Cardiomyopathy generally begins in the walls of the ventricles, although in serious cases it can also affect the atria. There are three main types of cardiomyopathy:
- dilated (also known as congestive)
- hypertrophic
- restrictive (which is less common).
There is also a relatively rare form called arrhythmogenic right ventricular cardiomyopathy.

What causes cardiomyopathy?

Although the cause is often unknown, both hypertrophic and dilated cardiomyopathy can be genetically linked congenital diseases that occur in more than one member of a family, even though some family members may not have any symptoms. Dilated cardiomyopathy can also result from a viral infection. Restrictive cardiomyopathy is usually due to another disease.

How will I know if I have cardiomyopathy?

Cardiomyopathy may not cause any symptoms so is sometimes only detected in later life. However, it is often diagnosed in babies or young children born with the condition, in whom symptoms are particularly serious. It affects about one in 500 people in the UK.

What is dilated or congestive cardiomyopathy?

Dilated cardiomyopathy may be inherited or caused by a viral infection or alcohol abuse. The heart muscle stretches and loses its elasticity, which makes the chambers of the heart (particularly the left ventricle) enlarge. This can cause breathlessness and chest infections, poor feeding and weight gain in children affected, congestive heart failure (see p.15) and arrhythmias (see p.18). Because the heart is enlarged, blood flows through it more slowly than normal and blood clots can develop. If your heart becomes very large, the mitral and tricuspid valves cannot close properly and the valves become regurgitant.

What is hypertrophic cardiomyopathy?

Sometimes hypertrophic cardiomyopathy is inherited, but often the cause is unknown. The heart muscle is abnormally thick, usually around the left ventricle but also sometimes around the right ventricle. Different parts of the muscle are affected in different forms of the disease, but often there is thickening of the septum (the muscle wall between the left and right sides of the heart), which can obstruct the flow of blood through the mitral valve, causing a heart murmur and mitral regurgitation.

The thickened muscle becomes stiff and unable to relax properly, so the heart cannot hold as much blood as normal and sends less around the body with each contraction than it should.

Hypertrophic cardiomyopathy may cause no symptoms for years or it can result in a sudden heart attack. If the flow of blood through the heart is obstructed (hypertrophic obstructive cardiomyopathy), it may cause dizziness, fainting, palpitations due to arrhythmia (see below), pain in the chest (angina) and possibly light-headedness or even blackouts.

What is restrictive cardiomyopathy?

Restrictive cardiomyopathy is usually associated with another disease, a heart attack or surgery that has caused scarring of the heart tissue. Although the thickness of the muscle and the size of the ventricles may be normal, the heart muscle stiffens and it becomes difficult for the ventricles to fill with blood between contractions. This can cause tiredness, swelling of the hands and feet and shortness of breath on exertion.

What is arrhythmogenic right ventricular cardiomyopathy?

This is a rare type of inherited cardiomyopathy in which the muscle in the right ventricle dies and is replaced by fat. It can cause serious arrhythmias or heart attacks. Symptoms sometimes develop in childhood and may suddenly get worse, or they can appear for the first time in adulthood, when there may already be congestive heart failure.

DISORDERS OF THE CONDUCTING SYSTEM – ARRHYTHMIAS

The heartbeat is controlled by an electrical signal that starts in a special group of pacemaker cells (also called the sino-atrial node) in the right atrium and passes across the atria. Another group of specialised cells between the right atrium and the right ventricle (called the atrio-ventricular or AV node) transmits the electrical impulse from the atria to the ventricles, which contract to produce the heartbeat. A normal heartbeat is between 60 and 100 beats per minute. When the rate or rhythm of the heartbeat is disturbed, an arrhythmia develops. If the heart beats too quickly, the arrhythmia is called tachycardia; if it beats too slowly, it's called bradycardia. Slowing of the electrical impulses through the heart causes heart block, which can develop to complete heart block if no impulses cross the ventricles at all.

How are arrhythmias caused?

Arrhythmias can be caused by:

- heart disease, such as coronary artery disease, diseases of the heart valves, congestive heart failure and infection of the tissue that surrounds the heart (the pericardium)
- diseases affecting the electrical system of the heart
- chemicals, such as alcohol and caffeine
- some medicines, including certain antidepressants
- ageing
- other diseases such as thyroid disease.

How do they develop?

Arrhythmias develop if:

- the heart's pacemaker fires at an abnormal rate
- another part of the heart takes over the pacemaker's role
- the passage of the electrical signal through the heart tissue is interrupted.

What conditions are associated with arrhythmia?

If the arrhythmia affects the atria, the ventricles can usually still beat normally. Arrhythmias starting in the ventricles often have more serious consequences. There are several conditions associated with arrhythmia.

- **Atrial fibrillation.** In this condition, the atria stop beating effectively and start to quiver. Blood collects in them, increasing the risk of a blood clot forming. If a blood clot blocks an artery in the heart, it causes a heart attack; if it blocks an artery in the brain, it causes a stroke; and if it blocks an artery in the lung, it causes a pulmonary embolism. Anticoagulants such as aspirin and warfarin may reduce this risk.
- **Ventricular fibrillation.** This occurs when a rapid heartbeat starts in the ventricles, which then stop beating altogether and start to quiver.
- **Stokes-Adams disease.** This is caused by an arrhythmia developing as the result of an electrical impulse being interrupted between the atria and the ventricles. It usually leads to marked slowing of the heart rate and to heart block. Fainting fits can occur if the blood flow to the brain is reduced.

- **Bundle branch block.** As an electrical impulse passes through the heart to produce the heartbeat, it travels to the ventricles via the two branches of a pathway called the Bundle of His. The speed of the impulse is normally the same in both branches, so that both ventricles contract at the same time. However, if one of the branches becomes blocked, the electrical signal takes longer to pass down it and therefore one of the ventricles contracts just before the other. Although this doesn't normally cause any symptoms – and is often only detected on an electrocardiogram (see p.45) – it does mean that a small area of the heart muscle may not be getting enough oxygenated blood. It's important to have regular check-ups if you have this condition so that any damage can be detected before it becomes serious.
- **Long Q-T syndrome.** This is an inherited disorder that usually affects children and young adults. The electrical impulse that starts a heartbeat is represented on an electrocardiogram by a wave, the different parts of which are identified by letters. The Q-T interval is the time between activation and inactivation of the ventricles. People with long Q-T syndrome have a longer interval than normal (although not necessarily all the time) and, although they may not have any symptoms, it can cause fainting and an abnormal heart rate or rhythm and is sometimes associated with deafness. Treatment is with beta-blockers or, in more serious cases, an implantable defibrillator (see p.97).
- **Wolff-Parkinson-White syndrome.** This occurs when there is an extra conduction pathway in the heart that causes the electrical signal to arrive at the ventricles too soon. If symptoms occur, they include palpitations, dizziness and fainting and can be treated with medication if required. Rarely, the condition leads to cardiac arrest. Serious cases may be treated by a procedure called ablation.

How will I know if I have arrhythmia?

Arrhythmias often don't cause any symptoms; however, if you have a low heart rate (bradycardia), you may get very tired, dizzy, short of breath, or may faint or feel light-headed. If your heartbeat is too fast (tachycardia), you may have similar symptoms as well as palpitations and chest pain (angina).

Women and heart disease

Traditionally heart disease was seen as a male disease, but after cancer, coronary heart disease is the second major cause of death among women in the UK today. It kills about one in five women and one in four men and it is the main cause of death amongst women over the age of 50. As women approach the menopause, their risk of developing heart disease starts to increase, and it continues to do so as they get older (see p.111). Hormonal changes at menopause increase the tendency to put on weight around the abdomen: the typical 'apple-shape' fat distribution associated with heart disease (see p.111). The following table shows some recent figures for the UK:

	Women	Men
Incidence of heart attacks per 100,000 population (age 30–69 years)	200	600
Total number of heart attacks per year (age less than 65)	20,000	66,000
Total number of heart attacks per year (all ages)	125,000	149,000
Number of new cases of angina per year	158,000	330,000
Incidence of heart failure per 100,000 population	120	140
Number of new cases of heart failure per year	30,000	63,000

The overall death rate from heart disease has fallen in recent years, but the rate of decline is less for women than for men. Although men are more at risk of having heart attacks than women and tend to have them at a younger age, women who have already had a heart attack have a higher chance than men of having another.

After the age of 55, women have higher cholesterol levels than men, and a low level of the 'good' HDL cholesterol (see p.111) appears to be a greater risk factor for women. Women are also more likely than men to have high blood pressure: 50 per cent of women over the age of 55 suffer from high blood pressure.

Are women protected from heart disease until the menopause?
On average, women tend to develop coronary heart disease ten years later than men. Pre-menopausal women may be less at risk because:

- They tolerate high blood cholesterol levels better than men. In pre-menopausal women oestrogens (female sex hormones) raise levels of 'protective' cholesterol and reduce 'bad' levels.
- Pre-menopausal women tend to have low iron stores because of menstrual losses. This is beneficial because excess iron may lead to damage by free radicals. Free radicals are an atom or group of atoms with at least one unpaired electron. This makes the atom or atoms unstable and highly reactive. It is thought that free radicals can damage cells, accelerating the progression of cardiovascular disease.

This doesn't mean that women are completely protected from heart disease until the menopause. Some groups of women, including those from low-income working families, those from south Asia, diabetics, those with familial hyperlipidaemia and those who are apple-shaped (having more fat around the waist) stand a higher chance of developing heart disease than others.

What if I have polycystic ovarian syndrome (PCOS)?
This is a condition which occurs when the ovaries have many small follicles containing eggs that have stopped growing. Symptoms may include excessive weight, acne and increased body hair or hair thinning. Because ovulation is not occurring, progesterone is no longer produced, although oestrogen levels remain normal. The risk of heart disease increases for all women after the menopause, but women with PCOS are at even more risk due to raised androgen levels, unhealthy changes to blood fats and obesity. In addition, 40 per cent of women with this condition develop Type 2 (non insulin-dependent) diabetes by the age of 40, which further increases the risk of heart disease. If you have PCOS, make sure your GP checks your blood fat levels and blood pressure regularly.

Do birth control pills cause high cholesterol?

The oestrogen and progesterone in the combined oral contraceptive pill do cause a slight alteration to the level of cholesterol in the blood, raising LDL levels slightly and lowering HDL levels. However, these changes are minor and are further reduced in users of the newest types of pills. Any changes in cholesterol level are also outweighed by detrimental factors such as smoking and obesity.

Do birth control pills increase my risk of heart disease?

No, but women over 35 who take birth control pills, who smoke and/or are overweight are at an increased risk of high blood pressure, thrombo-embolitic disease and pulmonary embolism. There have also been concerns raised about a possible increase in risk of heart disease from the injected contraceptive Depo-Provera. Researchers have suggested that women using Depo-Provera could be at risk of impaired function of the lining of their arteries. However, more research is needed as there is no evidence yet directly linking the injection to heart problems. If you are concerned, you should discuss your risk with your doctor.

Does HRT reduce my risk of getting heart disease?

This is an incredibly complex and much-debated area. Although some doctors think that HRT (which contains oestrogen, which protects against heart disease) helps to guard against heart disease, this has not been proved. Observational studies show that the risk of ischaemic heart disease may be reduced by up to 40 per cent in women who use HRT, but two recent trials in the US suggest that HRT doesn't prevent heart disease. At the moment, there is nothing to indicate that HRT should be taken primarily to protect your heart. If you have a family history of heart disease, you should discuss the relative risks and benefits of taking HRT with your doctor.

Are heart attacks different in women and in men?

Men are more likely than women to have a heart attack below the age of 50, after which the risk is about equal. However, a greater percentage of women than men die within a year of having a heart attack, and almost twice as many women as men have a second heart attack within six years of the first.

Audrey Phillips

My angina was diagnosed a long time ago; I think it must have been about 30 years ago. I didn't feel well and I had pains in my chest and for a time my GP said 'I think it's rheumatics' but after a time I had a test and they said I had angina, for which I had little pills to put under my tongue. But in my view my angina was a curious kind of angina because it didn't come when I walked up a hill or when I ran, it only came when I was very aggravated, and at the time I was very much aggravated by my supervisor – I was doing a PhD and I didn't get on with her.

I hadn't been getting attacks really, but they changed my medicine anyway. I think it was a fashion! They changed the under-the-tongue pills to a little bottle of a spray which you sprayed into your mouth, trinitrate, which I hardly used. My angina has come back a little bit more lately, though, as I'm getting older!

I don't think the doctors ever know what causes these things, but I know that my father was 40 when he died. I remember that Mummy used to say to me: 'Daddy's got very bad indigestion' and this went on for several weeks, then one Sunday morning when I'd gone to the park I came back and he was gone. I don't know any details, I was a little girl, they didn't tell me much, but apparently it was a pain like indigestion. It's a long time ago; to give you an idea of how long ago, my brother, who was born six months after that, is 72 now, and back then angina wasn't always recognised. Nowadays you hear of people suing when it hasn't been recognised but I heard that if you get the appropriate pills you can live for another 30-40-50 years! I think it depends on the type of angina and your age.

About six or seven years ago I had an angiogram and they said no, the artery wasn't blocked. My angina hasn't impacted much: I've travelled on holidays, and when my daughter was going to India a few years ago and she said come with me I did. I must have been 78; too old to go on my own. It was a very busy 14 days or whatever it was because every day we took a plane to another part of India! So I was quite capable of doing all those things and going up the steps of the temples and whatnot, so it hasn't really made any difference to me. Only now that I'm not so young as I was I never go an inch now without my little 'TNT'! Fortunately I don't seem to use it when I'm out much; it's like an insurance in a way and it gives you confidence.

How the NHS works

The majority of people who have heart disease can live quite comfortably at home. However, they will need to be looked after by the health services, and how and where that care is given will depend on a number of factors including the severity of symptoms, onset of new symptoms and the local health care system.

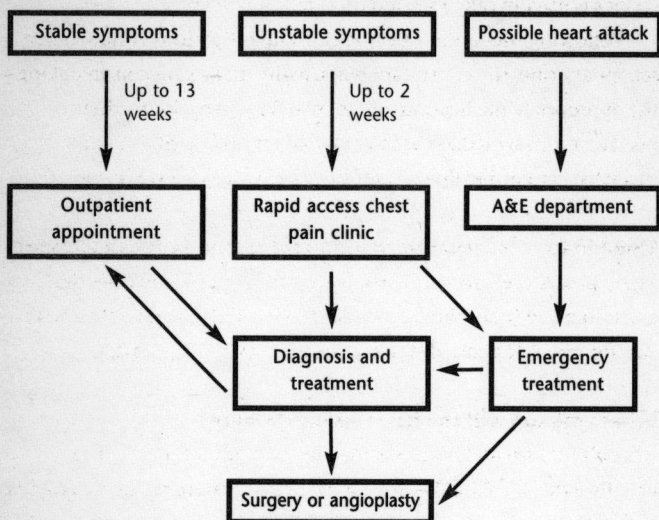

STABLE SYMPTOMS → Up to 13 weeks → Outpatient appointment

Unstable symptoms → Up to 2 weeks → Rapid access chest pain clinic

Possible heart attack → A&E department

Outpatient appointment → Diagnosis and treatment

Rapid access chest pain clinic → Diagnosis and treatment / Emergency treatment

A&E department → Diagnosis and treatment / Emergency treatment

Emergency treatment → Diagnosis and treatment

Diagnosis and treatment → Surgery or angioplasty

Emergency treatment → Surgery or angioplasty

STABLE SYMPTOMS

Most people living at home will be looked after by General Practitioners in the local surgery (care in the GP setting is called primary care). Most GPs are now well equipped to give high-quality care; many have registers that help them keep track of everyone who has heart disease and specialist nurses to help people to control their risk factors: help them to stop smoking and/or lose weight, encourage healthy eating, treat high cholesterol and make sure people are on the best medications. They will also identify people who need further investigation or treatment and send them to hospital either for a routine appointment or for urgent treatment.

What about the local hospital?

Many patients with heart disease have stable symptoms and can easily be looked after in the local hospital outpatient department. Following a routine referral to a consultant at the local hospital, you should be seen in the outpatient clinic in no more than 13 weeks. The doctors there will ask you about your symptoms and previous problems with your health and will organise various investigations (see p.44). Most local hospitals have consultants with specialist knowledge of heart disease, but many of these hospitals do not have the facilities for full investigation and treatment. The local hospital service is usually called secondary care.

Following the results of the various investigations conducted in secondary care, the consultant will usually make sure you are taking the appropriate medication, and may refer you on for further investigations which are usually carried out in hospitals with specialist cardiac facilities. These are called tertiary care hospitals.

Should I take someone with me to the outpatient department?

Many people feel anxious when going to an appointment with a consultant, so it may be a good idea to take a friend or relative with you for moral support and to take notes for you if necessary.

What training will the heart specialist have?

Consultants are doctors and surgeons who have a special and usually extensive knowledge of a particular system of the body. This makes them specialists in their field. A consultant is the most senior grade of cardiac specialist. Before becoming a consultant, your doctor will have had a general medical training which includes five years at university followed by one year as a house officer, before gaining registration with the General Medical Council. Cardiac consultants will then have spent two to three years as a senior house officer in various medical disciplines. They will have had a five- or six-year training in cardiology, passed a series of postgraduate examinations, and most will have performed medical research. Many have ongoing academic, research or managerial commitments. The consultant will also be responsible for a team of doctors who are training in cardiology.

Can I refer myself to a consultant without seeing my GP?

No: in the UK you always need to be referred by your GP for both NHS and private treatment unless you are admitted to hospital in an emergency for treatment in the Accident and Emergency (A&E) department. If you suspect you have a problem that requires specialist attention, go to your GP and discuss it with him or her.

What if my GP won't refer me to a consultant?

Your GP is only obliged to refer you to a consultant if he or she thinks it is appropriate. Your GP does not have to refer you on demand. If you want to see a consultant and your GP won't refer you, ask why. It may be that you have a condition that can be better treated in general practice. If you are unhappy with this decision, you can ask to see another GP in the practice for a second opinion.

How does my GP decide which consultant is best for me?

Your GP will base their decision on his or her existing knowledge of the consultant and the facilities at the hospital in which the consultant works. This will include feedback from other patients. Ask your GP for the name of the consultant to whom he or she is referring you, and why. A few hospitals ask GPs not to write to individual consultants, but to let the hospital appointments office allocate each referral to the most suitable consultant, or the one with the shortest waiting list. Tell your GP if you do not want this type of referral.

Can I choose which consultant I am referred to?

Yes, provided the consultant of your choice deals with the condition for which you are being referred. There are some limitations, however. If you are being referred via the NHS, the primary care trust (PCT, the local management group who are responsible for how the health budget is spent in your area) may only fund referrals to local consultants, but you can appeal to the PCT on this. Under new European Union directives, you have the right to be referred anywhere in the country if treatment is available for your condition. In some cases there may only be one consultant in your area that specialises in your condition and this will be the person you are referred to. If you are unhappy with this, ask your GP to refer you to a hospital in a different PCT.

Can I choose which hospital I am referred to if I hear of one that is better at treating my condition than others in the area?

Ultimately, the decision on which hospital you are referred to falls to your GP. If you express a preference for one hospital or one consultant over another, most GPs will take this into consideration when referring you and will try to refer you to the hospital of your choice. If the hospital of your choice is out of your local area, your GP may need to seek the permission of the PCT.

Why may my GP suggest another consultant/hospital?

There is often a huge variation in waiting times between hospitals to see a consultant. Your GP's first choice of consultant may have the longest waiting time and it may be better to accept the second or third choice rather than wait an unacceptable time.

How do I find out more information about the consultant I've been referred to?

Ask your GP to tell you about the consultant's experience and his or her reasons for referring you. The Dr Foster website (www.drfoster.co.uk) lists consultants by specialty and areas of expertise and gives further information about them. You could also ask your hospital for information about your consultant and a copy of the hospital prospectus, which will often include a short biography of all the consultants at the hospital.

How is a referral made?

Your GP will contact the hospital at which your consultant is based either by letter or by telephone and fax. Non-urgent referrals are usually made by letter and posted to the hospital. Your consultant will read the letter and decide the level of priority, based on its contents. An appointment officer will then allocate an appointment, details of which are sent to you by letter. If your referral is urgent, for example if you are at high risk of a heart attack, your GP will telephone the hospital to arrange an appointment and will send the referral letter by fax. Often you will be told the date and time of your appointment on that same day.

Do I have a right to see my referral letter?

Yes: if you feel your GP has not adequately conveyed the pain or discomfort you are experiencing or the effects your condition has on your quality of life, you should ask him or her to rewrite the letter stating these points.

Will I always see the consultant to whom my GP referred me?

There is a chance you will be seen by a trainee consultant (specialist registrar) or by a clinical nurse consultant, as it is impossible for any consultant to see every patient who has been referred to him or her. However, your consultant will actively supervise your care. Most consultants make a point of seeing the most complicated cases personally.

How long will I have to wait to see a consultant?

Government guidelines state that patients should have to wait no more than 26 weeks for an outpatient appointment. The waiting period varies between hospitals and between specialists, although the majority of patients are currently seen within 13 weeks. The Dr Foster website (www.drfoster.co.uk) and the Dr Foster *Good Hospital Guide* give waiting times at individual hospitals.

Is there any way I can speed this up?

Your GP may be able to help you to be seen more quickly, but only if there is a sound medical reason for it. If you have an urgent problem, you will be seen more quickly than people whose condition is less serious, so you should let your GP know if your condition gets any worse whilst you are waiting.

Also, you could:

- write to the consultant's secretary to say that you would be able to accept someone else's cancelled appointment at short notice
- ask to see a different specialist with a shorter waiting list – your GP should have a list of the waiting times for the different specialists in your area
- ask to be referred to a hospital outside your local area – this is sometimes possible if your PCT has an agreement with hospitals in other areas.

If I just turn up at hospital will I get to see a consultant more quickly?

The doctors who work in A&E departments cannot arrange outpatient appointments with consultants in other departments. Unless your condition is rapidly deteriorating and you need urgent treatment, do not just turn up at hospital.

What if I see a specialist privately?

You have the option of paying to have your first appointment privately, and then asking to be transferred back to the NHS waiting list for any treatment you need. This could cut down the wait for your first consultation, although you will then have to wait for any non-urgent treatment. Consultation fees vary around the country. Further information is given in the section on the private sector (see p.37–40).

If the appointment I've been given isn't convenient, can I change it?

Contact the consultant's secretary or the hospital's booking office as soon as possible to cancel it – the telephone number should be on your appointment card. Explain the situation and they should be able to change the appointment to a date and time that suits you better. Do not simply fail to attend: outpatient appointments are scarce and somebody else could use the appointment.

What if my appointment is cancelled or changed?

If your appointment is cancelled by the hospital, you should be contacted within seven days with an offer of a new appointment. You should not have an appointment cancelled more than once and you should be given an explanation as to why it has been cancelled or changed. It may be that the doctor you were scheduled to see will be absent. If the new date is much later than the original one, you should telephone the hospital booking office or the consultant's secretary to ask if alternative arrangements can be made to see you earlier. If it is important on medical or social grounds that you should not have a long wait, ask your GP to write on your behalf.

What if I miss my appointment?

Try not to miss your appointment as this will mean you have to wait longer. As soon as you realise you have missed your appointment, contact the hospital booking office or the consultant's secretary to let them know. Some hospitals may send you another appointment but others may assume that you have changed your mind about attending. If you are told that your GP needs to refer you again, ask your GP in person rather than leaving a message with the receptionist.

I don't like hospitals. Can I see a consultant anywhere else?

It may be possible to see your consultant at a community clinic: ask your GP. However, most consultants work in hospitals. This is because they are responsible for inpatient beds as well as outpatient clinics, and because their time can be used more efficiently if they are based in only one or two sites instead of having to travel around.

How long will my appointment last?

Most outpatient clinics are very busy, and appointment times vary from seven minutes to half an hour. It may take longer than this if you need to have any special tests.

Questions to ask your doctor

You should ask your consultant to explain clearly what is wrong with you and what can be done to improve your condition. If you are prescribed medication, make sure you understand what it is for, and when and how often you should take it. It is a good idea to write down a list of questions about your condition or anything else that worries you to take with you when you see your consultant. These questions may include:

- Do I really have the disease my GP thinks I have?
- What disease do you think I have?
- Can you explain that condition to me?
- What treatments are available?
- Which is the best treatment for me?
- What can I expect from the treatment?
- When is it going to work?
- How long will it take?

- Are there any side-effects?
- What is the short-term prognosis?
- What is the long-term prognosis?

What if I don't understand what my consultant says?

It is vital that you understand what the consultant says to you; if you don't follow what he or she is saying, calmly insist on having your condition explained further, and in plain English. If you are confused, say so and ask your consultant to slow down. Take notes during your appointment so you don't forget what you are told, or take a friend or relative with you who can take notes for you. At the end of your appointment make sure your consultant has given you a treatment plan and that you understand any follow-up procedures you may need to have. Ask your consultant when you will next see him or her again. If you have any questions in the meantime, write them down and raise them at your next consultation.

What should I do if I'm not happy with the consultant I have been sent to?

If you're unhappy with the specialist you have been sent to, you can ask your GP to refer you to another one. However, before you decide to ask for another referral, it is worth asking why your GP has chosen a particular consultant – it may be because he or she has particular expertise in the treatment of your condition. Your GP will either be able to explain why you are not receiving the treatment you expect or, if appropriate, can put your case to the consultant in a constructive way. If you're still unhappy about it, your GP could refer you to another consultant. When you have a serious illness, it is important that you are sure that you are receiving the best possible care. If you want to see a consultant outside your local PCT area, European Union directives give you the right to do so. You can also pay for a private consultation with the consultant of your choice.

Can I ask for a second opinion?

Yes. You have a right to be referred for a second opinion if you and your doctor agree that this is appropriate. Ask your GP to refer you to another consultant in the NHS, or consider asking for a referral to a private consultant who will be able to see you more quickly.

How will my GP monitor my care after I've been referred to a specialist?

After your appointment with the cardiologist (heart specialist), details of the results of the tests you have had and any treatment recommendations will be sent to your GP. Your GP will then co-ordinate your care, giving you advice on any risk-reducing lifestyle changes, carry out or organise any regular tests you need, and prescribe your medication.

What if English is not my first language?

If English is not your first language and you need an interpreter, get someone to inform the hospital when you receive the appointment. They may make arrangements to have an interpreter available at your consultation. There isn't a Government policy yet on this issue, so you will have to rely on what individual Trusts provide.

What if I can't wait for an outpatient appointment?

If you are suffering with chest pain which may be angina, and your GP feels that you can't wait a number of weeks for an appointment, he or she may refer you to a specialist clinic called a Rapid Access Chest Pain Clinic (RACP clinic). These have been established in many local hospitals and are staffed by doctors and nurses with expertise in diagnosing and treating heart conditions. They will be linked to facilities for some cardiac investigations and treatments. After a visit to an RACP clinic the doctors may be able to reassure you that the pain is not coming from your heart, or they may feel that you are suffering from angina, and refer you on to a specialist hospital for further investigations and treatment.

UNSTABLE SYMPTOMS AND HEART ATTACKS

Someone who is having a heart attack and is still conscious and breathing may have severe pain or a heavy, tight feeling in the centre of the chest (which may spread to the arms, neck, jaw, back or stomach), although a heart attack does not always cause severe pain. He or she may also be sweating and having difficulty breathing, and may vomit. Someone who is unconscious and does not respond to gentle shaking or questioning may be having a more serious cardiac arrest. In this case, the person will not be breathing and will not have a detectable pulse.

What should I do if I think I am having a heart attack?

First, dial 999 for an ambulance. Then, if you can, find an aspirin and chew it. Do not wait to contact your GP or try to make your own way to hospital: you must get medical treatment as soon as possible, and the ambulance crew will have the equipment to confirm the diagnosis and treat you. Ambulances give priority to anyone suffering from chest pain. The first concern of the ambulance crew will be to ease your pain and breathing, by giving you a morphine-based pain-killing injection and oxygen through a mouthpiece. The ambulance crew may be able to do an ECG (electrocardiogram, see p.45) to check your heartbeat and will measure your blood pressure and pulse too. They may put a small tube (called a cannula) into a vein in your arm in case you need to be given emergency drugs. As soon as your condition is stable, they will take you to the A&E department of a hospital as quickly as possible.

What will happen in the A&E department?

A&E departments are well staffed with doctors and nurses with expertise in the emergency diagnosis and treatment of heart problems such as severe angina or heart attacks. They will usually organise some tests and often start emergency treatment. If they feel you are suffering from a severe heart condition, they will usually transfer you from A&E to a coronary care unit (CCU). These are high-tech units with a high ratio of nurses to patients, and facilities to carefully monitor the heart and initiate emergency treatments.

What will happen to me in the CCU?

You will have your heartbeat monitored continuously. You will also be given an ECG to monitor your heart's electrical rhythm, a chest X-ray and blood tests to help doctors diagnose your condition. You may also be given an echocardiogram, an ultrasound scan to check the pumping action of your heart. After your stay there, the chance of you suffering from abnormal rhythms or complications is greatly reduced and you will then be transferred to a cardiology or general medical ward for a few more days until you are fit to go home. The Cardiac Rehabilitation Team will visit you there to tell you what you can do to feel better on leaving the hospital.

Will which hospital I go to influence my recovery?

Provision of heart services varies between hospitals and it may be that you will get better care in one rather than another in your area. The most important things to look for in the care of heart conditions are how soon after arrival the hospital performs thrombolysis and whether they have a cardiac rehabilitation unit. These factors could influence your recovery, and even your survival, so it is important to discuss your preferred hospital with your GP if you can when you are diagnosed with heart disease.

Is heart treatment for children the same as it is for adults?

No. The conditions that affect children's hearts are very different from those that affect adults. Children's heart services are very specialised and focused in a small number of hospitals. Many childhood heart problems are congenital and picked up at, or shortly after, birth. Depending on the severity of the problem, these are managed in specialist units which have paediatricians (children's doctors), specialist intensive care doctors, cardiologists, cardiac surgeons and specialist nurses.

The private sector

Almost all consultants who work in private hospitals also have NHS practices, and therefore the quality of treatment is likely to be much the same in both sectors. However, with private treatment, the consultant will be able to spend more time with you. You will also have the reassurance of knowing that an operation, should you require one, will be performed by your consultant, who will also oversee all aspects of your care before and after your stay in hospital.

What are the advantages of private health care?
The advantages of private health care include:
- avoiding long NHS waiting lists
- having your treatment at a time that suits you
- knowing you will be operated on by a consultant, who will also be responsible for your care
- having a single room with a private bathroom, telephone and television
- being offered a wider choice of food
- being able to have visitors at most times of the day.

Questions to ask
- Will my insurance cover all aspects of my treatment?
- If not, what is likely to cost extra and how much will this be?
- Will my insurance pay for any extra treatment I may have to have if there are complications?
- Does the hospital offer a package to self-funded patients which covers costs occurring through complications?
- Does the hospital have the appropriate facilities to cope with complications and emergencies?
- Are the resident staff capable of dealing with possible complications in the absence of the consultant?
- How will long-term or follow-up treatment be arranged?
- Does my insurance cover long-term or follow-up treatment?

What will happen if there are complications?

In most cases these will be treated in the private hospital, although if the facilities are limited, you may need to be transferred to an NHS hospital. You should check whether the hospital where you are to receive treatment has adequate facilities to cope with major complications of surgery. Most hospitals performing cardiac surgery have the facilities to treat most major complications. If you are concerned, discuss your concern with your surgeon.

How do I arrange to have private care?

Just as with NHS treatment, you'll have to be referred by your GP for private care. The referral procedures vary at different hospitals and for different consultants – your GP or the staff at the private hospital will be able to give you details.

If you have medical insurance, your insurers may only deal with certain private hospitals, although it may be possible for you to pay a premium to remove this type of restriction from your policy.

I want to go private but my GP won't refer me to the consultant/hospital of my choice. What can I do?

Ideally you should be referred for private treatment by your GP. If he or she won't refer you, you can ask to see another GP. If your GP agrees a referral is necessary you do have the right to be referred privately and to the hospital of your choice, although the hospital of your choice may not be equipped to give you the best treatment for your problem. If your GP suggests a different consultant or hospital, ask why. If you are not satisfied with the answer and your GP still won't refer you, then you can either ask to see another doctor in the practice, or change to another practice altogether.

Can I be a private patient in an NHS hospital?

Yes. Some NHS hospitals have facilities for private patients, often either a private wing or single rooms off a main ward.

Can I switch between private and NHS care?

Yes. You can see a consultant privately for assessment and then ask to be added to his or her NHS waiting list for surgery. However, this will not advance your priority on the waiting list. You can see a consultant on the NHS and then transfer to private care for your operation, should you require one. You can also have diagnostic tests done privately to reduce the time you have to wait for these.

How will I be able to access cardiac rehabilitation on the NHS if I have had my operation privately?

You should talk to your GP, who can put you in touch with the cardiac rehabilitation unit nearest to you, and any other support groups you need. There is no problem in transferring between private and NHS care at different stages of treatment.

What are the costs of private care?

The costs of different operations vary slightly between consultants and from hospital to hospital. If your private hospital has a system called 'fixed price care', you'll be quoted a figure that includes all the likely costs of your hospital stay. However, sometimes this doesn't include the fees for the consultant and anaesthetist, so make sure you understand exactly what is included in the fixed price and get a quotation in writing before you're admitted to hospital. Ask your consultant's secretary or someone at the hospital to confirm the details if you're unsure about anything.

A private consultation with a consultant will probably cost between £100 and £150. A consultation may not include investigations. The cost of the operation itself will depend on how long it takes, how complicated it is and how long you're likely to be in hospital afterwards. A heart bypass operation, for example, is likely to cost around £12,000. This will generally include the hospital costs, the surgeons and the anaesthetist's and other specialists' fees. You should check with your insurance company whether there is likely to be a shortfall between what your policy covers and the cost of your treatment.

What is private medical insurance?

Private medical insurance is an arrangement whereby, in return for a yearly fee to an insurance company, any private medical treatment you need is paid for by that company. There are many different levels of insurance cover and prices: some schemes only cover the cost of having a private bed in an NHS hospital for inpatient treatment, whereas others include all aspects of any type of medical care you may need. Some insurance companies will only pay for treatment at particular private hospitals, so you should ask your insurers about any restrictions they have. Insurance premiums increase as people get older, and there are often restrictions: for example, the cover may exclude treatment for a condition you already have. It is important that you understand what your insurance covers before you take out a policy and before you have any private consultations or treatment. Many people have medical insurance as part of their work package, in which case the company they work for pays the annual insurance fee. Your company secretary will be able to advise you about what their scheme covers if your employer pays for your insurance. The six major private health insurers are BUPA, Norwich Union Healthcare, PPP Healthcare, Royal Sun Alliance, Standard Life and WPA.

Diagnosis and treatment

Tests at the hospital

The tests you have will depend on your risk factors and symptoms and on what procedures can be done at your hospital or clinic – not all of them are available at all hospitals. Usually, the simple tests are done first and, if necessary, the more complicated ones afterwards. The following are the main investigative tests for heart disease:

Non-invasive tests
- Chest X-ray
- Electrocardiogram (ECG or EKG) – also called electrocardiography:
    - Exercise (or stress) ECG
    - 24-hour Holter monitoring – also called ambulatory ECG
    - Event recording
- Echo or echocardiogram – also called echocardiography:
    - Stress echocardiography
    - Doppler echocardiography
- Computed tomography (CT) – also called CAT scan:
    - Electron beam computed tomography (EBCT)
- Magnetic resonance imaging (MRI) – also called nuclear magnetic resonance (NMR):
    - Magnetic resonance angiography (MRA)
- Nuclear scanning – radionuclide imaging – also called radionuclide angiography:
    - Thallium test or myocardial perfusion scanning
    - MUGA test
    - Positron emission tomography (PET)
    - Single photon emission computed tomography (SPECT)

Invasive tests
- Cardiac catheterisation
- Coronary angiography – also called coronary arteriography (sometimes also carried as part of cardiac catheterisation)
- Electrophysiological testing
- Transoesophageal echocardiography (TOE)

What is the difference between a non-invasive and an invasive test?

A non-invasive test can be performed at low or no risk and, apart from the occasional need to insert a small needle into your arm, is done entirely outside the body, whereas an invasive test involves inserting an instrument into the body and may need a local anaesthetic or sedation.

Is there any risk in having an invasive test?

There are risks with some invasive procedures, but these are small when the tests are done by an experienced doctor. Very rarely, in cardiac catheterisation, the artery walls are damaged by the catheter and have to be repaired in an emergency operation. Also rarely, the coronary artery being treated becomes completely blocked during the procedure and a bypass operation then has to be done immediately. In a small percentage of patients it can be fatal. Before having an invasive test, make sure your doctor discusses any potential risks with you.

I understand some invasive tests involve the use of radioactive substances. Aren't these dangerous?

Radionuclide tests involve injecting a very small amount of a radioactive substance (called an isotope) into the blood. This radioactivity is less than the amount used for a chest X-ray and is therefore unlikely to cause you any harm, although pregnant and breast-feeding women should not have these tests.

NON-INVASIVE TESTS

What is an electrocardiogram (ECG or EKG)?

An electrocardiogram is a recording of your heart's electrical activity. It is recorded as a line traced on paper.

Why would I have an electrocardiogram?

An electrocardiogram can be done:

- as part of a routine check-up
- before surgery to help plan your treatment
- after surgery to help decide how much exercise you should be doing (an exercise ECG: see p.46)

- to diagnose chest pain
- to diagnose palpitations (Holter monitoring: see below).
- to detect problems with the heart rate or rhythm (arrhythmia)
- to detect a recent heart attack or one that occurred some time ago
- to see if the heart is enlarged.

How will an ECG be carried out?

Small sticky pads (called electrodes) attached to wires are placed on your arms, legs and chest to record the electrical activity at different distances from your heart. The wires are linked to an ECG recorder that produces a trace on paper in the form of waves, which provide information about the rate and regularity of your heartbeat.

Is it an accurate test?

Yes, but there are limits to its usefulness. Arrhythmias can only be detected if they occur spontaneously during testing, and therefore some people with heart problems can have a normal reading, and some people with no problems can have an abnormal one. Patients with angina may have a normal ECG between attacks.

What is an exercise ECG and how is it done?

An exercise ECG, also called an exercise stress test or exercise tolerance test, may be done if you only get chest pain when you exercise. The ECG is recorded while you are on a treadmill or stationary bicycle for about 15 minutes. The exercise you are doing may provoke ECG changes or an arrhythmia, making diagnosis easier.

You should not eat a heavy meal immediately before doing an exercise ECG and, if you are taking beta-blockers (which lower the pulse rate), you may be told to stop taking them for a day or two before your test.

A negative exercise ECG result after a heart attack is a sign that your risk of developing further problems may be relatively low, whereas a positive result indicates that your risk may be higher.

What is Holter monitoring and how is it done?

It is also called an ambulatory ECG. It will detect silent angina (ie without symptoms), palpitations and other problems that may not occur very often or only occur in specific situations, eg in bed.

For this you will need to wear a portable ECG recorder attached to a belt for 24 hours while you go about your normal daily activities at home – although you shouldn't have a bath or shower during the test period as it may wash off the electrodes! You will be asked to keep a diary, noting down what you do and at what time you do it as well as any symptoms you may have, such as palpitations or dizzy spells.

An event recorder is similar to a Holter monitor, but can be worn for a month or two if your problems don't occur daily. When your symptoms start, you attach the recorder to your wrist, finger or under your arm, and the recordings are stored until you are able to send them by telephone to the hospital for analysis.

What is an echocardiogram and why would I have one?

An echo or echocardiogram is an ultrasound heart scan to check the pumping action of your heart. It gives information about:

- the condition of the heart muscle after a heart attack or heart failure
- the heart valves in valvular heart disease
- heart disease in babies and young children
- heart defects in a fetus.

You may have an echocardiogram if your consultant thinks your heart is not pumping efficiently, especially if he can hear a murmur when he listens to your chest.

How is it carried out?

An echocardiogram involves sending sound waves through a small recorder held on your chest. These waves are bounced off the walls and valves of the heart like an echo (similar to the fetal scans used during pregnancy) and show the shape, texture and movement of the valves as well as the size of the heart's chambers in a picture on a screen. The test takes about an hour to do.

What is stress echocardiography and how is it done?

Stress echocardiography will show up any parts of your heart that are not contracting properly because of damage to the heart muscle. This test is done during or after physical exercise, such as walking on a treadmill or using a stationary bicycle. If you can't exercise for any reason, you may be given a drug to simulate the stress that exercise would put on your heart. This can show up problems that may only occur on exercise.

What is Doppler echocardiography and how is it done?

This type of echocardiography measures the rate of blood flow in different parts of the heart and provides information about how well the heart valves are working. It is done in the same department with the standard echocardiography machine.

What is computed tomography (CT) or CAT scan?

A CAT scan is an imaging technique that can be used to look at your heart and blood vessels, using a special computer to manipulate the X-ray images. There are several variations, such as electron-beam computed tomography (EBCT), which may be better at certain aspects of the investigation.

Why would I have one?

CT can see into areas that cannot be seen in regular X-ray examinations, making it possible to diagnose diseases of the heart and big blood vessels earlier and more accurately than other imaging tools.

How is it done?

For a CT scan, X-rays are taken of your chest while you lie on a special table as it travels through a large, hoop-shaped scanner. A computer then processes the X-ray images to give pictures of your body including your heart and main blood vessels.

What is magnetic resonance imaging (MRI)?

Magnetic resonance imaging measures the changes in the cells of the body caused by a high-powered magnetic field, and makes high-quality images of the heart using these changes.

Why would I have magnetic resonance imaging?

MRI is done to:
- examine the heart muscle
- measure the blood flow through the major arteries
- detect damage caused by a heart attack

- detect disease of the aorta and other large blood vessels
- detect valvular disease
- diagnose some congenital heart defects.

How is MRI carried out?

MRI takes about an hour to do. Like with CT, you lie on a special table as it passes through a short tunnel but, instead of involving X-rays, the scanner used for MRI is a large, powerful magnet, which produces three-dimensional, computer-generated pictures of the inside of your body. Because of the magnet used, this test cannot be done on anyone with an artificial pacemaker. The newer MRI scanners can also produce pictures like angiograms to show the coronary arteries (magnetic resonance angiography or MRA).

Why is cardiac MRI only available in a few hospitals?

Although MRI is now widely available, cardiac MRI is a new form and is still being evaluated, so it is quite rare. It seems useful for looking at the function of the heart, and in the future it could prove useful as a technique to assess the blood flow in coronary artery grafts, but at present it is not as accurate as the gold-standard method which is coronary angiography (see p.51).

What is radionuclide imaging and what is it for?

Radionuclide tests are done to assess:
- the supply of blood to the heart muscle
- any blockage in the coronary arteries
- how well the chambers of the heart are working
- damage to the heart after a heart attack.

The main radionuclide tests are the thallium test or myocardial perfusion scanning and the MUGA scan, each of which involves injecting a small amount of a radioactive substance into the blood. The radioactivity is detected by a 'gamma camera' and the blood flow to the heart muscle is seen on computer-generated pictures. There are several types of scan, each giving slightly different information to help your doctors decide on your diagnosis and what to do about it. Some of these tests are only available at very specialised hospitals.

What will happen to me in a thallium test (myocardial perfusion scan)?

The thallium test shows how much blood is reaching the heart muscle, and will probably be done while you are exercising on a treadmill or stationary bicycle (a thallium stress test). This test is better at diagnosing heart disease and provides more reliable prognostic information than an exercise ECG, and can also provide additional information to coronary angiography (see below). These tests are usually only used if an exercise ECG cannot be performed for clinical reasons or if the exercise ECG is inconclusive. It has been found that the exercise ECG is less sensitive for women in general so a thallium test may be used as well as an ECG.

What will happen to me in a MUGA scan?

MUGA stands for multi-gated acquisition. A MUGA scan is used to assess ventricular function (the heart's ability to pump). The isotope injected is technetium. After injection of the technetium a gamma camera is used to pick up the radioactivity given off. The pictures can then be analysed to look at the heart's function.

What other radionuclide tests are there?

Single photon emission computed tomography (SPECT) and positron emission tomography (PET) are types of radionuclide tests. They both involve the injection of a radioactive isotope and the detection of the emissions from this by different means to give information about the heart's function and blood supply. They are only available in a very few centres.

INVASIVE TESTS

What is cardiac catheterisation and why would I have it?

Cardiac catheterisation is used to:

- see how well the heart is working
- measure the blood flow and blood pressure within the heart
- measure the amount of oxygen in the blood
- detect narrowing of the coronary arteries (when it is known as coronary angiography)
- decide whether surgery will be of benefit to someone with angina.

Cardiac catheterisation provides additional data for cardiologists and surgeons. It is also used to exclude coronary artery disease. This test can be carried out on children and even newborn babies.

Coronary angiography (using catheterisation to produce a map of the arteries) is currently the gold-standard test for coronary artery disease. It allows a detailed look at the coronary arteries and the blood supply to your heart, so is an essential test to decide on whether to go ahead with angioplasty or coronary artery bypass grafting. The same technique is used for treatments such as angioplasty and stenting.

How will it be done?

You won't be able to eat or drink anything before you have this test, which takes about an hour and is often done as a day-case procedure, although you may have to stay in hospital overnight after it.

A thin plastic tube (catheter) about the width of the lead in a pencil is inserted into a blood vessel in your groin or arm after the area has been numbed with a local anaesthetic. The catheter is then gently moved under X-ray guidance so that it enters your heart or coronary arteries. Dye is injected through the catheter to show up any damage to the arteries on X-ray pictures. Some people get brief angina during the procedure, and you should tell the doctor doing the test if you feel any pain in your chest.

An ECG recorder measures your heart rate and rhythm throughout the procedure. X-ray films will be taken by putting a fluid that shows up on X-rays down the catheter and taking a series of pictures called angiograms. When the catheter is removed, if it was inserted through your arm, you will usually have a few stitches. If the catheter was inserted in your groin, pressure is applied to your leg for about ten minutes to prevent any bleeding.

Are there any side-effects?

You may find that you feel tired and a bit 'groggy' for a day or two afterwards, and you may have bruising and tenderness where the catheter was inserted.

Many hundreds of thousands of these tests have been done and serious complications are rare. Overall, one person in 2,000 dies as a result of this procedure and serious complications occur in about one per cent of people.

Your doctor will not recommend a catheterisation test unless he or she feels that the benefits outweigh the risk.

Can anyone have this test?

Yes, as long as it is clinically indicated. Coronary angiography is regarded as a routine investigation in patients with clinical features of angina. Priority of access to this test is usually based on symptom severity, exercise test performance and effectiveness of medical treatment. As it takes skill to perform, the Government has suggested that hospitals that do this test should perform at least 500 per year to ensure that the cardiologists have enough experience. This guide lists the hospitals that meet this target.

What is Transoesophageal Echocardiography (TOE)?

Like the standard echocardiogram, this test looks at the structure and function of the heart muscle and heart valves. It takes an ultrasound picture (echocardiogram) of the heart from inside the gullet (oesophagus). This picture is formed by very low-energy sound waves similar to the technique used to 'see' a baby inside a mother's womb.

It is generally only used where pictures obtained across the chest wall are of inadequate quality or detail. It is used to make a diagnosis of potential problems with the heart or aorta and to guide decisions about how to repair a heart valve that is known to be abnormal. It may also be used during an operation to check repairs to valves and how the heart is pumping.

How is it done?

You may be given a light sedative to help you relax before this procedure. A probe attached to a narrow tube is passed down your throat and into your oesophagus, which lies close to and behind your heart. The probe contains a tiny 'camera', which takes pictures of your heart and all its structures.

What are electrophysiological tests (EPS) and why would I have one?

If you suffer from palpitations it may be necessary to do an EPS to decide what abnormal rhythm is occurring.

As well as assessing the rhythm of your heartbeat, EPS testing can also be done to look at the effects of particular anti-arrhythmic drugs, which you will be given while the test is in progress. This is a useful way of deciding which drugs you should be given. These tests give more detailed information than a standard ECG, but they and ablation are only available at a few hospitals.

How will this test be done?

You will probably be given an injection of local anaesthetic before some very fine tubes (called electrode catheters) are inserted into a vein in your neck or just under your collarbone. These tubes are then pushed gently through into your heart to stimulate it and to record its electrical impulses, and an ECG is done to examine your heart's activity. The stimulation of your heart may make you feel as though you are having palpitations.

Sometimes, rather than inserting the electrode catheters directly into the heart, they are pushed through a nostril and into the windpipe, which runs past the heart between the mouth and stomach.

EPS can also be used in some patients to 'burn out' (ablate) the abnormal cells causing the palpitations, so making drugs unnecessary.

Are there any dangers?

The catheters can cause damage to the blood vessels, leading to bleeding, and, very rarely, can damage the pacemaker cells of the heart (see p.4), so that an artificial pacemaker has to be fitted. In doing the tests some serious rhythm disturbances may occur, needing a heart shock (defibrillation) to correct them.

What is a tilt table study and how is it done?

Tilt tests are sometimes done to find out why people are having fainting spells (syncope) and to decide which drugs they need.

While you lie on a special table, an intravenous line is inserted into one of your veins and a catheter is inserted into an artery to monitor your blood pressure. The table is then tilted to find out what happens to your heart rate and blood pressure at different angles.

Sometimes, different drugs are injected through the intravenous line to see which has the best effect.

What happens when all the tests are done?

When all the results are available, your cardiologist will be able to advise you on the most appropriate treatment depending on what exactly is wrong with your heart and how serious your symptoms are. He may decide to persevere with drugs, either the same as before or new ones. Perhaps your heart is OK and he can reassure you that your symptoms are caused by something else. He might refer you to another specialist if this is the case.

If the problem is not treatable with drugs, referral to another specialist such as a surgeon might be appropriate. If you need treatment for narrowed coronary arteries, either coronary angioplasty or coronary artery surgery (revascularisation) will be needed. If your heart valves are damaged, you may require valve replacement or repair.

Common drugs

There is a wide range of drugs used to treat heart disease. Some only treat the symptoms while others treat the underlying cause. Many of these drugs have more than one effect, and some are used in combination to obtain the desired result.

Each of your drugs will have two names: the 'generic' or chemical name and the commercial or brand name given to it by the manufacturer. Different manufacturers will give the same chemical drug a different name so some drugs will be known under a number of different names.

What should I know about the drugs I'm given?
Many drugs have side-effects and interact with other drugs. You should always read the leaflet that comes with the drugs and if concerned, check with your GP. Also check if you plan to take any other medicines, just to be on the safe side. Although all drugs have some side-effects most people will not experience them. The main groups of drugs and their principal actions are given below:

- **Cholesterol-lowering drugs**
  - Statins
  - Resins (also called bile acid-binding drugs)
  - Fibrates
- **Blood pressure-lowering drugs (antihypertensives)**
  - Beta-blockers
  - Diuretics
  - Calcium channel blockers
  - Angiotensin-converting enzyme (ACE) inhibitors
  - Angiotensin-2-receptor antagonists
  - Vasodilators
- **Drugs for angina (anti-anginal drugs)**
  - Nitrates
  - Beta-blockers
  - Calcium channel blockers
  - Potassium channel blockers
  - Antiplatelet drugs

- **Drugs for fluid retention (diuretics)**
- **Blood thinning drugs (anticoagulants)**
  Antiplatelet drugs
  Anticoagulants
  Thrombolytic drugs (clot-busters)
- **Anti-arrhythmic drugs**

Below is a description of some of the most commonly used drugs for treating heart disease. They are divided into different categories according to their uses, actions, cautions (possible reasons why you may not be prescribed the drug) and side-effects. In the descriptions below we have used the generic or chemical names.

CHOLESTEROL-LOWERING (ANTI-HYPERLIPIDAEMIC) DRUGS

Statins

Uses

To reduce the risk of heart disease by lowering the level of cholesterol in the blood. They should be considered for all patients with a blood cholesterol greater than 5mmol per litre and all patients who have had a heart attack, angina or coronary bypass surgery irrespective of their cholesterol level.

Common types

Atorvastatin, fluvastatin, pravastatin and simvastatin

Actions

These are the most effective cholesterol-lowering drugs. They act on the liver to raise HDL levels and/or lower LDL levels (see p.111).

Cautions

In the presence of liver disease, high alcohol intake, pregnancy or breast-feeding.

Side-effects

Constipation or diarrhoea; flatulence (wind), nausea or headaches. Rarely: muscle pain, tender or weak muscles or a rash.

Resins (also called bile acid-binding drugs)

Uses

To reduce the risk of heart disease by lowering the level of cholesterol in the blood. Statins are generally used first and these drugs are reserved for those people with specific problems or those who do not respond to statins (see above).

Common types

Cholestyramine, colestipol

Actions

They work by combining with bile acids in the gut and preventing their absorption. These acids are essential for proper digestion, so the liver breaks down blood cholesterol instead to make more bile acids.

Cautions

Generally pretty safe. May raise the level of triglycerides in the blood. The resins also interfere with the absorption of certain vitamins so supplements of Vitamins A, D and K may be required.

Side-effects

Since bile acids are not being absorbed by the gut, constipation is common. Occasionally diarrhoea and indigestion.

Fibrates

Uses

To reduce the risk of heart disease by lowering the level of triglycerides and cholesterol in the blood. Statins are generally used first for lowering cholesterol. These drugs are also used for lowering triglycerides or those who do not respond to statins (see above).

Common types

Bezafibrate, ciprofibrate, fenofibrate and gemfibrozil

Actions

Fibrates act through two mechanisms. Firstly they encourage an enzyme in blood vessels to break down a component required for cholesterol and secondly they encouarage the liver to excrete an essential cholesterol building block (sterol) into the bile. For this reason they should be handled carefully in people with biliary problems such as gallstones and pancreas problems.

Cautions

Generally pretty safe. May raise the level of triglycerides in the blood. The resins also interfere with the absorption of certain vitamins so supplements of Vitamins A, D and K may be required.

Side-effects

Since bile acids are not being absorbed by the gut, constipation is common. Occasionally diarrhoea and indigestion.

DRUGS FOR ANGINA, HIGH BLOOD PRESSURE AND HEART FAILURE

Beta-blockers

Uses

To reduce the amount of work performed by the heart and so reduce blood pressure and angina. There is little to choose between the drugs, although some are slightly better in some circumstances than others.

Common types

Acebutolol, atenolol, bisoprolol, carvedilol, metoprolol, nadolol, oxprenolol, sotalol

Actions

These drugs work by blocking the effect of the hormone adrenaline on the heart and blood vessels. Adrenaline tends to stimulate the heart to beat harder. These drugs reduce that effect so the heart beats slower and contracts less vigorously.

Cautions

They may precipitate heart failure in people with poor heart function because they make the heart beat less strongly. They may cause or aggravate asthma or wheezing because they narrow the air passages in the lungs, so are best avoided by people with asthma. In some people they may aggravate diabetes.

Side-effects

Fatigue, coldness of the hands and feet, nightmares and very occasionally impotence.

Diuretics

Uses

To reduce the build-up of fluid in the body. This has different effects in different circumstances. These drugs are used to lower blood pressure (sometimes combined with beta-blockers, ACE inhibitors, calcium channel blockers, or other drugs). They are also used in heart failure to remove fluid from the body and lungs, thereby reducing ankle swelling and making breathing easier (often combined with digoxin or ACE inhibitors and with beta-blockers).

Common types

Amiloride, bendrofluazide, bumetanide, frusemide, indapamide, spironolactone

Actions

They increase the amount of salt and water that is removed from the body in the urine, so you may find you are going to the toilet more often.

Cautions

Sometimes cause low potassium levels in the blood. They can raise the blood sugar level in diabetics, and they can make gout worse. Avoid buying salt substitutes instead of ordinary salt.

Side-effects

Nausea, headache, dizziness, rash, muscle cramps; in men, enlarged, painful breasts can occur with spironolactone.

Nitrates

Uses

Treatment of angina.

Common types

Glyceryl trinitrate (GTN) either as spray, tablets or skin patches, isosorbide dinitrate and isosorbide mononitrate

Actions

They open up the coronary arteries to the heart muscle. They also open up other blood vessels in the body which makes it easier for the heart to pump blood around the body.

Cautions

Very few. Low blood pressure. Can sometimes cause severe liver or kidney failure.

Side-effects

Mainly related to the opening up of the blood vessels: throbbing headache, flushing and feeling faint when standing suddenly.

Calcium channel blockers

Uses

Angina, high blood pressure and some irregular heart rhythms.

Common types

Amlodipine, diltiazem, felodipine, nicardipine, nifedipine, nimodipine, verapamil

Kate Rogers

My high blood pressure first came to light when I was 30 and I was having my daughter, not when I was carrying her but when I went into labour. My blood pressure was dangerously high: pre-eclampsia. She was born by an episiotomy and forceps delivery. My blood pressure was so dangerously high that I wasn't moved off the labour table for hours. I was given all sorts of drugs, which meant that I couldn't breastfeed. They gave me an injection to take the milk away. I was sedated, so I didn't see Mary for three days after I had her. They just took her away. I gave birth at 4pm and it must have been midnight when they moved me onto the ward. I was given barbiturates. Of course, they don't do that any more: this was twenty-seven years ago. And then, of course, you make your recovery and go home, but nobody ever bothered to check my blood pressure, so I never realised that it was still high.

After my husband died I was working on a gynaecology ward and I was letting a student nurse do practice on me, taking my blood pressure. She read it out and I told her she'd done it wrong and made her do it again. She got the same reading: 240 over 160. It was checked by a doctor and I was told to pack my bag and go home! I went to my doctor and he put me on diuretics. Again it wasn't managed very well and nobody kept on checking my blood pressure, but it seemed to have gone down.

I suppose it was probably about two years later that I had a bit of a 'keep-fit' campaign; the local gym was offering free membership if you worked at the hospital. They give you a cursory check when you sign up and the guy took my blood pressure and said that he wasn't prepared to do an exercise programme for me until I'd seen my doctor. The doctor checked me and put me on beta-blockers. By this time I was working in the training department of the hospital and I had a new doctor and I went along every month to have my blood pressure checked, but it didn't seem to be going down. I asked 'Why? Is it because I'm overweight?' And he said, 'No, you could do with losing half a stone but it's not that.' He couldn't find a reason despite doing blood tests. So I was on the beta-blockers for about two years and my blood pressure started to creep up again. So he doubled the dose and I went off my head! They sent me loopy! Actually, my boss had to take me to one side, and she said, 'Some of the girls have noticed, and I've noticed, that you're not exactly yourself at the moment...' I went to the doctor and he said that they don't suit everyone. So he stopped the drugs, they were not controlling the hypertension properly anyway, and told me to take two weeks off and rest. I said I'd write my own sick note but he said no, he knew what I was like! In the end I stayed off for a week. He said, 'You're to get out of bed at ten every day, read the papers, go for walks.' And the very next day after I stopped the drugs I felt normal again.

So now I'm on an ACE inhibitor – enalapril, 10 milligrams. I was started on 5milligrams but my blood pressure started creeping up again so the dose was increased. About a year ago it was creeping up again, but then so was my weight, and I know these things are linked. I've never felt particularly ill with it. I've had headaches, but everyone in my family has bad heads. And I've never had dizzy spells or fainting. It's just one of those things you learn to live with.

Actions

These drugs restrict the amount of calcium entering the muscle cells in the walls of the arteries, making them relax and widen. This means more blood reaches the heart muscle, which in turn can pump blood around the body more easily through the widened arteries. Some calcium channel blockers slow down and steady the heart rate.

Cautions

Vary between drugs. Generally heart failure, recent heart attack or slow heart rate.

Side-effects

Mostly minor – headaches, flushing, faintness, dizziness, indigestion, nausea, vomiting, swollen ankles or constipation (with verapamil).

Potassium channel openers

Uses

Treatment of angina.

Common types

Nicorandil

Actions

Nicorandil opens up the body's blood vessels including the coronary arteries to the heart muscle.

Cautions

Similar to calcium channel blockers. Avoid in heart failure, recent heart attack and low blood pressure.

Side-effects

Transient headache particularly when the drug is first started, flushing of the skin and dizziness.

Angiotensin-converting enzyme (ACE) inhibitors

Uses

ACE inhibitors have a valuable role in treating high blood pressure and heart failure.

Common types

Captopril, cilazapril, enalapril, lisinopril, perindopril, ramipril

Actions

They open up the body's blood vessels so that the blood pressure drops. This also means the heart can pump blood with less effort, which is helpful in heart failure.

Cautions

Should always be started at a low dose then escalated according to response. May cause low blood pressure with faintness in patients on diuretics or patients with heart failure. They should be used with caution in people with generalised vascular disease because of possible hidden kidney disease, which can be made worse by ACE inhibitors. Kidney function should be monitored before and after commencing ACE inhibitors treatment. Avoid during pregnancy.

Side-effects

Commonly a dry cough. May also affect the kidneys.

Angiotensin-2-receptor antagonists

Uses

These drugs have a similar role to ACE inhibitors in treating high blood pressure and heart failure. Also called angiotensin II inhibitors.

Common types

Candesartan, eprosartan, irbesartan, losartan, telmisartan, valsartan

Actions

They open up the body's blood vessels so that the blood pressure drops. This also means the heart can pump blood with less effort, which is helpful in heart failure.

Cautions

Similar to ACE inhibitors. May cause the blood potassium level to rise, particularly in the elderly. This should be checked before and after commencing treatment. Avoid during pregnancy.

Side-effects

Mostly mild and similar to ACE inhibitors. Tiredness; can lower blood pressure too much when first used. Losartan and valsartan are more likely than the others to cause a dry cough.

BLOOD-THINNING DRUGS

Antiplatelet drugs

Uses

To prevent blood clots forming in the blood vessels that feed the heart muscle; to reduce the risk of dying after a heart attack and of having a first or further heart attack or stroke; to control angina and reduce the risks from having an irregular heartbeat (atrial fibrillation); following coronary artery bypass surgery.

DRUGS COMMONLY USED FOR TREATING HEART DISEASE

Drug	Type	Action
Acebutolol	Beta-blocker	*Reduces heart work and rate*
Alteplase	Thrombolytic	*Dissolves clots*
Amiloride	Diuretic	*Increases urine with loss of salt and water*
Amiodarone	Anti-arrhythmic	*Controls atrial and ventricular heart rhythm*
Amlodipine	Calcium channel blocker	*Opens up coronary arteries, lowers blood pressure*
Aspirin	Antiplatelet	*Prevents small blood clots in arteries*
Atenolol	Beta-blocker	*Reduces heart work and rate*
Atorvastatin	Cholesterol lowering	*Reduces blood cholesterol*
Bendrofluazide	Diuretic	*Increases urine with loss of salt and water*
Bezafibrate	Anti-hyperlipidaemic	*Lowers cholesterol and triglycerides*
Bisoprolol	Beta-blocker	*Reduces heart work and rate*
Bumetanide	Diuretic	*Increases urine with loss of salt and water*
Candesartan	Angiotensin-2-receptor antagonists	*Opens all arteries, lowers blood pressure*
Captopril	ACE inhibitor	*Opens all arteries, lowers blood pressure*
Carvedilol	Beta-blocker	*Reduces heart work and rate*
Cholestyramine	Cholesterol lowering	*Reduces blood cholesterol*
Cilazapril	ACE inhibitor	*Opens all arteries, lowers blood pressure*
Ciprofibrate	Anti-hyperlipidaemic	*Lowers cholesterol and triglycerides*

Clopidogrel	Antiplatelet	*Prevents small blood clots in arteries*
Coestipol	Anti-hyperlipidaemic	*Lowers cholesterol*
Dalteparin	Anticoagulant	*Thins blood, slows blood clotting*
Digoxin	Anti-arrhythmic	*Controls atrial heart rate*
Diltiazem	Calcium channel blocker	*Opens up coronary arteries, lowers blood pressure*
Dipyridamole	Antiplatelet	*Prevents small blood clots in arteries*
Enalapril	ACE inhibitor	*Opens all arteries, lowers blood pressure*
Enoxaparin	Anticoagulant	*Thins blood, slows blood clotting*
Eprosartan	Angiotensin-2-receptor antagonists	*Opens all arteries, lowers blood pressure*
Felodipine	Calcium channel blocker	*Opens up coronary arteries, lowers blood pressure*
Fenofibrate	Anti-hyperlipidaemic	*Lowers cholesterol and triglycerides*
Flecainide	Anti-arrhythmic	*Controls atrial and ventricular heart rhythm*
Fluvastatin	Anti-hyperlipidaemic	*Lowers cholesterol*
Frusemide	Diuretic	*Increases urine with loss of salt and water*
Gemfibrozil	Anti-hyperlipidaemic	*Lowers cholesterol and triglycerides*
Glyceryl tinitrate	Nitrate	*Opens up coronary arteries*
Heparin	Anticoagulant	*Thins blood, slows blood clotting*
Indapamide	Diuretic	*Increases urine with loss of salt and water*

Irbesartan	Angiotensin-2-receptor antagonists	*Opens all arteries, lowers blood pressure*
Isosorbide	Vasodilator	*Opens up arteries, improving blood flow*
Isosorbide dinitrate	Nitrate	*Opens up coronary arteries, lowers blood pressure*
Isosorbide mononitrate	Nitrate	*Opens up coronary arteries, lowers blood pressure*
Lignocaine	Anti-arrhythmic	*Controls ventricular heart rhythm*
Lisinopril	ACE inhibitor	*Opens all arteries, lowers blood pressure*
Losartan	Angiotensin-2-receptor antagonists	*Opens all arteries, lowers blood pressure*
Metolazone	Diuretic	*Increases urine with loss of salt and water*
Metoprolol	Beta-blocker	*Reduces heart work and rate*
Metopropol	Beta-blocker	*Reduces heart work and rate*
Mexiletine	Anti-arrhythmic	*Controls ventricular heart rhythm*
Nadolol	Beta-blocker	*Reduces heart work and rate*
Nicardipine	Calcium channel blocker	*Opens up coronary arteries, lowers blood pressure*
Nicorandil	Potassium channel opener	*Opens up coronary arteries*
Nifedipine	Calcium channel blocker	*Opens up coronary arteries, lowers blood pressure*
Nimodipine	Calcium channel blocker	*Opens up coronary arteries, lowers blood pressure*
Oxprenolol	Beta-blocker	*Reduces heart work and rate*
Perindopril	ACE inhibitor	*Opens all arteries, lowers blood pressure*

Phenindione	Anticoagulant	*Thins blood, slows blood clotting*
Pravastatin	Cholesterol lowering	*Reduces blood cholesterol*
Procainamide	Anti-arrhythmic	*Controls atrial and ventricular heart rhythm*
Propafenone	Anti-arrhythmic	*Controls atrial and ventricular heart rhythm*
Quinidine	Anti-arrhythmic	*Controls atrial and ventricular heart rhythm*
Ramipril	ACE inhibitor	*Opens all arteries, lowers blood pressure*
Reteplase	Thrombolytic	*Dissolves clots*
Simvastatin	Anti-hyperlipidaemic	*Lowers cholesterol*
Sotalol	Beta-blocker	*Reduces heart work and rate*
Spironolactone	Diuretic	*Increases urine with loss of salt and water*
Streptokinase	Thrombolytic	*Dissolves clots*
Telmisartan	Angiotensin-2-receptor antagonists	*Opens all arteries, lowers blood pressure*
Ticlopidine	Antiplatelet	*Prevents small blood clots in arteries*
Tinzaparin	Anticoagulant	*Thins blood, slows blood clotting*
Valsartan	Angiotensin-2-receptor antagonists	*Opens all arteries, lowers blood pressure*
Verapamil	Calcium channel blocker, anti-arrhythmic	*Opens up arteries, improving blood flow. stabilises heart rhythm*
Warfarin	Anticoagulant	*Thins blood, slows blood clotting*

Common types

Aspirin, clopidogrel, dipyridamole and ticlopidine. In hospital more powerful intravenous versions may be used to prevent clots forming at the site of coronary angioplasty.

Actions

These drugs prevent small blood cells called platelets sticking together and forming clots in the blood vessels that supply blood to the heart muscle (coronary arteries). Such clots can cause severe angina or a heart attack.

Cautions

Use aspirin with caution if you have a history of indigestion, stomach ulcers or kidney trouble (clopidogrel may be better). Notify your doctor if you get indigestion when taking aspirin. Antiplatelet drugs should usually be stopped a few days prior to heart surgery.

Side-effects

Aspirin can cause nausea, vomiting and indigestion and sometimes stomach ulcers. The ulcers may bleed if severe. Clopidogrel and dipyridamole can cause an upset stomach or heartburn and sometimes a rash, nausea, diarrhoea or constipation.

Oral Anticoagulants

Uses

Long-term treatment to prevent or dissolve blood clots anywhere in the body. Clots may occur in the heart if the heart rhythm is irregular (atrial fibrillation) or on artificial heart valves or even in the deep veins of the leg after surgery.

Common types

Warfarin and phenindione by mouth or heparin, dalteparin, enoxaparin, tinzaparin by injection

Actions

Warfarin and phenindione stop the formation of the protein fibrin, which is one of the constituents of blood clots. They take about 48 hours to begin working and increase the time it takes for your blood to clot. Heparin, dalteparin, enoxaparin, tinzaparin are given by injection and work almost immediately.

Cautions

Recent surgery or liver or renal disease. Pregnancy or breast feeding. Regular blood tests to ensure dose is within recommended range.

Side-effects

Severe bleeding. Too high a dose can cause continued bleeding from cuts, nosebleeds, bleeding gums, heavy menstrual bleeding. Warfarin, in particular, interacts with a number of other drugs and alcohol which can enhance its bleeding effect.

Thrombolytic drugs (clot-busters)

Uses

Given by injection as soon as possible after a heart attack.

Common types

Alteplase, reteplase, streptokinase

Actions

These drugs dissolve blood clots in the coronary arteries to restore blood flow through a coronary artery blocked by clot.

Cautions

A recent stroke or surgery that has increased the risk of bleeding.

Side-effects

Severe bleeding. Too high a dose can cause continued bleeding from cuts, nosebleeds, bleeding gums, heavy menstrual bleeding. these drugs interact with a number of other drugs and alcohol which can enhance their bleeding effect.

ANTI-ARRHYTHMIC DRUGS (TO CORRECT HEART RHYTHM)

Uses

To regulate the heartbeat; to treat disturbances in the heart rhythm. Each of heart's two main pumping areas – the atria and the ventricles – can beat irregularly. Some drugs stabilise the atria, some the ventricles and some act on both.

Common types

Verapamil acts on the atria; lignocaine and mexiletine stabilise the ventricles; amiodarone, flecainide, procainamide, propafenone and quinidine act on both. Some beta-blockers act on both although they are most commonly used to treat atrial arrhythmias. Digoxin is used to strengthen the heart muscle and slow the heart rate, and is often used in heart failure.

Actions

These drugs act in a complicated way to influence the way that electricity is transmitted between the cells of the heart.

Cautions

These drugs tend to reduce the force of the heartbeat and should therefore be used cautiously on patients with heart failure. Special care should be taken if two or more are used together.

Side-effects

Can cause even worse arrhythmias.

- **Amiodarone:** nausea, headaches, dizziness, stomach upsets, loss of appetite, dry mouth, blurred vision, difficulty with night glare, eg car headlights; can also make the skin very sensitive to sunlight. Very rarely causes problems with the thyroid gland, liver, lungs.
- **Digoxin:** loss of appetite, nausea and sometimes vomiting, diarrhoea, breast pain, fainting, palpitations; too high a dose can make everything appear to have a yellowish tinge.

Are there any new drugs available?

Few new drugs have been developed recently but some trials show that more aggressive use of current medication – particularly statins, clopidogrel and the angiotensin-2-receptor antagonists in hypertension can reduce the risk of recurrent heart attack and angina in some individuals.

However, new research published by *The Lancet* medical journal suggests that heart attacks and strokes could be cut by at least one third by tripling the number of patients on cholesterol-lowering drugs (statins).

The protective effect of statins comes on top of that offered by the drugs that lower blood pressure and heart rate. Taking these drugs in combination and quitting smoking might reduce the risk faced by high-risk patients by as much as 80 per cent.

Dos and don'ts of taking your medication

- **Do** be patient while the right drug at the right dose is found for you: people react differently to different drugs and to different doses so you may have to try a few before finding the best one.
- **Do** let your doctor know if you have any new problems, as these could be side-effects of the drug(s) you are taking or due to the dose being too high.
- **Do** take your medication exactly as prescribed.

- **Don't** take any other drugs that you have not been prescribed – even apparently harmless medications that you can buy at a chemist – without first asking your doctor or a pharmacist. Some common 'over-the-counter' drugs can interact with the drugs used to treat heart disease and/or make them less effective.

Coronary artery disease

Your GP may be able to tell if you have coronary artery disease from the symptoms you describe and from what you say about your family history and lifestyle. Your doctor will listen to your heart to check its rate and rhythm using a stethoscope, measure your blood pressure and assess your general condition and check for diabetes.

Are there any tests my GP can do to check for angina?

The tests he will do will depend on the answers you give, but if he thinks there is a possibility of heart disease, he will want to know your cholesterol and triglycerides levels (risk factors for coronary artery disease), blood sugar level (in case you have developed diabetes), kidney function (risk of raised cholesterol) and haemoglobin level (anaemia makes the symptoms of coronary artery disease worse). Blood tests will give him this information.

What will my GP do if I have angina?

Your GP will prescribe medication to control your symptoms. He or she will also give you advice about what to do when you have an angina attack and about any lifestyle changes you can make to reduce your risk of further problems. If your angina is unstable or does not respond to the treatment, you may be referred to a cardiologist (heart specialist) for tests.

What drugs will my GP give me for angina?

Nitrates, supplied as a spray or tablets, are the most common drugs prescribed for angina. You may also be given aspirin. Beta-blockers, calcium channel blockers and other drugs for diabetes, high blood pressure and high cholesterol will be given as appropriate.

What happens if the treatment does not work?

If your GP feels the diagnosis is certain or at least very likely and you do not get better, he or she may decide to refer you to a cardiologist. If you've tried different drugs (and different combinations) to find which suit you best, but your symptoms are not getting any better, your doctor or the specialist may suggest you think about having further tests with a view to having an operation. The investigations needed and the operations that can be done to treat different heart conditions are described in this and the next sections.

What is revascularisation?

'Revascularisation' means making the blood vessels wider or bypassing blocked or narrowed arteries with grafts. Revascularisation treatments include:

- coronary angioplasty with or without stenting
- coronary bypass surgery.

ANGIOPLASTY

Coronary angioplasty (also called balloon angioplasty or Percutaneous Transluminal Coronary Angioplasty [PTCA]) is an invasive procedure in which the walls of the narrow arteries are opened up with a tiny balloon. This may avoid the need for a major operation, though not all narrowings are suitable for this procedure, particularly if several blood vessels are involved or the lesions are long and complex. The aim of angioplasty is to improve the blood flow to your heart muscle. The treatment has developed rapidly since it was first introduced in 1977, and it is now a common treatment for coronary artery disease. More than 20,000 of these procedures are carried out each year in the UK.

Why would I be given angioplasty?

You may be offered angioplasty if you have angina (see p.10) that is affecting your quality of life and leading to a risk of heart attack and your coronary arteries are suitable. You may also be offered it if you have just had a heart attack, to try to open the artery up and reduce the damage to your heart muscle.

Why might I be considered unsuitable for angioplasty?

You may not need to have angioplasty if you have mild coronary artery disease that can be controlled by drugs and changes to your lifestyle, such as getting more exercise, eating a good diet and giving up smoking.

A bypass operation will be more suitable if several of your coronary arteries are narrow or blocked, or if the narrowings are very long. The risk of them closing down again after angioplasty may be so high in this situation as to make the procedure a waste of time.

Who will perform my angioplasty?

Angioplasty is a skilled technique that must be done by a cardiologist experienced in this sort of intervention.

What does the procedure involve?

The cardiologist inserts a thin, hollow tube called a catheter through a small cut in the skin (usually in the groin) after it has been numbed with a local anaesthetic. The catheter is then passed over a fine wire, which is used to guide it into a coronary artery. A dye is also injected into the artery and a sequence of X-rays (angiogram) is taken to show the blood vessels and plaques, in order to help the cardiologist guide the catheter to the areas of blockage. When the catheter is in position in the coronary artery, the balloon at its tip is inflated so that it pushes the walls of the artery apart and flattens and breaks up the plaques. A device called a stent may also be deployed to hold the area open, thereby reducing the likelihood of recurrence of the narrowing. More recent developments with drug-eluting stents may extend this benefit further. These are stents which have been coated with a drug, which releases slowly to further help prevent the arteries re-narrowing. At present they are not widely available on the NHS. It is possible for the patients to pay the extra to have these stents used; if you think you might be interested in this option, discuss it with your cardiologist. Then another set of X-rays is taken to make sure that the blood flow has been improved. If it hasn't, the procedure can be repeated before the catheter is removed.

How long does it take?

Although angioplasty is similar in some respects to cardiac catheterisation, it can take much longer to get the catheter into the correct position.

Are there other forms of angioplasty?

Yes. In atherectomy (which is less common), a rotating shaver (rotablation) or laser at the tip of the catheter cuts away or vaporises the plaques. These procedures are not widely available, and it is not yet known whether they have any advantages over balloon angioplasty with stenting.

What is a stent and why would I be given one?

Stents are small tubes made of stainless steel mesh left in the artery to keep the walls open. Stents can increase the chances of success of angioplasty by giving support to the artery walls and helping to stop them narrowing again.

What is the success rate of angioplasty?

According to the British Heart Foundation, angioplasty is successful in at least 90 per cent of cases. After angioplasty with a stent three per cent of patients will have narrowed arteries again (restenosis) within six months.

What are the possible risks and complications?

In about two per cent of people, an artery becomes completely blocked during angioplasty, in which case an emergency bypass operation may have to be done to prevent the heart being damaged. Although the risk is small, it will be discussed with you beforehand to prepare you for the possibility of emergency action having to be taken.

There's also a very small risk of having a heart attack or stroke or of dying: about five people in every thousand (0.5 per cent) die within 30 days of having angioplasty. These complications depend to some extent on people's general health before they undergo the procedure, and your fitness will be taken into account in making any decision about your treatment.

Very rarely, the balloon or guide wire damages the artery wall, which has to be repaired immediately in an open-heart operation.

Less serious complications include allergic reactions to the dye used to show up the blocked artery on X-ray, and re-blockage of the artery, either shortly afterwards or several months later.

If I have a stent, will it reduce the risk of complications?

Having a stent will reduce your risk of having to have emergency bypass surgery (see p.75). It will also reduce the chances of your treated arteries narrowing again, which occurs in about three per cent of cases within six months – compared with about 33 per cent of people before stents were used routinely.

If I have angioplasty, will I avoid having a heart bypass operation?

Maybe. For many people, angioplasty is a less traumatic alternative to bypass surgery. However, people who have angioplasty are more likely to get angina again than those who have bypass surgery. Most then have to decide whether to have angioplasty again or to have a bypass operation. This will depend on the state of your coronary arteries at the time.

What treatment will I receive afterwards?

If you have a stent in place, you will probably have to take antiplatelet drugs such as aspirin or clopidogrel to prevent blood clots forming around it. You should not have much pain, if any, but you can take painkillers if you do. You may also need to continue to take any drugs you were taking before the procedure to help reduce your risk of further coronary artery disease, although some of these may be changed.

What are the advantages of angioplasty over coronary bypass surgery (CABG)?

Angioplasty is done under local anaesthetic, is a less traumatic procedure and recovery takes a few days rather than months. However, there is a higher chance of recurrent symptoms and the need for further treatment.

CABG (see p.79) is a major operation involving a general anaesthetic and it takes some time to recover, though the long-term results, particularly with an arterial graft to the major artery known as the left anterior descending, have been shown to be vastly superior to angioplasty, with far fewer cases of recurrence.

What are the drawbacks of angioplasty?

Because angioplasty simply stretches the walls of the affected coronary arteries rather than bypassing them altogether, there is a chance your symptoms could return if the treated segment of an artery narrows again. If the treated arteries re-narrow, or different arteries are affected by atherosclerosis, you may be able to have angioplasty again or you may end up having coronary bypass surgery anyway.

If the consultant cardiologist advises referral for coronary bypass surgery, what questions should I ask?

You may want to ask:

- Are there any other drugs I can take before resorting to surgery?
- Why do I need to have this operation rather than angioplasty?
- How much difference will it make to my health and survival if I don't have the operation?
- Why have you chosen this particular surgeon?

What type of surgery will I have?

This will depend on what is wrong with your heart. If tests show that one or more of your arteries is in danger of becoming completely blocked, thus increasing your chances of having a heart attack in the near future, you may be advised to have an angioplasty or a coronary artery bypass graft (CABG). If your problem is a faulty valve, you might need either a valve replacement or repair. It is possible that you might need both repair and replacement. (see p.85).

Operations may be required to deal with certain other forms of heart disease or with congenital heart disease in children (see p.103). Sometimes the lining of the sac that contains the heart (pericardium) becomes thick and rigid, interfering with the action of the heart (constrictive pericarditis), and needs to be removed. Some people with coronary heart disease and who have suffered a heart attack may develop extreme weakening of the heart muscle which forms a bulge (aneurysm), reducing the ability of the heart to pump blood, and this may need to be removed.

How long will I have to wait?

This will vary depending on how serious your condition is. You may have to wait for up to the current maximum waiting time of nine months. However, since July 2002, patients who have waited more than six months are eligible to be offered a choice to move to another NHS hospital with a shorter waiting list, to a private hospital or even a hospital abroad, all paid for by the NHS.

Is there anything I can do to speed things up?
You could talk to your GP to find out if there is another heart surgeon at another hospital in your area or within another PCT area who has a shorter waiting list. If you can afford it, there is also the option of private treatment, but do discuss the pros and cons of this with your GP and specialist before you make a decision. Not all private hospitals have the special equipment and trained staff needed for open-heart surgery. It can also be very expensive.

You should also tell your doctor immediately if your symptoms get any worse or change in any way, so that steps can be taken to try to arrange for your operation to be done sooner.

How does the treatment in the UK measure up to other countries?
The results of heart surgery in the UK compare well with those in other countries. Survival rates are as good as or better than in the USA and Germany. Many other countries do not have national results for us to compare with. Waiting times for surgery are too long but are rapidly improving.

What questions should I ask my surgeon about my treatment?
It is important you are fully informed about any procedure that you are to undergo. Relevant questions may include the following:
- Are there any alternatives to surgery?
- What are the benefits of the operation compared with not having it done?
- Who is going to carry out the operation?
- How many times has the surgeon carried out this procedure?
- What is the mortality rate of the patients for this procedure?
- What is the rate of complications for the surgeon?
- How many of these operations does the hospital do?
- What is the mortality rate for the unit?
- What is the rate of complications for the unit?

- What are the risks involved and what do you do to minimise these?
- How long is the expected recovery time?

CORONARY BYPASS SURGERY (CABG)

The word bypass is used for two different aspects of heart surgery. Firstly it is an abbreviation of 'cardiopulmonary bypass'. This is the heart-lung machine that keeps you alive while the operation is going on. Secondly it is also used to describe coronary artery bypass grafts.

Coronary artery bypass grafting (CABG) is a type of open-heart surgery done to re-route blood around the blocked coronary arteries. It involves using blood vessels from somewhere else in the body (usually an artery from just under the chest or a vein from the leg) to provide a route around the blocked coronary artery. There are various methods of performing the operation with or without using a heart-lung machine. In 75 per cent of cases currently performed, the heart is stopped during the operation and a heart-lung machine keeps the blood circulating round the body.

Operations on the beating heart using special retractors without using the heart-lung machine are increasing in frequency and may be particularly beneficial in patients with significant aortic disease, patients with cerebral arterial disease and those with renal problems.

What is the purpose of CABG and why would I be offered it?

The aim of CABG is to give the blood alternative routes to reach the heart muscle that avoid the narrow or blocked coronary arteries. This can have two main benefits. Your angina should disappear or at least be greatly improved. For some patients there is a good chance that they will live longer than if they did not have the operation. You may also be offered CABG if you have had unsuccessful angioplasty or further damage has occurred to other coronary arteries after a successful procedure. Finally, if you are having an operation for heart valve disease and are found to have coronary artery disease as well, you will probably be offered simultaneous bypass grafts.

Are there different types of bypass surgery?

There are some types of bypass surgery, called minimally invasive or limited-access surgery, which do not involve cutting open the chest and breastbone, but these are only done at a few centres. Like CABG, using a heart-lung machine they re-route the flow of blood around the blocked arteries to improve the supply of blood and oxygen to the heart, but the techniques used mean very small incisions. They are not suitable for all patients.

MIDCAB is one type of minimally invasive surgery which can only be done if no more than two arteries need to be bypassed. The surgeon can see the operating site through a cut made just above the artery that is going to be bypassed.

Although these operations may prove to be less invasive than CABG – and they certainly avoid the need to make a large incision in the chest and to cut through the breastbone – they still need to be done under a general anaesthetic, and there is not yet enough evidence to show whether they will eventually be able to replace the standard operation.

What is used for the bypass grafts?

The most common types of conduit used in heart bypass surgery are an artery from the inside of your chest wall (internal mammary artery), an artery from your forearm (radial artery) or a length of vein from your leg (saphenous vein). If the left anterior descending artery (LAD) on your heart requires a graft, it is usual to use the internal mammary artery, unless there are specific reasons not to use it. The reason for this is that it has much better long-term results than if veins are used for this vessel.

There is good evidence that arterial grafts last longer than vein grafts, and that grafts from the internal mammary artery to the LAD last best of all. Vein grafts are known to develop signs of disease after ten years or so and for this reason may need to be replaced.

Will I be offered a bypass even though I haven't had a heart attack?

Bypass operations are occasionally done as emergency procedures following a heart attack, but in most cases they are offered to people with stable angina which is not responding to treatment, for protective reasons in high-risk narrowings, for uncontrolled angina or to people who have several very narrow or badly affected coronary arteries.

You may be advised to have coronary bypass surgery if you've had tests that indicate you have a high risk of having a heart attack in the near future or if your coronary arteries are so narrow or damaged that angioplasty is unlikely to be effective.

How effective is CABG?

It gives 95 per cent success in providing immediate relief from angina; in many of the remaining five per cent of patients their angina is improved or easier to control with medication. About seven in every ten patients who have a bypass operation get relief from angina that lasts for at least five years. The remainder find that the bypass improves their angina.

What are the possible risks and complications of CABG?

There are many complications that can occur after any type of operation, such as infections (particularly chest or wound infections), pain and bruising. Breathing deeply and coughing frequently will help prevent you getting chest infections.

Over 28,000 people have coronary artery bypass surgery in the UK each year. The most serious risk, although a relatively rare one, is that of dying after a bypass operation: about 3 in every 100 patients die within thirty days of a first operation. This risk of dying is dependent to some extent on how serious your heart disease is, how many coronary arteries were affected and how badly, and your general level of fitness before surgery. Some people can develop an irregular heartbeat (arrhythmia), bleeding, or blockage of the graft. There is a risk of heart attack or stroke during the operation or in the immediate post-operative period, and there is a risk in some susceptible patients of gangrenous bowel, kidney failure, pancreatitis, bleeding duodenal ulcers, deep vein thrombosis or pulmonary embolism (blood clots on the lung). Diabetic patients may experience instability in their diabetic control and are more prone to wound infections. Also, because cigarettes affect breathing, smokers have an increased risk of developing serious complications. Some degree of memory loss occurs in up to 5 of every 100 patients, but this usually improves within six months or so.

How likely am I to develop new coronary artery disease?

Although the diseased coronary arteries have been bypassed, it is still possible to have recurrence of angina. This may be due to blockage of one or more grafts or to the development of disease in previously unaffected coronary arteries. The risk depends on the length of time since the operation, the sort of graft used and how well your risk factors for coronary disease are controlled. Continuing to smoke after surgery is one reason why angina might recur. Roughly 40–50 per cent of patients will have some angina ten years after the operation.

Am I likely to need another bypass operation?

It is possible. A minority of patients will require repeat surgery, usually several years after their original operation, though the number of patients needing this is falling because the internal mammary artery has come into regular use and treatment for the underlying causes of the problem are improving.

Is there anything I can do to get help myself?

Taking the right drugs long-term is essential. But one of the most important ways to recover from heart disease and reduce the risks of further heart disease is to join a cardiac rehabilitation programme (see p.125). This involves structured training, advice and help in planning a healthy, low-fat diet to help reduce your cholesterol and blood pressure levels, controlling your weight, getting enough exercise and stopping smoking.

Are there any medicines I should avoid before surgery?

Patients should not take any medication that is not administered by a nurse prior to surgery. Some anti-anginal medications may need to be stopped before your operation – you will be advised by your surgeon or anaesthetist which these are. If you are taking diuretics or diabetes medication, do not take them on the day of surgery unless you are given them by the nurses. If you are taking warfarin, you will need to stop at least three days prior to admission as advised by your doctor. Aspirin and clopidogrel should be stopped five days before the operation. Check with your specialist about the correct way to stop your medication.

Heart valve disease

Some people are born with valve defects (congenital defects), which may cause no symptoms for many years. Other people develop valve problems later in life (acquired defects) following an infection such as rheumatic fever that affects the lining of the heart (a condition called endocarditis) or the valves themselves. Rheumatic fever is now rare, but because its effects often only come to light after 20–30 years, it's still the most common cause of serious valve problems in adults. The heart valves, especially the aortic valve, may also stiffen and narrow in old age, which can lead to blockage of the flow of blood through the heart.

How will heart valve problems be detected?

Some people don't know they have a valve problem until their doctor hears a 'heart murmur' when listening to their heart with a stethoscope. (However, murmurs can also sometimes be heard in normal hearts.) Symptoms may not develop for up to 20 years after valve disease has been diagnosed. People with known valve disease have regular assessment by a cardiologist and possibly tests to make sure that any developing problems are detected early. If your doctor suspects you have a valve defect, you may have the following tests (see pages 44–54 for details):

- An electrocardiogram
- An echocardiogram
- A chest X-ray
- Cardiac catheterisation.

How is it treated?

In many cases, the symptoms are minor and don't need to be treated. But even if valve problems don't cause any serious symptoms to begin with, they can put a strain on the heart muscle. Some people need to take drugs to control their symptoms or have surgery to repair or replace a damaged valve.

Can I be treated by drugs alone?

Although drugs can't cure valve defects, they can often control the symptoms.

- **Water tablets (diuretics)** relieve the collection of fluid in the lungs (lung congestion) and abdomen.
- **Digoxin** improves the heart's pumping efficiency.
- **ACE inhibitors** improve the flow of blood to the heart muscle and reduce its workload.

But if these drugs do not make your symptoms better or you have more serious problems, you may need surgery to repair or replace a damaged valve.

I've been taking drugs for my valve disease, but my doctor has suggested I now have an operation. Why is this?

The check-ups and tests you've been having may have brought to light a worsening of your condition (possibly following an infection), or your medication may not be controlling your symptoms as well as it was. If your heart is being put under an increased strain, it is important for the defect to be repaired before it causes irreversible heart damage.

Are there any precautions I need to take before surgery?

If you have any type of valve disease, your heart valves are susceptible to infection and you should therefore take antibiotics before having any dental or surgical treatment.

How long will I have to wait for surgery?

Your position on the waiting list will depend on the seriousness of your condition, although valve disease is usually more serious than routine coronary artery disease and should be treated in less than six months.

Can I speed things up?

If your symptoms get any worse, you should tell your doctor, as it may be possible to bring your appointment forward. You could let the surgeon's secretary know that you can accept someone else's cancelled appointment at short notice, or you could ask your GP if there is another surgeon who could do your operation sooner.

What surgery will I have?

If you have a leaky mitral valve that is not very badly damaged, it may be possible for it to be repaired, but if another one (or more) of your valves is affected, it will probably need to be removed and replaced. The surgeons may not know what is needed until he or she starts to operate. Operations for valve problems normally involve open-heart surgery, a heart-lung machine and a general anaesthetic.

There are several different ways of dealing with a diseased heart valve. Which you have will depend on which valve or valves are diseased and what exactly is wrong with them. The possibilities are:

Mitral valvuloplasty

If your valve doesn't open properly (stenosis), a catheter can be inserted through a small cut made in your groin after the area has been numbed by local anaesthetic. The catheter is then threaded through an artery and up into your heart, where a balloon at its tip is inflated inside the narrowed valve to stretch it. Further treatment may be necessary if the valve eventually narrows again.

Valve replacement

If the valve cannot be repaired, it will need to be replaced. This is particularly true of diseased aortic valves, which can only rarely be repaired. It is more common to be able to repair the mitral and tricuspid valves, but these also may need to be replaced if they are severely damaged.

Valve repair

The mitral and tricuspid valves can often be repaired to correct leakage or open up a narrowed valve.

What types of replacement valves are available?

'Biological' replacement valves can be from another human heart (homografts) or from the heart valves of an animal, usually a pig (xenografts). More often nowadays heart valves are made from the pericardial tissue of a pig. Pig valves are specially treated to make them stronger and to prevent them causing an immune reaction and being rejected.

There are also mechanical valves available, which are made of pyrolytic carbon, often in a metal ring.

What are their pros and cons?

Although mechanical valves last longer than biological valves, blood tends to clot around them and patients have to take anticoagulants indefinitely (see p.87) and have regular blood tests (about every six to eight weeks) to make sure they're getting the right dose. With biological valves, anticoagulants either only have to be taken for four to six weeks after surgery or can be avoided by the use of aspirin only, particularly in elderly patients.

Some people don't like the clicking noise made by artificial valves as they open and close, although most soon get used to the sound. Modern models are usually quieter.

Biological valves tend to wear out more quickly than mechanical ones and need to be replaced, which may make them less suitable for younger, active people.

How long will my replacement valve last?

A biological valve may have to be replaced after about ten years (80 per cent last at least ten to 12 years). Mechanical valves tend to last indefinitely unless they become infected or clotted.

How will the doctor decide which type of valve is right for me?

Your doctor will discuss the options with you and make a decision based on various factors, including:

- Your age
- The work you do
- Your level of physical activity
- How well your heart is working
- The size of the diseased heart valve
- How many valves need replacing
- Reasons you might not be able to take anticoagulant drugs
- Whether you need to take anticoagulants for other reasons
- Your personal preferences.

What are the possible risks and complications?

The complications are very similar to those after coronary surgery. For single valve replacements the risk of dying is around three to eight per cent but it depends on which valve and how ill you are beforehand. The risk of dying rises to eight to ten per cent when more than one valve has to be replaced. A special risk in valve surgery is of infection of the valve. This is rare but very serious when it happens. It may mean the operation has to be done again.

There is a risk of blood clots forming around your new valve (particularly if it is a mechanical one) so it is important that your anticoagulant treatment is set at the right level. If you are taking anticoagulants and the level is wrong there is also a risk of bleeding. If you had a valve infection before your operation, you will need to complete a six-week course of antibiotics.

If I have a mechanical valve, why will I have to take anticoagulant drugs for the rest of my life?

People with mechanical heart valves have an increased risk of suffering from potentially fatal blood clots on the valve.

Which drug will I have to take and how does it work?

Warfarin is the main anticoagulant drug and it regulates blood clotting. It reduces blood clotting by interfering with vitamin K, which plays a vital role in producing blood-clotting factors. Warfarin is taken as a daily tablet. It requires a expertise for your specialist to get the dose exactly right, and regular monitoring with blood tests is vital. If blood clots are not prevented, you can be at risk of a stroke, and if you have too high a dose, you are at greater risk of heavy bleeding and a possible haemorrhage. If you already have a blood clot, warfarin cannot dissolve it, but may prevent it from getting larger.

What do the blood tests show?

Blood tests done at an anticoagulation clinic or using a self-testing device monitor the International Normalised Ratio (INR), a measure of how much longer it takes the blood to clot when someone takes an oral anticoagulant.

Is there anything I need to do?

You should try to avoid extremes of activity, as they can affect how much the dose of warfarin reduces the clotting of your blood. Alcohol and some drugs such as antibiotics can affect the dose of warfarin needed, and you and your GP must be careful what you take.

Michael Kidron

When anybody asks me how I am, I always say, 'Ask my doctors.'
I've had two GPs over the last 50 years and I'm now so aware of
my condition there are very few weeks that I don't go. I have
almost everything you can imagine! I've had a heart valve
replaced, twice. I have what I think they call 'vascular disease' –
in other words, no blood in my toes! I've had a pacemaker for
two, maybe three years.

I think my first valve replacement must have been in 1988 or
1989, and the second one about ten or eleven years after that.
Having to re-replace valves is not expected but it's very likely.
The first was non-kosher, because it was a pig, or it might have
been a cow, and the second one was a human one, and I didn't
enquire whether or not they sent out a special party to hunt
sufficient numbers so that the actual valve would fit! After my
second heart operation I went to a rehabilitation class: we went
on machines, like cycling machines and walking machines, and
we walked around and did exercise.

When I was diagnosed as needing a pacemaker, I went to my
consultant, and when he asked, 'How are you?' I said I felt
pretty lousy and he looked at me and said, 'You are.' And then
he touched my chest and in a magical way knew what to do, put
me into hospital and had the pacemaker done. I don't worry
about it but I'm very conscious of it, you know, when I have a
shower or something like that and I dry myself and I've got this
bloody thing …

I've had lots of hospital stays, and it's changed. When I first
went into hospital here you went in for a time and so you could
bond slightly with the nurses and, you know, you had a social
time. Whereas now it's in, out, procedures … horrible. Another
interesting thing is the effect of the doctor's gender, or the
patient's gender on the doctor. You know, sometimes I think it's
a very bad idea that I have a woman doctor because I find her

attractive, and I don't want to lose her respect, so I don't complain about little things that might be important, whereas with a male doctor I couldn't care two hoots: 'Doctor, I couldn't cut my nails last night – what do we do about it?!'

My kids will be eight in January and the fact is that I can't play with them like an ordinary father. I can't do anything boisterous or very physical. They don't worry about it, but they're conscious of it because their mum tells them, you know, do this, don't do that, don't leave your toys on the floor because he'll trip over them and ... you know, various things like that. So those are areas that are quite difficult. But, you know ... one gets on with it.

I don't find that I'm constantly conscious of my heart, but I'm getting lazier and lazier, it takes me longer and longer to get dressed, not because I wear anything more elaborate but because it just takes time ... and I tend to 'pursue a posture' longer than I should!

My doctor says I have a mitral valve prolapse. What is this and what treatment will I need?

The mitral valve lies between the left atrium and left ventricle of your heart and has two flaps. In mitral valve prolapse, one or both of these flaps is slightly deformed and the valve is enlarged and unable to close properly, leading to leakage. Often, a heart murmur is the first sign that anything is wrong.

You probably won't need any treatment for this condition, although if it becomes severe, it may require surgery. A prolapsed mitral valve is a potential site of infection, and you will have to take antibiotics before having any dental procedures or surgery. A few people with mitral valve prolapse have angina or an arrhythmia (see p.18), which can usually be controlled by drugs.

If I need both bypass grafts and a valve replacement, will I need two operations?

No. Both will be done at the same time. The risk of the combined operation is higher than for either alone but less than having two separate operations.

Heart transplants

The first human heart transplant was done in South Africa in 1967 by Dr Christiaan Barnard. Although the patient died about 18 days later from pneumonia, the operation offered new hope to people with severe, untreatable heart disease.

What is a heart transplant?
A heart transplant is a major operation to remove the diseased heart and replace it with a healthy heart from someone whose brain is dead.

Why would I need a heart transplant?
If you have untreatable, irreversible heart failure and are at risk of dying, you may be eligible for a heart transplant. Your heart failure may be due to serious coronary artery disease, damage to your heart muscle, viral heart infection, disease unsuccessfully treated by a bypass operation, valve disease or congenital heart disease.

What factors determine whether I am eligible for one?
Before you are accepted for a heart transplant, a team of surgeons, cardiologists, nurses, social workers and transplant co-ordinators will assess you by considering:
- Your general health and fitness for major surgery
- Whether you have any other condition (such as emphysema or kidney or liver problems) that would rule out a transplant
- Whether you smoke
- Whether you're willing to take drugs for the rest of your life to help prevent the transplanted heart from being rejected by your body
- Whether you have any disease or addiction that would prevent you tolerating the anti-rejection drugs.

Are there any factors that would prevent me from being considered?
There are only a few things that would prevent you being considered for this operation. They include:

- Recent cancer
- An incurable form of an infection such as tuberculosis (rare), HIV infection, hepatitis B and C etc.
- Serious lung, kidney or liver problems that would increase the risks.

How long would I have to wait to get a heart transplant?
You may have to wait several years until a suitable donor is found. The waiting lists for heart transplants are long and donors are relatively rare. The most seriously ill patients are put at the top of the waiting list.

To be suitable, a donor has to have the same blood group as you do and be roughly the same size. Because a heart begins to deteriorate after about four hours when disconnected from the circulation, the donor will have to have died at a hospital within four hours' travelling distance from your transplant centre.

What does a heart transplant involve?
A heart transplant is a major operation which involves the use of a general anaesthetic. You will need to be placed on a heart-lung machine to keep you alive during the operation, and your heart will be detached from all its blood vessels and removed from your body. These vessels will then be re-attached to the donor heart, which may need to be electrically shocked to start it beating again. You will be given drugs to stabilise your heart rate and blood pressure and will then be taken to the intensive therapy unit (ITU) to recover.

What are the main complications possible after a heart transplant?
Rejection of the new heart, and infections occuring because the drugs used to combat rejection reduce your resistance are the main complications possible.

What drugs will I have to take and how long will I have to take them?
To stop the body rejecting the new heart, you will have to take a type of drug called an immunosuppressant for the rest of your life. Immunosuppressant drugs interfere with the body's immune

response and prevent the new heart being rejected. The most commonly used immuno-suppressant is cyclosporin, which you may be given in combination with another immunosuppressant drug and a steroid.

Are there any contraindications to cyclosporin?

This drug cannot be taken by anyone who is pregnant or breast-feeding. Also, you may not be able to take cyclosporin, or may need to have a lower dose, if you have or have had:

- Liver or kidney disease
- High blood pressure
- Treatment with an immunosuppressant or radiation therapy
- A serious, chronic medical condition.

What are the side-effects of cyclosporin and is there anything I should know about it?

Cyclosporin can cause:

- Kidney problems
- Increased blood pressure
- An allergic reaction, which may involve difficulty in breathing, swelling of the tongue, face or lips, or a rash
- A cough or fever
- Excessive tiredness
- Pain when urinating
- Nausea, vomiting or diarrhoea
- Unaccountable bleeding or bruising
- Seizures
- Tremors
- Numbness
- Loss of appetite
- Increase in body hair growth
- Bleeding or other gum problems.

You must let your doctor know immediately if you experience any of these effects. Because some of them can be serious, you will be closely monitored, particularly if you had kidney or liver problems before your operation.

Is there anything I need to avoid when taking cyclosporin?

You should not eat grapefruit or drink grapefruit juice, use an oral contraceptive or take calcium channel blockers while you are taking cyclosporin, as these all increase the level of the drug in the patient's blood possibly to a toxic level.

You should also make sure you tell your dentist you are taking cyclosporin and should never take any kind of medicine or over-the-counter drugs that you haven't been prescribed without first checking with your doctor.

How will cyclosporin affect my immune system?

Because the drug suppresses the immune system, you will be more susceptible to infections. Although urinary tract infections (which are common after many types of operation) are usually not very serious, wound infections and pneumonia can be life-threatening. You should tell your doctor immediately if you develop any of the following symptoms:

- Fever
- Sore throat
- Stomach pain
- Bleeding or bruising
- Pale stools
- Dark urine
- Sores in your mouth.

Also, if you develop a persistent cough, let your doctor know, as the immunosuppressant drugs can also make you more prone to a chest infection, which can be difficult to treat and potentially dangerous.

What are my chances of surviving?

About 85 per cent of people survive for a year after a heart transplant, and about 69 per cent of them are still alive after five years.

What about artificial hearts?

Artificial hearts have been implanted for some years but are still early in their development. Early models needed an external power source but newer ones are fully implantable. They still need some external batteries but there are no wires crossing the skin. In the UK they are not widely available.

Arrhythmias

What tests will I have for an arrhythmia?

Your GP can refer you to a specialist cardiologist who will arrange for you to be given any of the following tests, which are explained in detail on pages 44–54, in order to make a diagnosis.

- An electrocardiogram – possibly Holter monitoring and/or an exercise stress test
- A tilt table test
- An echocardiogram
- Cardiac catheterisation
- Electrophysiological testing.

What is the treatment for arrhythmias?

This will depend on the exact arrhythmia you have. Your symptoms will usually be controllable by medication (see p.69), although more serious arrhythmias may need a pacemaker or defibrillator to control your heartbeat (see p.96).

What happens if I don't have treatment for my arrhythmia?

If you have a serious arrhythmia such as ventricular tachycardia and don't have any treatment, you may run the risk of having a heart attack or stroke (blockage of a blood vessel in the brain) and possibly even dying.

What is a missed heartbeat?

A 'missed heartbeat' is really an extra irregular beat caused by the ventricles contracting too soon and interrupting the normal rhythm of the heart. There is then a pause while the heart gets back into its normal rhythm. Although usually harmless, the extra beat can cause more serious rhythm disturbances if it occurs often.

My GP says that my missed heartbeats are due to anxiety and won't give me any tests. Can I insist on having some?

You can always ask for a second opinion.

Does drinking coffee cause arrhythmia?

Caffeine increases the heartbeat and can cause tachycardia.

What is a pacemaker?

A pacemaker is a battery-driven device that is implanted in the chest and sends out electrical impulses to help correct an irregular heart rhythm. Although pacemakers are usually used to increase the rate of an abnormally slow heartbeat (bradycardia), they can also help steady an irregular heartbeat. Pacemakers are sometimes used externally as a temporary measure, for example if heart block occurs after heart surgery.

Why would I need one?

If the electrical impulse from your atria does not reach your ventricles (heart block) they can still continue to contract, but because your heartbeat is slow, less blood is pumped from your heart. This can cause breathlessness, fainting or blackouts. A pacemaker can control the contraction of the right ventricle (a single-chamber pacemaker) or of both the right atrium and right ventricle (a dual-chamber pacemaker).

How do pacemakers work?

The pacemaker comprises a power supply (normally a lithium battery) and electronic circuitry contained in a sealed, metal unit a bit smaller than a matchbox and weighing about 20–50g (1–2oz). It has either one or two electrode leads attached to it (a single-chamber or dual-chamber pacemaker, respectively), which are placed in the heart. These electrodes conduct electrical impulses from the battery to help the heart pump at a normal rate.

Are there different sorts of pacemaker?

Yes, several different types:

Fixed rate

These stimulate the heart with an electrical current at a fixed rate.

Demand pacemakers

These can pace at a variable rate depending on need. They can sense physical activity and increase the heart's rate just like the body normally would (rate-responsive).

Anti-tachycardia pacemakers

These can sense a rapid heart rate and use extra pacing beats to get the heart back into a normal rhythm.

Single-chamber pacemakers

These only pace either the atria or more usually the ventricles.

Dual-chamber pacemakers

These pace both the atria and ventricles with a short delay between them. This mimics the normal electrical impulse in the heart and sometimes helps the heart beat more efficiently.

What is an implantable defibrillator? Why would I need one?

A rapid heartbeat that starts in the ventricles (ventricular tachycardia) is a serious condition, particularly if the ventricles stop beating altogether and start to quiver (ventricular fibrillation). In this case your heart will stop pumping blood and you could die suddenly unless you receive immediate treatment.

An implantable defibrillator will monitor your heartbeat and control the irregular heart rhythm of ventricular tachycardia or ventricular fibrillation. Leads from the defibrillator are placed inside your heart to detect the heart's rhythm. They are connected to a small generator, which will be implanted under the skin of your chest or abdomen. Each time an abnormal rhythm occurs, the defibrillator sends out small electrical shocks to correct it. Sometimes a larger shock is necessary if the heart has gone into ventricular fibrillation, as there can be no delay in dealing with this.

How is it different to a pacemaker?

A pacemaker makes the heart beat faster so that it can pump enough blood to meet the body's needs. Some types control the heartbeat all the time, others only provide a tiny electrical charge when it slows below a certain rate. Although defibrillators (also called automatic implantable cardioverter defibrillators, or AICDs) are similar devices, they are used to slow a rapid heartbeat (ventricular tachycardia) or, if the heartbeat becomes so fast that the ventricles start to quiver (ventricular fibrillation), they give the heart an electric shock to restore its normal rhythm and rate. They usually have a pacemaker function built into them in case the heart stops after the defibrillation shock.

How do I know which one is right for me?

Your doctor will decide which type of pacemaker is best for you by taking into account the type of arrhythmia you have and the activities you want to be able to do. This decision will also depend on whether your heart needs an occasional 'kick start' to increase its rate or regular pulses of electricity to keep it beating fast enough.

Although individual requirements vary, these are the types of pacemaker that are most likely to be used in different conditions:

- Single-chamber pacemakers connected to the right ventricle are for arrhythmias that affect the electrical conduction (heart block)
- Single-chamber pacemakers connected to the right atrium are for problems affecting the heart's natural pacemaker but when there is no heart block
- Dual-chamber pacemakers are for when there is heart block but no problems affecting the heart's natural pacemaker.

How can I make sure I get the most advanced type?

Your cardiologist will give you the most appropriate type for your disease. This may not be the most advanced type as you may not need all the features of the latest models.

How long will I have to wait to have one?

This will depend on your symptoms and the seriousness of your disease but should not be more than a few weeks.

How is a pacemaker implanted?

Your pacemaker will probably be implanted through a vein (transvenous implantation). A small cut is made in your shoulder or at the base of your neck and, using X-rays as a guide, an electrode lead is inserted into a vein and threaded through into the appropriate chamber of your heart. This lead is then attached to the pacemaker, which is placed in a flap between your skin and chest muscle. The device is then tested and adjusted if necessary. The procedure only takes about an hour and is done under local anaesthetic.

An alternative is epicardial implantation, which is a surgical procedure to attach the electrode lead to the surface of the heart (the epicardium). The pacemaker itself is then placed under the skin in your abdomen.

Is the procedure to implant a defibrillator different from that for a pacemaker?

Most modern defibrillators can be implanted through blood vessels (transvenous implantation) in a minor procedure similar to that used for implanting a pacemaker, although surgery is still necessary on rare occasions.

What are the risks and complications of having a pacemaker inserted?

Although pacemaker implantation involves only minor surgery, it has the same types of risk as any type of operation, including an allergic reaction to the anaesthetic, infection and bleeding.

There's also a small risk of air leaking into your chest from your lungs during the procedure, but you'll be given X-rays before you leave hospital to check whether this has happened.

Occasionally, a pacemaker misfires, causing an irregular heartbeat. If you feel such palpitations, you should go to the A&E department of your local hospital or ring your cardiologist, so that your pacemaker can be checked.

After you've had a pacemaker inserted, you may still need to take anti-arrhythmic drugs (see p.69) to help maintain a normal rhythm.

What precautions should I take when I have a pacemaker?

Pacemakers are well protected by their metal case and can detect and filter out most types of external electrical activity. With a few exceptions (see below), the appliances you use in your home are unlikely to cause any problems. However, some people may come into contact with devices that produce strong electrical or magnetic fields and can interfere with the pulse generator, for example during their work. The main things to avoid are:

- the large magnets used in stereo loudspeakers (stay at least half a metre away)
- the magnets used in junkyards
- the powerful magnets used for MRI scans (see p.48) and some other medical tests and procedures
- arc-welding equipment (this gives out pulses that can turn your pacemaker off)
- power-generating equipment

- power plants
- working on a car engine while it's running.

If you use a mobile phone, always hold it to the ear on the side away from your pacemaker. Don't keep it in a pocket over your heart and make sure it is never closer than 15 cm (6 inches) to your pacemaker, even when it is turned off. The antenna on your mobile phone should never touch your body.

It is safe to use microwave if you have a pacemaker, as long as your microwave is less than ten years old.

You should tell medical staff that you have a pacemaker or defibrillator before you have any tests or treatment such as radiation therapy, and should also let your dentist know.

Although you can do most types of sporting activity, you shouldn't take part in any contact sports.

What is a temporary pacemaker?

A temporary pacemaker is sometimes used as an emergency measure, for example to treat heart block following a heart attack or tachycardia occurring as a side-effect of some drugs. It can also relieve symptoms before a permanent device is implanted.

What is a biventricular pacemaker?

Biventricular pacemakers control the pumping action of both ventricles, whereas standard pacemakers control the pumping action of either the right ventricle or the right ventricle and right atrium. Biventricular pacemakers help the ventricles to contract simultaneously and allow the left ventricle to pump more effectively. They are implanted in the same way as standard pacemakers.

Will my pacemaker or defibrillator set off alarms?

Although your pacemaker or defibrillator may set off security alarms, it shouldn't be damaged by the security systems used, for example, in airports. However, airport screening systems can cause temporary interference and you should tell security staff that you have a pacemaker or defibrillator so that a special arrangement can be made for you. The metal detector systems at the entrances to shops, libraries etc. may detect the pacemaker but won't do you any harm.

How often will the batteries need to be replaced?

Pacemaker batteries are designed to last six to ten years, defibrillator batteries anywhere from three to eight years. How long they last will depend on how much they are used. Both devices have a safety mechanism to warn you and your doctor well in advance (about six months) when the battery is starting to run low. You will have regular appointments to check the battery, but should let your doctor know immediately if you have any dizziness, fainting spells or chest pain so that the device can be checked.

What happens when my battery needs changing?

When your battery needs to be changed, the pacemaker will be removed in a procedure similar to the implantation operation, and a new unit will be put in its place. The electrode leads will probably be left as they are, or adjusted slightly if necessary. You may stay in hospital for a day or two or the operation may be done as a day case.

How often will I need my pacemaker or defibrillator checked?

Pacemakers are designed to work for several years, but you will have to have regular check-ups, probably every three to 12 months, to make sure the device is working properly. How often will depend on the type of pacemaker you have and how well it is functioning. It is now sometimes possible for pacemakers to be monitored by sending data from them to the hospital over the telephone. At each appointment, the battery will be tested and the effects on your heart will be checked so that any developing problems can be detected in good time.

What is a pacemaker registration card and do I need to have one?

A pacemaker registration card contains details of your pacemaker; it's useful to have one to show to your dentist or medical staff before you have any type of treatment so that any necessary precautions can be taken to avoid your pacemaker being damaged.

Will I be able to lead a normal life with a pacemaker?

Most people find their pacemakers comfortable and are able to lead active, normal lives and take part in sporting activities other than contact sports.

If you have a defibrillator, it is sensible to avoid doing anything that could put your life at risk should you collapse, for example, climbing up ladders or scaffolding or doing potentially dangerous sporting activities alone.

You may want to wear a Medic Alert bracelet so that, if you ever need emergency treatment, the medical staff will be aware that you have a pacemaker implanted.

Will I need to have a pacemaker/defibrillator for the rest of my life?

Almost certainly.

Congenital heart disease

'Congenital' means 'born with' – though the problem may not always be apparent at birth. The heart is a very sophisticated and complex pump. It develops very early on in pregnancy (it starts out as a straight tube) and by 12 weeks is fully formed and already pumping.

How common are congenital heart defects?
Approximately 8 in every 1000 babies born have a heart defect – some very simple which do not need any treatment, and at the other extreme, major defects for which the child will need a series of operations.

Can they be treated?
The results of treatment have improved dramatically over the years (the first open-heart surgery was in 1952), and now the great majority of children survive to adulthood.

Where can I get further information?
There are so many different types of congenital heart defects and treatments that it would be impossible to list them in enough detail in this book. The Children's Heart Federation (www.childrens-heart-fed.org.uk) is the umbrella organisation representing all the parents' groups. The British Heart Foundation (www.bhf.org.uk) website has a lot of useful information. GUCH (Grown Up Congenital Heart Patients) is an organisation for teenagers and adults with congenital heart disease and their website (www.guch.demon.co.uk) has a wealth of information. In this guide we provide you with information on main units treating children.

Having surgery

What will happen in hospital before I have my operation?
You will either be admitted to the cardiac surgical ward of the hospital the day before your operation or come to a pre-operative admissions clinic to have any remaining medical tests.

What tests will I have done?
Many of the tests you have will have been done before but must be rechecked in case they have changed. When you are admitted to the hospital ward, a doctor/nurse practitioner will ask you some questions, examine you, and check your details and the following tests:

- Blood tests to check your kidney and liver function, blood group, blood count (for anaemia, infections etc.) and blood clotting
- A chest X-ray
- An ECG (see p.45)
- A test to check your breathing (not all hospitals routinely perform breathing tests)
- If you have been on warfarin, he or she will have to check the level in your blood on admission, even if you stopped taking it several days before.

Who will be looking after me during my stay in hospital?
You will be visited on the ward by members of the medical team who will look after you while you're in hospital. These might include:

- The nurses who will be responsible for your care, from the wards, theatre and intensive therapy unit
- The surgeon who will do your operation and his assistants
- The anaesthetist – to discuss the anaesthetic and painkilling drugs you will be given, any allergies you may have, etc.
- A physiotherapist – to show you the breathing and coughing techniques you will need to use after your operation, particularly if you are a smoker
- Someone from the cardiac rehabilitation team – to discuss how you can help yourself to make a fast and complete recovery.

What is 'informed consent'?

Before your operation, you'll be asked to sign a consent form, which must also be signed by the doctor who has explained it to you. In signing this form, you are confirming that you understand exactly what your operation involves and agree to any necessary emergency procedures being carried out. You must be completely happy that you know all you need to know about the operation. If there is anything on the form you don't understand or are unhappy about, you must discuss this with the doctor before you sign it.

What does a heart-lung machine do?

In 75 per cent of cases, heart bypass surgery is done after the heart has been stopped temporarily, either electrically or by the injection of a solution with a high potassium content. A heart-lung machine is used to take over the work of the heart and provide oxygenated blood to the body's organs.

Who will be in the operating room with me?

Several specialist nurses and doctors will be involved in your operation, including:

- The surgeon and his assistants
- A cardiac anaesthetist
- A perfusionist – a specialist qualified in looking after the blood flow of patients when heart-lung machines are used
- Several surgical nurses
- Various technicians to look after the equipment in the theatre.

How do I know I won't be mixed up with another patient and have the wrong operation?

When the operating theatre porters collect you from the ward for your operation, the nurse on the ward should confirm who you are and what operation you are having. If this is not done in your presence, tell the porters your name and what you are in for and ask them to check that they are collecting the right person. Again, while you are in the anaesthetic room but before you are given the anaesthetic, ask the anaesthetist to check that the operating theatre staff have the correct information about you.

Will I be conscious when I go into the operating theatre?

If you are having a general anaesthetic, you will be put to sleep in a small room that leads into the operating theatre. If you are having a local anaesthetic, you will be conscious in the operating theatre. If you are anxious about this, talk to your consultant – you may be able to have a sedative to keep you calm. Drapes may be arranged so that you will not be able to see the operation being done.

Where will I be taken after my operation?

After a procedure such as angioplasty, you'll be taken to a recovery room so that you can be watched closely for a few hours. After more complicated procedures you will be taken to a special unit staffed by doctors and nurses who are experienced at looking after post-operative cardiac patients. This may be called an intensive therapy unit (ITU), an intensive care unit (ICU), or a cardiac recovery unit. These special units have the high nurse staffing levels and sophisticated medical equipment needed to monitor your progress for the first 24–48 hours after your operation.

What will happen when I come round from the anaesthetic?

The drugs used for your anaesthetic will make you sleep for a few hours – possibly until the next morning. When your doctors are happy that you are stable and not bleeding, they will allow you to wake up. You will have various tubes attached to you to help your doctors monitor your body's function, including:

- An endotracheal tube that passes through your mouth into your lungs and is attached to a ventilator, which breathes for you during and immediately after the operation. This will be removed as you wake up and are able to breathe for yourself
- A urinary catheter inserted into your bladder. This drains the urine and allows the amount you produce to be measured – an indication of how well your kidneys are working
- A couple of chest drainage tubes (the number varies) through which fluid can drain out, alerting the staff in case you are bleeding
- Several intravenous lines (tubes inserted into veins), through which you can be given any fluid and blood you require
- A tube in an artery in your wrist, to monitor your blood pressure

- A tube in your neck, to check the pressure of blood entering your heart. This can help tell how well your heart is working and allows blood samples to be taken easily and painlessly
- Possibly a nasogastric tube, inserted through your nostril and leading into your stomach to drain it and help stop you feeling sick
- A device on your finger or ear that measures the level of oxygen in your blood (oximeter).

Will I be in any pain?

You can expect to have some pain for a few days after your operation, but you'll be given medicine by the nurses to relieve it, either by injection or tablets. If you feel any pain or discomfort, tell the nursing staff, who can adjust your medication.

When will the tubes be taken out?

You should be able to come off the ventilator and be able to breathe normally as soon as you are awake enough. The other tubes will gradually be removed, with the aid of painkillers, over the next couple of days, as soon as your body becomes able to function normally without them.

Where will I go when I leave the ITU and what will happen?

If everything has gone well, you will return to a cardiac surgical ward the day after your operation. If you are recovering more slowly, you may be transferred to a high dependency unit before returning to the ward.

A physiotherapist will visit you in the ITU to show you how to take deep breaths and to get rid of any fluid in your lungs by deep breathing exercises and coughing. When your condition is stable and your doctor is sure that you're not in any immediate danger, you will be taken to a cardiac surgical ward or a high dependency unit. Your breathing will continue to be checked and you will probably be able to start eating and drinking again. When you are able to drink enough to keep up your fluid level, the intravenous lines will be removed. You may get indigestion or a bloated feeling in your stomach for a few days, until your digestive system settles down again.

Modern anaesthetics don't usually cause as much nausea and vomiting as the older ones used to, but you will have been under the anaesthetic for a long time so if you do feel sick, there are tablets and injections you can be given. You may have constipation for a few days, but if necessary you can be given a mild laxative.

When will I be able to walk again after my operation?
Most people can get out of bed and walk around the ward with the help of a nurse and physiotherapist on the day after their operation. Don't try to get up without help, as you will probably feel quite faint to begin with. As the days pass, you will gradually be able to walk a little further.

When will my stitches be taken out?
Some surgeons use stitches that gradually dissolve and therefore don't need to be removed. If your wounds have been closed with non-dissolvable stitches or with clips, a nurse will take these out before you go home, along with any stitches holding your chest drains in place.

At the end of surgery, either wires or sutures will have been inserted to hold the bone together and allow it to heal. These will remain in place permanently and rarely cause a problem. The wires are stainless steel, do not rust and will not affect airport security scanners. The wounds will heal and other stitches will dissolve over a period of three to six weeks.

What will my relatives be told?
Your relatives will have been warned about all the tubes and monitoring equipment you will be attached to after your operation and that you will be asleep for the first few hours and breathing with the aid of a ventilator. They will also be told that they can ring the ward at any time to find out how you are and will be able to visit you when you are on the cardiac surgical ward, although you are likely to be very tired and their visits should be kept short for the first few days. If you agree they may also be given more detailed information about your condition.

How long will I be in hospital?

After angioplasty you may be able to go home later the same day or the next morning, and will not be in hospital for more than a couple of days. However, if you have had angioplasty as an emergency treatment during a heart attack, you will probably have to stay in hospital for a few days. Similarly, after having a pacemaker fitted you will have to stay in hospital for one or two days and can probably return to doing your normal activities after two to four weeks.

More complicated operations require longer stays. Most people stay in hospital for between five and ten days after heart bypass surgery or eight and ten days after valve surgery. After a heart transplant you can expect to stay in hospital from two to three weeks after your operation if you suffer no complications.

What needs to happen before I can go home?

Before you go home, a doctor will examine you and do some tests to ensure everything is OK. Your physiotherapist will make sure that you can walk up and down stairs safely.

Hospital staff will also want to be sure that there will be someone at home to help look after you for the first couple of weeks. If there is no one who can stay with you, arrangements can be made for a district nurse and/or home help to visit you regularly for a few days.

A cardiac rehabilitation nurse may visit you on the ward (although this service is not universally available) to give you advice and information about any rehabilitation programmes or heart support groups in your area. It is a Government requirement, set out in the National Service Framework (NSF) for coronary heart disease that all eligible patients are referred for rehabilitation on discharge from hospital. You will be given enough medication to last you for several days and a letter for your GP with details about the drugs you need (which your GP will prescribe for you) and any other information concerning your treatment.

What you can do

Fortunately, there are a lot of things that you can do to reduce the risk of heart disease including giving up smoking, keeping your weight and your alcohol and salt consumption down, taking exercise and learning to manage stress. Your GP can treat your high blood pressure with drugs, which will probably have to be taken indefinitely. Once your blood pressure comes down, so does your risk of heart disease.

Very often, there is no obvious cause of high blood pressure (essential hypertension), but being overweight, eating too much salt, drinking too much alcohol, smoking, stress and not getting enough exercise all raise blood pressure levels.

There are many risk factors in ischaemic heart disease that are unavoidable, but knowledge of them can help develop preventative measures.

- **Age.** The arteries become less elastic with age, which increases the risk of developing ischaemic heart disease and high blood pressure.
- **Gender.** Although ischaemic heart disease is more common in men than in women below the age of 65, it is now a major cause of death amongst older women in Britain (see 'Women and heart disease' p.21).
- **Family history.** Some genetic (inherited) factors can increase people's risk of developing ischaemic heart disease, such as having a naturally high cholesterol level or high blood pressure. These risks are greater if you have one or more close relatives (mother, father, sister or brother) who had a heart attack before they were 60.
- **Race.** Some ethnic groups are more likely to suffer from heart disease. Afro-Caribbean people are more at risk of developing high blood pressure, and south Asian people have a greater risk of developing diabetes (see below), both of which are risk factors for heart disease. People of south Asian descent have a much higher death rate from heart disease (46 per cent higher for men and 51 per cent higher for women) than the rates for the UK as a

whole, whereas those of Afro-Caribbean descent have a 25–50 per cent lower death rate from heart disease. They are, however, more liable to suffer from stroke.

- **Body shape.** People with an 'apple shape', that is extra weight around their waists (called central obesity), particularly men, have a greater risk of heart disease than people with a 'pear shape' or extra weight around their hips, because the apple shape makes the heart work harder than it should. This shape also accelerates atherosclerosis. Body shape tends to be inherited, but central obesity can also be caused by a condition known as insulin resistance, which leads to diabetes.

- **Diabetes.** People with diabetes have three times the normal risk of developing heart disease. Diabetes affects the nerves involved in sensing pain, so if you have diabetes, you may have silent ischaemia without being aware of it. Diabetes commonly affects people with 'apple-shaped' fat distribution and those of south Asian origin.

- **Lung disease.** People with diseases that affect the lungs also have an increased risk of developing heart disease.

- **Social group/occupation.** Manual workers (such as builders) are three times more likely to die early from heart disease than non-manual workers (such as lawyers), and this rate is falling faster for non-manual workers, thus increasing the difference. Wives of manual workers have nearly twice the risk of wives of non-manual workers. Although there are some genetic reasons too, socio-economic grouping (and 'Westernisation' in general) accounts for the fact that Afro-Caribbeans and Asians living in the UK are more likely to suffer from heart disease than the UK population as a whole.

Risk factors that can be avoided or reduced:

- **Build-up of cholesterol.** The liver produces cholesterol from the saturated fats in food. Too much of this type of cholesterol in the blood causes fatty deposits to build up in the coronary arteries, leading to atherosclerosis and the risk of heart disease. You should aim to have a low level of low-density lipoprotein (LDL) cholesterol (found in foods containing saturated fats) and a high level of high-density lipoprotein (HDL) cholesterol (found in foods containing unsaturated fats). Most people have high cholesterol levels due to preventable lifestyle factors such as a diet high in saturated fats, too much alcohol or increased stress levels. If your cholesterol levels are high despite a good diet or because you have an inherited disease, such as familial hyperlipidaemia, an underactive thyroid or kidney failure, your GP will give you cholesterol-lowering drugs such as statins (see p.56) as well as dietary advice to help. There are two ways of developing high cholesterol level: through cholesterol you take in via your diet and through the cholesterol that your body manufactures. Thus, even if you eat a healthy diet and are thin, you can still have a high cholesterol level. This is particularly true in some families where it is hereditary. The longer you have high cholesterol, the higher the risk of you developing heart disease. If you reduce your cholesterol level when you are young by just ten per cent, there is a 54 per cent reduction in the incidence of heart disease when you are older. This reduction drops to just 27 per cent if you don't change your dietary habits until you are 60 and only 19 per cent if you reduce your cholesterol when you are 80.

- **Being overweight.** If you are overweight you have a direct risk of heart disease or stroke, and an increased risk of developing diabetes in middle age. Fat builds up around the heart, making it work harder than it should, and for every extra stone you put on, blood has to be pumped along an extra 20 miles of veins and arteries. Because carrying around extra weight makes you tired, it also makes it harder to exercise.
- **Lack of regular exercise.** The heart is a muscle and responds like any other muscle to exercise, becoming stronger and healthier with regular activity. Exercise, particularly aerobic (cardiovascular) exercise, helps the tissues of the body to extract oxygen from the blood, reduce the amount of fats in the blood and increase the metabolic rate – all of which mean a healthier heart.
- **Smoking.** Cigarette smoke contains carbon monoxide and nicotine, which have harmful effects on the heart. Nicotine stimulates the body to produce adrenaline, which increases the heartbeat and raises the blood pressure temporarily, increasing the risk of blood clot formation. Carbon monoxide cuts the amount of oxygen the blood can carry around the body to the heart, which can lead to chest pain and angina. So when you

smoke, your heart is having to work harder and yet is getting less oxygen. Smoking also hardens the arteries, making them less flexible and increasing the risk of developing aortic aneurysms.

- **Poor diet.** If your diet is poor, you are more likely to become overweight and to have raised cholesterol and blood pressure levels than someone who eats healthily.
- **Drinking too much alcohol.** Moderate drinking can help protect against heart disease, but heavy, regular drinking and binge drinking poison the heart muscle, making alcohol a definite risk factor. In general, the more you drink, the higher your blood pressure becomes.
- **High triglyceride level.** Triglycerides are the most common type of fat in the blood and are produced in the liver. There is more medical debate about triglycerides than about cholesterol, but a high level of triglyceride encourages blood to clot, and so is associated with an increased risk of a heart attack and stroke.
- **Stress.** How and whether stress contributes to the development of heart disease is not entirely clear. However, stress causes the liver to release cholesterol into the blood along with adrenaline, which affects the immune system. It is also associated with high blood pressure.

What can my GP do to help me?

Your GP remains responsible for your care and, even after you have seen the consultant, will often work with him or her as a team and will continue to look after your other health needs.

You should have your cholesterol level tested regularly by your GP, at least once every five years for adult men and women past the menopause, to spot any changes. It is measured by a blood (or fingerprick) test (measurements are in millimoles per litre of blood – mmol/l). As levels vary from day to day and at different times of the day, a fasting measurement (ie a measurement taken after a period without food) will usually be needed. The target level is 5 mmol/l of total cholesterol and less than 3 mmol/l of LDL cholesterol.

Alternative treatments

Is there any evidence that complementary medicine can help people with heart disease?

Complementary medicine includes a lot of the diet and lifestyle advice given to people with heart disease, such as stress management and relaxation techniques, which do seem to help reduce some of the symptoms of heart disease. Your GP may also be able to give advice on which complementary medicines may be helpful.

Can complementary medicine prevent heart disease?

If you already have problems that may lead to heart disease, you will need drugs to deal with them effectively.

Can complementary therapies cure heart disease?

No. Although dietary advice, exercise and stress management techniques, acupuncture and vitamin supplements may help to prevent further damage to the heart and arteries, there is no evidence to suggest they can reverse damage that has already occurred.

Are there any dangers in taking complementary medicines?

It is possible that having too much of certain substances in your body (such as iron) can do more harm than good, so check with your doctor first. Some herbal preparations, such as St John's Wort, ginseng and ginkgo biloba, interact with other medications or can have side-effects including raised blood pressure and bleeding. Consult your GP before taking any of these or reducing the dosage of any medicines you have been prescribed.

Can food supplements make a difference?

Daily Vitamin E supplements have been shown to reduce the risk of a heart attack for people who already have atherosclerosis, and there have been suggestions that dietary supplements of folic acid and Vitamin B may help reduce damage to the artery walls. Antioxidant Vitamins A, C and E, which are found in fresh fruit and vegetables, may help to protect against heart disease as they reduce the effect in the body of molecules called free radicals, which cause chemical reactions that can damage cells, including those in the heart. Other supplements that may be of help include Vitamin D, magnesium, Vitamins B12 and B6 and grape seed extracts. However, it is not yet known whether vitamin supplements have the same effect as eating these substances naturally occurring in foods.

Are there any herbal remedies that can help my heart disease?

Hawthorn has long been considered a potent heart tonic. It relieves the chest pain of angina, lowers high blood pressure, helps the heart to pump more efficiently in people with heart disease and can correct an irregular heartbeat.

Are there any side-effects?

Hawthorn is widely regarded as one of the safest herbal preparations. Side-effects may include nausea, sweating, fatigue and skin rashes, but these are rare. Hawthorn appears to be safe to use with drugs prescribed for heart disease; you may even need less of some heart medications while you are taking it.

What is ginkgo biloba for?

This popular herbal medicine is promoted as a memory booster and it is thought to help protect the heart.

Are there any side-effects or dangers?

Unprocessed ginkgo leaves, including teas, contain potent chemicals that can trigger allergic reactions, so make sure you select standardised extracts (GBE) in which the allergens have been removed during processing. Rarely, ginkgo can cause irritability, restlessness, diarrhoea, nausea or vomiting, but these effects are usually mild and transient. People starting to take the herb may also notice headaches during the first day or two. If side-effects are troublesome, discontinue ginkgo or reduce the dosage.

Are there any treatments that will lower my blood pressure?

Some people use acupuncture to help lower their blood pressure. Scientists at the Medical College of Georgia in the US discovered that practising transcendental meditation daily significantly lowered people's blood pressure by keeping the blood vessels open.

Can transcendental meditation help with stress?

Studies support evidence suggesting that stressed people and those prone to mood swings are at greater risk of heart disease. Transcendental meditation helps people to remain optimistic.

I have heard that soya can lower my cholesterol – is this true?

There is evidence that regular intakes of soya can help to lower cholesterol. However, unless you are vegetarian, it is unlikely that anyone would eat enough soya to have a significant effect, but every little may help.

I have heard garlic can help prevent clogging of the arteries. Is this true?

There does seem to be some evidence that taking a daily garlic supplement can reduce your level of cholesterol.

Is there anything I can take after heart surgery?

Arnica is often recommended to help reduce bruising after heart surgery – although there is no clinical evidence that it is effective – and Vitamin C helps wounds to heal.

What is chelation therapy?

Chelation therapy is normally used to treat poisoning by heavy metals such as lead and mercury. It involves injecting into the blood a synthetic amino acid called EDTA, which combines with the metal so that it can be passed out of the body in the urine.

As the plaques that develop in the arteries in atherosclerosis contain calcium, it has been suggested that chelation therapy might be able to remove the calcium from these deposits, so that plaques break up.

Does it work?

Although some people have reported an improvement in their general health after chelation therapy, it is more likely that this is due to the lifestyle changes, such as giving up smoking and improving their diet, which are also encouraged by the therapists using this technique. Scientific studies of the effects of chelation therapy on atherosclerosis have not provided any evidence that it is more effective than a placebo, ie injecting a fluid that does not contain EDTA.

Does chelation therapy have any harmful effects?
There is a danger that chelation therapy can have harmful effects on the heart, respiratory system and kidneys – such as causing cardiac arrhythmias, respiratory arrest and kidney failure – and its use has also been linked to deaths.

Will I be offered it on the NHS?
As there is no scientific evidence that chelation therapy works, it is not available on the NHS. Most people who offer this treatment privately recommend up to 30 treatment sessions (each lasting two to four hours) in the first month, followed by one treatment per month thereafter, so it is expensive.

Are any complementary therapies offered on the NHS?
Complementary therapies are not usually offered to heart patients on the NHS.

Rehabilitation

Recovering from surgery

What are common problems after surgery and what can I do?

- Loss of appetite, indigestion and constipation are normal for a few days after surgery, but will gradually improve as you start to move around and your digestive system settles down. Try to eat something at each meal.

- Tiredness after open-heart surgery may last up to six weeks.

- Reduced sense of taste: many people have a metallic taste in their mouth or find that all food either tastes the same or is tasteless. This problem will disappear with time.

- The general anaesthetic can cause nausea or sickness, but tablets or injections will help relieve this.

- Sore throat and loss of voice due to bruising of the tissues by the tubes in your mouth – will settle down after ten to 14 days.

- Some pain, stiffness and discomfort in your chest and shoulders are also normal, but will gradually improve.

- Suddenly feeling hot and cold, and night sweats, may occur until your temperature regulation settles down again.

- Some people worry about the wound in their chest opening up again, but the stitches or clips used to close it are strong enough to keep it secure even when you cough.

- There may be a small amount of discharge from the wound (which may be blood-stained) for a few days. If this is heavy, your dressing will need to be changed regularly by a doctor or nurse when you are in hospital, or by a district nurse who will visit you once you're at home again.

- Swelling of the leg and ankle is common after coronary bypass surgery if a vein has been removed from the leg; this can be reduced by wearing a special support stocking.

- Most people have days when they feel a bit depressed or anxious and some have very vivid dreams or nightmares, both of which will pass in time.

- Visual disturbances such as blurred vision, spots before the eyes and visual hallucinations may occur. It is advisable to wait three months before having your eyes tested.

- Memory loss of varying degrees and difficulty concentrating can occur, but usually last no more than about six months.

What kind of drugs will I be given?

After any kind of heart surgery, you may have to take one or more of the drugs listed on page 55–71 (some of which you may already have been taking) to lower your risk of having more problems in the future. After a heart transplant, you'll have to take an immuno-suppressant drug to stop your new heart being rejected (see p.92).

How long will it be until I am up and about?

You'll probably be helped to get out of bed by a nurse and physiotherapist on the day after your operation and will be able to sit on a chair. You will gradually be encouraged to walk a little further around the ward over the next few days including up and down stairs. Once you're at home again, you should take it easy for the first two or three days, moving around inside your house no more than you did in hospital and having plenty of rest.

After this, you can start to do more exercise, possibly going out for a short walk with someone else if the weather is good enough. You may feel discomfort in your chest, neck, back and shoulders to begin with, which is normal as the muscles and bones in your chest heal. Painkillers will help you to increase your level of activity gradually but steadily. Any shortness of breath will also improve in time.

What should I be looking out for when I go home?

You may have days when you feel depressed, anxious and even bored, but you shouldn't worry, as these are normal reactions to a major operation, which will gradually get better. However, if you still feel depressed after a couple of months, you should discuss this with your doctor, who may arrange counselling or other therapy for you.

Do remember that you should try to increase your activity gradually and steadily, and don't push yourself too hard. Also, don't exercise after a heavy meal or outside when it's very hot or cold.

Some pain and discomfort are inevitable as your wounds heal, and it is common to feel numbness and sometimes itchiness in a leg wound in the weeks after the operation. Let your doctor know if you develop any of the following signs:

- severe shortness of breath
- palpitations that get worse or that start for the first time
- dizziness
- heavy sweating or fever
- swelling or an oozing discharge from your wound.

How should I care for my wound?

Caring for your wound after you have been discharged from hospital consists of simple cleansing with soap and water a couple of times each day. You don't need to cover the wound with a dressing unless it is oozing, which shouldn't go on for more than a few days after the operation. Strangely, more people suffer problems from a leg wound due to heart bypass surgery than from the chest wound. Swelling around the incision in your leg is often present for about three months following surgery, until the other veins have taken over the job of the missing vein. To reduce swelling:

- Keep your leg elevated any time you are not exercising. Try to keep your ankles above your knees and your knees above your hips. This helps extra fluid in your legs become reabsorbed.
- Wear support stockings.

Can I wear my bra after the operation?

You should wear a bra if possible from the second day after your operation, as the muscles supporting the breasts will have been divided whilst opening the chest. If you find the bra is uncomfortable over the wound, try placing a pad under it to stop it rubbing.

Will my scar fade?

Yes. Initially the scars may not look very pleasant, but they will fade over a period of months, although they will not disappear completely.

My heart races and skips a beat. Should I be worried?

This can happen and should not hinder your recovery. If this has been detected during your time in hospital, you will have been prescribed tablets that control your heartbeat. If it becomes a noticeable problem at home, however, tell your GP. Remember that coffee, alcohol and other stimulants can lead to an increased heart rate (see p.19).

I have a persistent cough, which gets worse at night. Why is this?

A physiotherapist will show you how to do deep breathing and coughing exercises after your operation to make sure your lungs are fully expanded and kept clear of fluid. You may feel anxious about breathing deeply because of the wound in your chest, but it is important to do the exercises you are shown. Even so, you may find that you cough, particularly at night when you are lying down and breathing more shallowly. If you become shorter of breath, you should see your doctor, as you may have developed a chest infection.

Why do I have to take water tablets?

Water tablets (or diuretics) help reduce swelling due to the collection of fluid in the body after heart surgery by increasing the amount of urine. They may be used in combination with digoxin and/or ACE inhibitors and with beta-blockers to treat heart failure (see p.58).

Getting back on your feet

Following a period of recovery, most people find that their lives can continue pretty much as normal after a heart attack or heart surgery. Most people are able to return to their normal jobs. It will probably take about two or three months for your body to get over the heart attack or the operation.

However, after a heart attack, if your heart has been more seriously damaged, you may continue to feel a bit breathless and tired and suffer from attacks of angina after this time. You should tell your doctor if you develop any of these symptoms or if they get worse. After coronary artery surgery you should no longer suffer from angina, although some people (around five to ten per cent) still have some.

You will probably have to take some drugs, for example to control your blood pressure or cholesterol levels or to help prevent blood clots forming, possibly indefinitely. You may also need to take a serious look at your lifestyle – the amount of exercise you do, your eating, smoking and drinking habits – and make some changes to reduce your risk of further heart problems (see p.110).

Anger, frustration, guilt and depression are just some of the emotions you – and members of your family – may experience, but these are normal after any life-threatening event or major surgery and they will pass in time. If they continue for more than two or three months, you should ask your doctor's advice about ways to deal with them.

Many people find that their experience makes them take stock of their lives and think about what is really important to them. Some take up new hobbies and activities following heart surgery. Whatever your reaction, patience, a positive attitude and a sensible approach to your health should enable you to lead a full and active life. Don't try to do too much to start with, but build up your physical activity gradually and learn to relax and to avoid or deal with stress.

What is cardiac rehabilitation and should I join a programme?

The aim of cardiac rehabilitation programmes is to help people with heart disease or who have had heart surgery to make as full a recovery as possible. They are useful for people with all types of heart disease, whether it is mild or severe, and usually involve exercise, relaxation techniques and lifestyle advice. The evidence shows that cardiac rehabilitation programmes dramatically improve people's life expectancy after a heart attack or heart surgery, reducing deaths by as much as 20–25 per cent over three years. You may be asked to join a cardiac rehabilitation programme if you have:

- stable angina
- congestive heart failure
- a heart attack
- angioplasty
- a coronary bypass operation
- a heart transplant
- a heart valve replacement
- a pacemaker.

A rehabilitation programme can improve the function of your heart and your quality of life, reduce your risk factors for further heart disease and help you feel optimistic about your future. Even if you are severely limited by your heart condition and can't do much exercise, you will at least start to regain your confidence.

When will I find out about the programme?

If you're having heart surgery, someone from the cardiac rehabilitation team may visit you before your operation and again before you leave hospital to tell you about the rehabilitation programme you can join and to give you advice about how to speed your recovery. If you haven't already been invited to join a programme, ask your GP for details of any that are run in your area.

Will cardiac rehabilitation be available at my hospital?

Cardiac rehabilitation programmes should be available to everyone (see p.126). However, they are not run by all hospitals. If there isn't one at your hospital, ask your doctor for details of any that are available in your area or of any heart support groups that may run similar programmes.

What are the NHS recommendations concerning cardiac rehabilitation?

The NSF for Coronary Heart Disease has published the goals that should be met by all cardiac rehabilitation services. Briefly, these are that every hospital should ensure:

- that more than 85 per cent of people discharged after a heart attack or coronary revascularisation should be offered cardiac rehabilitation.
- that one year after discharge, at least 50 per cent of patients should be non-smokers, exercise regularly and have a body mass index less than 30 kg/m^2 (ie not be seriously overweight).

The NSF recommends that cardiac rehabilitation should begin as soon as possible after admission to hospital, continue through the early discharge period and the rehabilitation programme, and extend to ensure that the best possible health is maintained in the long term.

What should I expect from my rehabilitation?

Rehabilitation programmes typically run for about six to 12 weeks, and you should join one as soon as possible after a heart attack or heart surgery (see above), for one or two sessions per week. Many people find cardiac rehabilitation programmes useful because in them they don't have to worry about how much exercise they should be doing, and can ask questions as problems arise.

Rehabilitation programmes vary from hospital to hospital, but most involve the following:

- An exercise programme tailored to your specific needs and abilities (you may have an exercise ECG [see p.46] to assist with this).
- Counselling to make sure you understand what your disease involves and how best to manage it.
- Advice about how to reduce your risk factors, such as giving up smoking, losing weight if necessary, eating healthily and controlling diabetes.
- Advice about returning to work.
- Emotional support.
- Someone to talk to about depression, stress, sexual problems and the need for social support.

Your own particular needs will be taken into account when your programme is planned. Perhaps the most important factors in its success are your motivation and the amount of effort you put into it.

Who will I see as part of my rehabilitation?

Arrangements will be made for you to see anyone who can help you during your rehabilitation. The rehabilitation team will probably include:

- nurses
- physiotherapists
- occupational therapists
- dieticians
- psychologists
- job counsellors
- doctors.

When will I start cardiac rehabilitation and how long will the programme be?

You should be able to join a cardiac rehabilitation programme about four to six weeks after surgery, and will probably go once or twice a week for six to eight weeks, although some programmes last longer than this. The sessions may take place at your local hospital or at a centre near you.

Should my partner/family be involved in the rehabilitation process?

Ideally partners should be equally involved in the rehabilitation process as it will help them understand your needs. Family and friends can help by giving you support and any practical assistance you may need.

Who will co-ordinate my care once I have left hospital?

Your GP will co-ordinate your care after you have left hospital. Always talk to them if you're concerned about anything. If you aren't given details about a cardiac rehabilitation programme before you leave hospital, your doctor will also be able to advise you about this. You will also be given a follow-up appointment to see the surgeon a few weeks after your discharge.

Will I be offered counselling as part of my rehabilitation?

Many people with heart disease experience some degree of anxiety and depression, and some may lose their confidence and self-esteem. These are normal reactions, but they do need to be talked through with a trained counsellor. Although medication can help someone with depression in the short term, it should be avoided if possible and should only be taken while arrangements are being made for you to see a counsellor.

You will almost certainly be offered counselling as part of a rehabilitation programme, and should not be embarrassed to take advantage of it to discuss any fears or anxieties you have, however trivial they may seem.

Is there any other support available to me?

The British Heart Foundation is a good independent source of information, advice and support. The Foundation employs seven cardiac support advisers, whose role is to promote and encourage patient support groups. Contact the British Heart Foundation (see p.248) for details of a support group in your area. There are many local support groups, for example, British Cardiac Patients Association Zipper Clubs or other local groups.

There are local heart support groups in many areas, which give people recovering from a heart attack or heart surgery and their families the chance to talk to people who have had similar experiences. Some of these groups also run exercise classes and organise talks on medical and general topics.

Why do I have good and bad days rather than making a steady improvement?

It's normal to feel depressed and disheartened on some days and more optimistic and positive on others. Having a heart attack or heart surgery is a stressful event and, although you may be glad to get home again after having been in hospital, many people find it a worrying time too, because they no longer have the security of all the monitoring equipment and trained staff.

Your recovery will be a gradual process and sometimes the improvement you're making may seem imperceptible. Don't expect to make too much progress too fast, but be realistic and persevere. If you still feel depressed after a couple of months, talk to your doctor about counselling to discuss what's causing it. And remember, the good days will start to outnumber the bad in time.

Could my medication be contributing to my depression?

Some of the drugs you may have been prescribed can cause tiredness and some have other minor side-effects that may be affecting the way you feel and contributing to your depression. Tell your GP about your concerns, as it may be possible for you to be given another drug that doesn't have these effects.

What steps can I take to avoid further heart problems?

The steps you take to lower your risks of further heart problems after a heart attack or surgery are called secondary prevention. They should help you to live longer, improve your quality of life and make it less likely that you will need further medical treatment such as angioplasty or bypass surgery. You need to stop smoking, watch your diet and take plenty of exercise. If you have high blood pressure, diabetes or high cholesterol level you will need to take the appropriate medication to make sure they are under good control.

What medication am I likely to be on and why?

Your drug treatment will depend on your specific problems. Some drugs have more than one effect, so you may be given any of these:

- An angiotensin-converting enzyme (ACE) inhibitor after a heart attack or to help control your blood pressure
- Aspirin, or another antiplatelet drug such as clopidogrel, to help stop blood clots forming, or
- An anticoagulant, such as heparin or warfarin, if you are not able to take aspirin for any reason
- A beta-blocker (for at least six months) to help control your heart rate and rhythm, lower your blood pressure and manage angina
- A cholesterol-lowering drug, probably one of a group of drugs called the statins
- A calcium channel blocker, such as nifedipine or verapamil, to help control your heart rate and/or reduce your blood pressure
- A diuretic, such as frusemide or spironolactone, to treat heart failure and/or control your blood pressure

- An anti-arrhythmic drug, such as digoxin or amiodarone, to control the rhythm of your heart
- A nitrate to relieve or prevent angina attacks
- A drug to reduce your blood pressure, such as an alpha-blocker, methyldopa or moxonidine.

Will this be different from the medication I'm already taking?

If your blood pressure, blood sugar and cholesterol were well controlled before your operation or heart attack, you will probably continue on these drugs, but if not you may be given others in place of or as well as these.

I always feel sick after taking my tablets. Is there anything I can do to help this?

Yes. Try taking the tablets after food, but do not do this if the label tells you to take them before food. Tell your GP. He or she may be able to change them to something that does not upset your stomach.

How will my lifestyle be affected?

For the first few weeks after a heart attack or surgery, you will have to take things fairly easily and gradually increase the amount you do.

When you have recovered from your heart attack, you will be able to do most of the things you want to do – swimming, bicycling, walking, jogging, gardening and having sex – although you will probably be advised not to do sports such as playing squash or weightlifting. You should avoid going out in very cold weather or walking at high altitude or after a heavy meal. The important thing is to learn to recognise when you have done enough and to stop if you become breathless or get pain in your chest. Do not push yourself too hard. After your wound has fully healed, you should be able to do anything you want to, but if you do feel chest pain, tell your doctor.

When will I be able to go back to work?

After angioplasty most people can return to work within five to seven days, although if your job involves heavy manual labour, you will probably need to wait a bit longer. After a heart attack, if your job does not involve any strenuous activity, and you have made an uncomplicated recovery, you will be able to go back to work from four to 12 weeks or about two months after heart surgery. About 50 per cent of people who have had valve surgery are able to go back to work within three months and 80 per cent within a year, most of them to their previous jobs. However, if your job involves heavy manual labour, you will have to wait for at least three months, so talk to your GP first.

Questions to consider before returning to work
- How physically strenuous is your job?
- How stressful is your job?
- Does your work involve long hours or overtime?
- Will it be possible to arrange to work flexible hours?
- Can you change to part-time working?
- How will you deal with talking about your experience to workmates or colleagues?

To find out more about your employment rights and/or answer questions about safety and health at work, contact your cardiac nurse, GP, personnel officer or a cardiac support organisation.

Questions to ask your doctor
Your GP can give you advice about what you can do to lower your risk of further problems. Everyone is different, so do not worry if the advice you are given is different from that given to someone else who has had a heart attack or heart surgery. Questions may include:
- What regular physical activity is suitable for me?
- What is my ideal weight?
- Are there any diet and exercise programmes that are particularly appropriate for me?
- Do I need to take an aspirin daily to help prevent blood clots?
- Can you recommend any methods to help me stop smoking?
- What can I do to help control my blood pressure and cholesterol levels?

Are there any tests I should ask my GP to do?
Your GP can do a test called a fasting lipid profile to measure your cholesterol level and should check your blood pressure regularly, although how often will depend on how elevated it is and how well it is responding to treatment.

Dr Robin King

In 1998 I woke up in the middle of the night with a horrendous pain in my chest. I called out to my wife, who was in the first stages of frontal lobe dementia, to help. We rang up an emergency doctor who said, 'Go and see your GP in the morning.' We later realised that this was the first heart attack.

In mid-December we had some friends to stay and when it happened again we were persuaded to call an ambulance. This was my second heart attack. I went into hospital, had all the treatments, the drugs etc. I recovered, went home and the same night I had another heart attack. So I spent the Millennium in hospital, which was fine with me as I never wanted to celebrate the damned thing in the first place! While I was in I had the usual treadmill test and an angiogram and the cardiologist suggested I have an angioplasty. At this point I decided to go private, and my treatment has been private from then on.

The cardiologist did the angioplasty, found one blockage and put a stent in it. He found another blockage and tried to stent it but it was just after a bifurcation and he couldn't stent it – the stent just kept slipping round the healthy bit of the artery. I came out of hospital and went home, but some time later I had another slight pain in my chest, in the middle of the day, with some sweating and difficulty breathing. I got an ambulance straight away, but it was diagnosed as unstable angina – not another heart attack, thank God!

My cardiologist, Simon Joseph, who has since become a close personal friend, suggested I go into hospital for another angiogram, perhaps because of the angina. He came into my room to give me the results and said, 'I think a bypass is necessary – I have a surgeon outside who can do it for you.'

So I had a single bypass. All these people boasting about their triple and quadruple bypasses – they're lucky to have enough arteries to support them! I've only got one! Still, I'm lucky to have 30 per cent of my heart working – some people only have ten.

I always felt very well prepared and there was no difference between NHS and private as Simon was my cardiologist for both types of treatment. One thing that was important, though, was the courtesy. Simon always insisted that his students refer to patients as 'gentlemen' or 'ladies' no matter who they were.

So in April 2000 I had CABG and then I went home and cared for my wife. She had had a lumpectomy for breast cancer some years earlier, but died of a secondary tumour in her liver. It was better really, rather than waiting for the dementia … We were lucky, we had 50 years of wonderful married life then three years of looking after her. It's relevant to my heart condition, as the stress was obviously having an effect. For example, I remember one night, she was up and down, up and down, something wrong with the corner of the duvet, until I finally shouted at her to leave the duvet alone, and you know, it's not a tone I liked to use, but that's how stressful it was.

After the first six months of grieving for her I definitely began to feel better. We had moved house before she died in order to be closer to my daughter and son-in-law. I felt so much better I went round and decorated the whole house!

But I used to have bad angina. On my scale, it was a five out of ten, where one is bearable and ten is dead. It was really, really unpleasant. But since my life has changed, removing the stress of my wife's illness, among other things, it has disappeared, showing that heart disease is a lot to do with stress. I have four times as much energy now. Instead of mowing the lawn in two bites, now I mow the lawn, prune the trees and wash all the windows!

When will I be able to drive again?

If you have made an uncomplicated recovery after a heart attack or surgery, you should be able to drive again after about four weeks. If you have had a pacemaker fitted, you must not drive for at least a week after (longer if you have any symptoms) and should let the DVLA know before you start to drive again.

If you have had a heart attack or any surgery other than that to implant a pacemaker and you have an LGV or PCV licence, you will not be able to drive for at least six weeks. You will have to have an exercise test before driving again, so contact the DVLA before returning to LGV (large goods vehicle) or PCV (passenger-carrying vehicle) driving. If you have an LGV or PCV licence and you have had a pacemaker implanted, you will not be able to drive for three months and will have to renew your licence every three years and attend a pacemaker clinic at regular intervals.

However, if you have recurrent ventricular arrhythmias for which a defibrillator has been implanted, you may not be able to drive again in the UK. Your case will have to be considered by the DVLA. If you have been given a defibrillator for less serious heart problems, you will have to wait at least six months before driving.

Will it affect my car insurance?

After any heart surgery you should check with your insurance company to make sure that your insurance is still valid. The British Heart Foundation has a list of insurance companies where you can get information about this.

When can I go on holiday?

After your heart operation you may find it helpful to go on holiday. A restful holiday in the UK is fine at any time, but doctors suggest you don't fly anywhere for a minimum of six weeks following an operation. Some airlines say that if a journey is essential following an uncomplicated heart attack, you may fly as early as two weeks afterwards. Follow the advice of your doctor, airline and travel insurance company and check your holiday insurance – you may need a letter from your doctor to validate it.

If you are taking warfarin, you need to inform the anti-coagulation clinic of your plans so they can advise you of the appropriate dose to take whilst on holiday, and remember to protect your scar from the sun with at least factor 25 sun cream as it will burn more easily than your normal skin.

You should take precautions to reduce the chance of developing a blood clot in the leg (deep vein thrombosis – DVT). Wear your compression stockings when travelling and take your aspirin regularly before travelling.

How will my condition affect my relationship?

Although you will probably be afraid of overdoing it and making your condition worse, your partner may be even more anxious than you are, and so may be over-protective, making you feel frustrated or dependent. It is important not only that you both get advice about what you can and cannot do, but also that you talk to each other about how you feel so that your relationship is not affected.

And don't forget that it may not only be you who feels tired and occasionally depressed in the early days of your recovery. Your partner may also get run down and have emotional highs and lows and will need time to relax and take stock.

When can I have sex again?

There is a myth that people who have had a heart attack or heart surgery have to give up sex. You can have sex again when you feel well enough, although you will probably be advised to wait two or three weeks after a heart attack and about four weeks after an operation if your recovery has been uncomplicated. A good yardstick is when you can walk about 300 yards on level ground or climb two flights of stairs without getting chest pain or becoming breathless. You should be able to have a normal sex life, although if you are recovering from heart surgery, you will need to make sure that you are in a comfortable position and avoid putting pressure on your chest wound or restricting your breathing.

Anxiety may make things a bit difficult to begin with, so it is a good idea to prepare yourself by making sure you are relaxed and comfortable, waiting one to three hours after a meal and first taking any medicine you have been prescribed. Don't forget that your partner may also feel anxious. If you do have any problems, talk to your doctor, who may change your drugs or be able to give you advice.

Are there things my partner should be aware of?

Your partner may be even more anxious than you are about you having another heart attack or hurting yourself after heart surgery, and may try to do too much for you. You should both have had the chance to talk to your doctor about what you can and can't do.

You may be a bit irritable or depressed in the early stages of your recovery, and it may help your partner to deal with this if he or she knows that it is a normal reaction and will soon pass.

Try to make sure that your partner understands the reason for any hesitancy you feel about having sex and knows that he or she is not to blame if you experience any problems because of anxiety or the drugs you are taking.

I have difficulty sleeping at night. Why is this?

One possibility is that your sleep pattern may have become disturbed by unfamiliar routines during your stay in hospital. Sometimes it is due to some ongoing wound discomfort, and a painkiller before going to bed might help. Alternatively, sleeplessness is often a symptom of anxiety, stress or depression. It might help if you learn some relaxation and deep breathing techniques. If the difficulty continues, talk to your doctor about counselling or therapy to help you deal with the emotional distress that is causing it.

I am so tired all the time. Is there anything I can do about it?

It is normal to feel tired after a major operation or heart attack, but this feeling should gradually improve over the weeks as you get your strength back. If it doesn't, discuss it with your doctor. Make sure that you are not trying to do too much too soon, and that you pace yourself and learn to stop doing things before you get breathless or feel any chest pain. You may be having too many visitors, which is likely to tire you out in the early stages of your recovery, so make sure that you have enough time to rest.

How much exercise should I do?

You should build up the exercise you do very gradually until you are doing at least half an hour of aerobic exercise three to four times a week, which could be split into two 15-minute sessions. Aerobic exercise includes brisk walking, cycling and swimming. It increases your heart rate and breathing and exercises your heart. Five to six weeks after the operation, you may be walking two to three miles at a good pace. Cycling and swimming can be introduced after about eight weeks if your wounds have fully healed.

Don't push yourself too hard, and always work within your own limits, stopping if you have any chest pain or feel breathless. Also, remember to carry prescribed medicines with you when exercising. You will find that you can gradually do more and more as the weeks pass.

Should I avoid certain kinds of exercise?

Don't do anything that involves heavy lifting for the first few weeks of your recovery. People with heart disease should not do isometric exercises, such as weightlifting and press-ups, or play games like squash. Regular exercise is much better for your heart than intermittent bursts of activity. If you are in doubt about anything that you want to do, ask your doctor or the professionals assisting you on your cardiac rehabilitation programme first.

What kind of diet should I follow?

After a heart attack or heart surgery, you may be able to talk to a dietician about what you should be eating and you can certainly ask your GP or cardiac rehabilitation team for advice. A healthy diet will help you to control your weight as well as your blood pressure and cholesterol levels. The main points to bear in mind are:

- Eat at least five portions of fruit and vegetables a day
- Eat oily fish or fish oils once or twice a week
- Eat less fat
- Eat more starchy foods
- Eat less salt
- Keep to a healthy weight.

I get palpitations a couple of days after drinking heavily. Why is this?

One of the effects of alcohol is to cause an irregular heartbeat, which is probably why you get palpitations. Alcohol also interferes with the anticoagulant medication many people have to take after a heart attack or heart surgery, and so can be dangerous.

How much alcohol can I safely drink?

Drinking too much alcohol is also a direct risk factor for heart disease. The effects of alcohol are exaggerated by any sleeping tablets, tranquillisers or painkillers you may be taking. You should therefore drink no more than about a pint of beer or two glasses of wine a day.

What about smoking?

Smoking is one of the major risk factors for heart disease. Smoking after a bypass operation increases the risk of the grafts failing or new disease developing to give you your angina back again.

Will lowering my stress level really make a difference?

Stress causes some of the same symptoms as heart disease – such as tiredness, palpitations, breathlessness and chest pain – and makes the heart beat faster and the blood pressure rise. Therefore reducing your stress can certainly help to reduce the workload on your heart and circulation.

Frequently heard 'facts'

Research has shown that people's beliefs and misconceptions about their health affect the way they look after themselves. It is therefore important for the myths surrounding heart disease and the causes of heart attacks to be dispelled, so that you can take the necessary steps to reduce your risks of developing problems or of making any existing problems worse. Heart disease is largely preventable, and many people could reduce their risk of being affected by it simply by making the lifestyle changes described on pages 111–112.

You're more likely to die from cancer than from heart disease.
False
Heart disease is the main cause of death in the UK (and in many other Western countries) and, despite the huge advances made in its treatment in recent years, it is also still responsible for a significant amount of illness and disability. It causes more deaths each year than all types of cancer combined. Recent American statistics indicate that the average life expectancy would increase by nearly ten years if all the main types of heart disease were eliminated.

If you suffer from angina, you should stop doing any type of physical exercise.
False
Exercise and physical activity are an important part of the treatment of the symptoms of angina. If your angina attacks are brought on by exertion, you probably feel that doing as little physical activity as possible might prevent them occurring. However, this will only lead to you becoming less fit, which makes it more likely that you will have an attack of angina whenever you do exert yourself, thus reinforcing your reluctance to exercise. Also, giving up a physical activity you enjoy because you have developed angina could lead to you becoming depressed, and thus increase your symptoms.

You will gradually learn how much and what type of activity you can do without triggering an attack, and your doctor will be able to discuss this with you and give you any necessary advice.

If you survive a heart attack and make a full recovery you now have the same chance as anyone else of having another.

False

Your risk of having another heart attack is greater than normal, particularly if you're a woman (women have a 31 per cent chance of having a second heart attack within six years, compared to 23 per cent for men). You also have an increased risk of developing angina, heart failure or even of dying suddenly and should take the steps described on pages 111–112 to reduce this risk and improve the health of your heart as much as possible.

Red wine is good for people with heart disease.

True

It certainly appears to be the case that a moderate amount of alcohol – one or two units a day (one unit = half a pint of beer or lager, or one small glass of wine or a small measure of spirits) – reduces the risk of developing heart disease or having a heart attack, but this is true for all types of alcohol, not just red wine. Red grape juice is unlikely to have the same effect, because it is the flavonoids in alcohol that seem to be responsible. Flavonoids are antioxidants, which are thought to reduce the effect in the body of molecules called free radicals. These molecules cause chemical reactions that can damage cells, including those in the heart, and it has been suggested that they play a part in heart disease, amongst other problems. It isn't really known how alcohol exerts its beneficial effect, although it does raise the level of 'good' HDL cholesterol (see p.111) in the blood.

It is safe to drink alcohol while taking heart medication.

True in some cases

It is usually all right as long as:

- the label on the bottle does not say 'avoid alcohol'
- your doctor has agreed that alcohol will not affect your illness
- you only have one or two drinks and do not drink to excess.

Viagra increases your risk of having a heart attack.

True

You must not take Viagra unless you have a healthy heart, as it affects your blood pressure. The nitrates in medications such as those taken for angina (see p.59) react with chemicals in Viagra to make the blood pressure drop suddenly. This can cause dizziness, fainting or even a heart attack or stroke. Make sure you speak to your GP before taking it.

Smoking low-tar cigarettes will reduce your risk of heart disease.

False

The two most harmful substances contained in any type of cigarette smoke are carbon monoxide and nicotine. Carbon monoxide starves the muscles of oxygen, including the heart muscle. Nicotine stimulates the body's production of adrenaline, which makes the heart beat faster and increases the blood pressure, both of which put a strain on the heart.

Smokers are twice as likely as non-smokers to have a heart attack and are more likely to die as a result of it. Smoking is also the greatest risk factor in sudden death from heart disease: it is estimated to be responsible for about 20 per cent of deaths from heart disease amongst men and 17 per cent amongst women.

Your risk of having a heart attack is dependent on the amount you smoke and on the age at which you started to smoke. Giving up smoking is probably the most important step you can take to reduce your risk of getting heart disease or of having a heart attack.

Smoking cigars or a pipe is less harmful than smoking cigarettes.

Partly true

Your risk of dying from heart disease is increased if you smoke cigars or a pipe, although possibly not to the same extent as it is if you smoke cigarettes. The harmful substances described above are also present in the smoke from cigars and pipes and it is not possible to avoid inhaling any smoke at all.

Stress causes heart disease.

Possibly true

Although there is no evidence that heart disease is caused by stress, it does seem that if you already suffer from angina, excitement or distress can trigger an attack. Stress makes your blood pressure increase and your blood vessels constrict, which, if you have coronary artery disease, can cause plaques in the arteries to break loose and block the flow of blood to the heart, resulting in a heart attack (or a stroke if they block the arteries to the brain). Stress also tends to make people drink, smoke and possibly eat more than normal – all of which are risk factors for heart disease.

Depression increases the risk of heart disease.
Possibly true
Although the link between depression and heart disease is unclear, it does seem that people who have suffered from clinical depression (particularly men) have an increased risk of developing heart problems – sometimes many years later. Long-term depression seems to be less of a risk, possibly because people learn to adapt to the stress it causes. Women seem to be less likely to develop heart disease associated with depression, perhaps because they deal with it in a different way. Depression can increase your blood pressure, cause an irregular heartbeat and possibly even a heart attack, but studies indicate that the risks appear to be greater for men over the age of 70 when they experience depression for the first time. It is also possible that people who become (and remain) depressed after a heart attack may be at increased risk of having another, although some doctors dispute this.

Loud noises can bring on a heart attack.
True in some cases
It is very unlikely that being startled by a sudden noise will cause you to have a heart attack – unless you already have severe coronary artery disease or another serious heart problem. A sudden loud noise can increase your blood pressure and make your arteries constrict, which could result in a heart attack if plaques already present in your coronary arteries break off and block the flow of blood to your heart.

Drinking tea reduces the risk of having a heart attack.
Possibly true
Tea contains flavonoids (a type of antioxidant also present in alcohol, see above) and various studies have suggested that drinking one or more cups of tea a day can help reduce the risk of having a heart attack.

Certain types of sexually transmitted disease can trigger heart disease.

True

Studies have shown that the bacteria chlamydia, which can infect the reproductive and urinary tracts of both men and women, can trigger an autoimmune response in some people that may cause inflammation of the heart muscle. There appears to be a protein in chlamydia that stimulates the body to launch an immune response, which can also be directed at a similar protein in heart muscle. As chlamydia infections are common and not all people who suffer from them develop heart disease, it is possible that vulnerable people have a particular gene that makes them susceptible.

Complaints and legal action

If you are unhappy with the care you have received in hospital or from any of your doctors on the NHS, you have a right to complain. It is best to complain as soon as possible – certainly within six months. If you have been treated privately, you should refer to your private hospital's complaints procedure.

How do I complain about the treatment I am receiving from my GP?

In the first instance, you may want to complain directly to the person concerned, or if you don't feel able to talk to him or her, with a member of staff such as the nurse. Doctors take complaints against themselves or other members of their practice very seriously, and most complaints can be dealt with satisfactorily within the practice itself. If this is not the case and you're not happy about how your complaint is dealt with, you can take it further by making a formal complaint (see p.146). Serious complaints, about a criminal act such as sexual assault, should be reported to the police immediately.

What should I do if I am unhappy about my hospital stay?

It is always best to talk to a doctor or nurse immediately, as most problems can be sorted out on the spot. If your complaint isn't dealt with satisfactorily, ask to speak to a more senior member of staff. If you are still not satisfied, you may choose to make a formal complaint.

To whom should I complain?

If possible, speak to someone close to the cause of your complaint – this may be a doctor, nurse, receptionist or anyone you think is appropriate. Hopefully they will be able to sort it out or arrange for someone else more senior to speak to you.

What if I do not feel able to speak to someone?

Each Trust has a special team to deal with complaints – write to the Complaints Department. The reception staff or the ward clerk should have a leaflet giving details.

How soon should I complain?

If you have a concern, you should complain as soon as possible – the longer it is after the event, the more difficult it is to sort out a complaint.

How will the hospital react if I complain?

The NHS in general, and your local hospital in particular, will welcome your complaint if it helps them improve services – staff want to provide you with the best care. However, they are human and things do not always go according to plan.

Will complaining affect any further treatment I might have?

Your views are important to those providing your healthcare. It is only by knowing what they are that services can be tailored to the needs of patients. It is your right to complain if you feel you have been treated poorly or unfairly, and you should never be afraid that it will affect your treatment or the services you can expect.

What should I do if I feel my complaint is being ignored?

If you have been treated by the NHS and feel your complaint still has not been dealt with to your satisfaction, you may wish to make a formal complaint to the NHS Trust's chief executive. The first step in doing this is to contact your local Patient Advisory and Liaison Service (PALS). These are the local watchdog bodies which were set up in 2002 to replace Community Health Councils. They are there to give you on-the-spot confidential advice and support. Each Trust has a PALS team – they can listen to concerns, help sort out problems or simply provide information. A friend or relative could contact PALS on your behalf, although they must have your written permission to discuss your case.

Local Resolution is the first stage of a formal complaint, carried out by the Complaints Manager in hospitals and the practice manager at your GP's surgery. PALS will help you draft a letter, helping you describe clearly and concisely what your complaint is and explain what you want done about it. If you agree, PALS can arrange a meeting to try to resolve matters as quickly as possible. If you still aren't happy with the response, the Complaints Manager can carry out further investigations on your behalf.

The following questions will help you to focus:

- Who are you complaining about?
- Where do they work?
- Who do they work for?
- What are you complaining about?
- When did it happen?
- What are your main concerns?
- What do you hope to achieve from making a complaint? An apology? An explanation? Action to put things right? Compensation?

Where else can I get help and advice about making a complaint?

At any point in the process you can also contact other organisations for help and advice. You can get more information about making a complaint by phoning NHS Direct on 0845 4647 or checking their website on www.nhs.direct.nhs.uk

Another source of support is the Patients Association. You can discuss your problem with a trained volunteer adviser on their helpline 0845 608 4455 between 10 am and 4 pm Monday to Friday. All calls are charged at local rate. Alternatively, you can email them with details of your experience at www.patients-association.com

What if I am unhappy with the response from the NHS Trust?

You will receive a letter in response to your complaint from the Chief Executive. If you are not happy with this, you should write back explaining why. If you are still not happy with the response, you can request an independent review within 28 days. You will receive details of how to do this with the Trust's formal response to your complaint. The Complaints Officer or PALS can give you the address of the closest Independent Convenor in your area who can review your complaint. The Convenor can ask the Complaints Manager to re-investigate, and where necessary can set up an Independent Review Panel to try to resolve your concerns. The panel will talk to all concerned and produce a short report which will be sent to you and the Chief Executive of the NHS Trust.

Note that if the problem concerns the treatment you have received in hospital, you need to complain within six months of your stay in hospital or, if it only became apparent later, within six months of your becoming aware of it. A written complaint to the NHS Trust should be acknowledged within three days and you should be informed of the outcome of the hospital's investigation within 20 days, although this doesn't always happen.

I'm still not happy. Is there anything else I can do?

If you're still not happy, you can contact the Ombudsman (Health Service Commissioner), who acts independently of both the NHS and the Government. However, you can only involve the Ombudsman if you've already followed the complaints procedure described above and have written evidence of doing so. It is useful to get some help from PALS in preparing your case for the Ombudsman. It is not necessary to involve a lawyer. The website www.health.ombudsman.co.uk contains a form which you can print out and use if necessary. Alternatively, telephone or write to: The Health Service Commissioner for England, 11th Floor, Millbank Tower, London SW1P 4QP. Tel 0845 015 4033.

Why not just sue the hospital/doctors/nurses?

Most people say they only want an explanation and an apology and an assurance that the same thing will not happen to someone else. The complaints process should be able to provide these things. However, some patients feel they deserve compensation (money) for injury they have received. Although a 'no fault' compensation system has been proposed for the UK (and already exists in some countries) this is still under debate. The legal process is rather complicated. For the moment, to receive compensation, a patient has to prove negligence. The case is heard in a civil court and therefore the standard of proof is the 'balance of probabilities' rather than 'beyond reasonable doubt' as in the criminal court.

What do you mean by negligence?

This is a legal term and the onus is on the claimant (patient) to prove it. First a 'duty of care' has to be shown – that is the standard of care that should have been given by the doctor, nurse or other hospital staff. Then you have to show that there has been a 'breach of duty' – that the standard of care given was less good than it should have been. The standard against which care is judged (when judging a doctor) is what 'a responsible body of medical opinion' would have done. It is important to note that this is the 'ordinary' not the best (you cannot expect perfection). It is important to note that a genuine mistake is not negligence.

If the doctor was negligent, do I get compensation?
No, not necessarily. You have to prove that the harm you suffered was the direct result of the 'breach of duty of care' and this is not always the case.

I think that doctors cover up for each other!
Our court system is an adversarial one – this means that each side fights hard, not only to defend their own side but also to find fault with the other side's case. So things can get very unpleasant. In many areas of medicine, care is based on opinion rather than evidence, and so doctors will have genuine differences of opinion over what was best. This adversarial legal system means that doctors often seem to be reluctant to apologise for fear of admitting that something went wrong – even though their defence organisations encourage them to apologise if mistakes are made.

How does this affect the NHS?
Billions of pounds of NHS money meant for patient care are used both in defending cases and in paying compensation. The Bristol Royal Infirmary report concluded that the present system was not fair for either patients or staff – the Department of Health is currently conducting a review of the medico-legal process.

I feel I have been treated well – is there any point in saying so?
Most patients feel this way and tell the staff before they leave – this is always appreciated. Trusts have recently started doing surveys of patients chosen at random to see how well they are doing and the results help to balance the information gleaned from complaints. If you feel you have had particularly good treatment, then write to the Chief Executive and say so – this will be fed back to the staff and is good for morale.

Your local services and specialists

How to use the data

NHS CARDIAC UNITS

Indicates what type of surgery is available at the cardiac unit – adult cardiac (C), adult thoracic (T) and/or paediatric cardiothoracic (P) surgery.

This tells you if the hospital has a CT (computed tomography) scanner on site. These produce sophisticated X-rays for bone and soft tissue.

This tells you whether the hospital has an MRI (magnetic resonance imaging) scanner, which are considerably better than normal X-rays for imaging soft tissues.

This tells you if the hospital has both a CT and an MRI scanner.

The most commonly used and effective treatment for a heart attack is thrombolysis. This is the use of clot-busting drugs to dissolve the blood clot blocking the artery. These drugs (streptokinase, alteplase and reteplase) are given by an infusion directly into a vein. The key point about thrombolysis is that it should be undertaken as soon as possible, and ideally within an hour of a heart attack (although it may still be of benefit up to 12 hours later). Because the effectiveness of thrombolysis reduces rapidly with time, much emphasis has been placed on reducing 'door-to-needle' time, ie the time from arriving in hospital to being given a clot-busting drug. The Government's National Service Framework (NSF) sets a door-to-needle target time of 30 minutes. To meet this target it is important that the assessment of all patients with chest pain occurs rapidly and that an ECG is performed within minutes of arrival in hospital.

Coronary angiography is a relatively specialised procedure and carries a small risk of serious complications. Centres performing these procedures should carry out a relatively large number of them to allow the medical team to gain experience. The NSF states that centres performing coronary angiography should aim to perform 500 cardiac catheterisations per year by at least two operators. This icon indicates which hospitals meet the first of these standards.

Waiting times and volumes

This data is derived from Hospital Episode Statistics for the year ending March 2001, and relates to Trusts in England, rather than individual hospitals. However it should be borne in mind that in almost all Trusts, cardiothoracic surgery usually takes place in one main hospital or centre.

Waiting times shown for England are for a first outpatient appointment with a cardiologist or cardiothoracic surgeon. The figure given is the percentage of people seen within the target time of 13 weeks from the time of the GP's referral. Waiting times for Wales relate to the quarter ending September 2002 and show the percentage of people seen within three months from time of referral. Where these are not available, '-' appears. Waiting times and volumes were not centrally available for the unit in Northern Ireland.

Remember that the waiting time you experience will depend upon the urgency of your condition, so you may be seen much more quickly if this is necessary. Also, as average waiting times are falling, there is a good chance that your hospital will have better waiting time performance at the time you read this. However, the numbers do give an indication of which hospitals are likely to have longer or shorter waiting times than other hospitals.

We have not given any inpatient waiting times because changes to the way waiting times are managed has made available information no longer relevant. In particular, the government has introduced a new initiative under which anyone waiting more than six months for heart surgery is given the option of going to another hospital – NHS, private or even abroad – to have their operation sooner.

The volumes shown for each procedure are defined as:
Frequent – ie performed at least once a month. As an example, this means that units would perform over 200 coronary angioplasty procedures a year, thereby meeting the NSF annual target of 200.
Very high – ie performing approximately 650–1,500 coronary angioplasty procedures per year.

For units in Scotland we have provided volumes and the average waiting time (in days) for these procedures. This data relates to discharges where the procedure carried out was the main one. Volumes include both elective and emergency cases. These figures were provided by NHS Scotland for the year ending March 2002.

Mortality rates
We give figures on mortality rates for two procedures – coronary artery bypass graft (CABG) and aortic valve replacement. For each procedure we give two figures. The first is a standardised mortality ratio which indicates whether the death rate is higher or lower than would be expected given the profile of the patients treated. A figure of 100 indicates a mortality rate in line with expectations. A figure of 200 would indicate a rate twice what was expected. The degree of statistical confidence in the significance of the figure depends on a range of factors, such as the number of patients treated. We indicated whether we can say with 95% confidence that the result is significantly higher than average (H), lower than average (L) or in the average range (A). The mortality ratios are calculated by Imperial College of Science Technology and Medicine and are adjusted to take account of the age, sex and length of stay of the patient, as well as whether or not the patient was an emergency admission, an elective admission or a transfer. They cover the three years to March 2001.

We also give the underlying raw mortality rate, expressed as a percentage of the patients treated who did not survive the operation. These figures are taken from the Society of Cardiothoracic Surgeons' National Adult Cardiac Surgical Database Report 2000/01. These figures are calculated on the year to March 2001.

List of cardiothoracic surgeons

This indicates the cardiothoracic surgeons working at the unit. Surgeons have been allocated to their primary NHS hospital. For details of their sub specialties, special interests and research interests please see the cardiothoracic surgeon index on page 233.

PRIVATE HOSPITALS

(C/P/T) See explanation on page 152.

(CT) See explanation on page 152.

(MRI) See explanation on page 152.

(X) See explanation on page 152.

(!) This indicates that the hospital accepts urgent admissions.

(♥) We tell you if the hospital has physiotherapists trained in cardiac rehabilitation.

Volumes

Figures for the number of angiography, angioplasty, CABG and pacemaker procedures performed were reported directly by the hospitals.

Cardiothoracic surgeons at private hospitals

For a list of cardiothoracic surgeons please refer to the private hospital surgeon listing on page 244. Further information about them can be found in the cardiothoracic surgeon index on page 233. Please note that surgeons may work at more than one private hospital but in most instances have been allocated to their primary private hospital.

DISTRICT GENERAL HOSPITALS (DGH) IN ENGLAND, WALES AND NORTHERN IRELAND

See explanation on page 152.

See explanation on page 153.

This tells you if the hospital has a coronary care unit. These are specialised wards in hospitals where patients who have had heart attacks are nursed. They are also used for patients recovering from heart bypass surgery and for anyone who is seriously ill with a heart condition. The main attributes of a CCU are the specialised training of its nursing and medical staff, and the monitoring equipment that is available.

This tells you if the hospital has an intensive therapy unit which provides very high levels of care for the most seriously ill patients. Higher standards of equipment and staffing are provided and patients can be kept on ventilators.

Waiting times

Outpatient waiting time for cardiology – see explanation page 153. This information was not available for district general hospitals in Northern Ireland.

Angiography

We tell you if angiography is available at each district general hospital.

SCOTTISH DISTRICT GENERAL HOSPITALS (DGH)

See explanation on page 152.

See explanation on page 153.

See explanation on page 156.

See explanation on page 156.

Volumes and waiting times

Figures for the number of procedures performed in Scottish district general hospitals relate to the year ending March 2002. This and the average waiting time (in days) for these procedures were provided by NHS Scotland. This data relates only to discharges where the procedure was carried out as the main one. Volumes include both elective and emergency cases. Average waiting time does not include any patient undergoing a procedure as an emergency case. Where this information was not available, '-' appears. Where a procedure is not carried out at a particular hospital, 'n/a' appears.

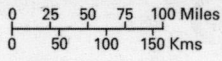

| 0 | 25 | 50 | 75 | 100 Miles |
| 0 | 50 | 100 | 150 Kms |

Aberdeen

Edinburgh
Glasgow

Newcastle upon Tyne

Middlesbrough

Belfast

Blackpool
Bradford
Liverpool   Manchester
Sheffield

Leeds
Kingston
upon Hull

Nottingham
Leicester
Birmingham   Coventry
Cambridge

Oxford
Swansea
London
Harefield
Cardiff   Bristol

Southampton
Brighton

Plymouth

NHS cardiac unit index

Barts and The London NHS Trust

St Bartholomew's Hospital
West Smithfield
London EC1A 7BE
Tel 020 7377 7000

This trust provides services at both
St Bartholomew's and the London
Chest Hospital. The range of standard and specialist cardiology and
cardiothoracic surgery services
include non-invasive investigations,
cardiac catheterisation and interventional cardiology, pacemaker inser-
tion, ablation and use of implantable defibrillators, valve repairs and
replacements, CABG, adult congenital heart surgery and open and
video-assisted thoracic surgery.

WAITING TIMES

Cardiology: outpatient	98%
C/T surgery: outpatient	100%

VOLUMES

Angioplasty	Very high
Aortic valve replacement	Frequent
Mitral valve replacement	Very high
Pacemaker	Very high

MORTALITY RATES

Aortic valve replacement	68A
Aortic valve replacement	3.1%
CABG	92A
CABG	1.2%

SURGEONS

Andrew S Cohen, Stephen J
Edmondson, Patrick G Magee, Alex
R Shipolini, Rakesh Uppal, Ian Weir,
Kit Wong, Alan J Wood

Birmingham Heartlands Hospital

Bordesley Green East
Birmingham
B9 5SS
Tel 0121 424 2000

Adult thoracic surgery is performed
at this unit.

*For information about cardiac surgery
services in Birmingham, please see
entry for Queen Elizabeth Hospital
(p.171).*

WAITING TIMES

Cardiology: outpatient	85%
C/T surgery: outpatient	100%

VOLUMES

Volume data not applicable

SURGEONS

Francis J Collins, Youssef F Khalil-
Marzouk, Pala B Rajesh, Richard S
Steyn

Blackpool Victoria Hospital

Whinney Heys Road
Blackpool
FY3 8NR
Tel 01253 300 000

This hospital provides a specialist regional service for cardiothoracic surgery. Around 1,000 open heart operations and 120 major thoracic procedures are performed each year, including oesophageal surgery (excluding cardiopulmonary transplantation). Approximately 2,500 angiographic procedures and 450 angioplasties are also carried out, and 500 pacemakers inserted. Echocardiography is used extensively in the department.

WAITING TIMES

Cardiology: outpatient	55%
C/T surgery: outpatient	100%

VOLUMES

Angioplasty	Frequent
Aortic valve replacement	Frequent
Mitral valve replacement	Frequent
Pacemaker	Very high

MORTALITY RATES

Aortic valve replacement	121A
Aortic valve replacement	8.2%
CABG	79A
CABG	2.4%

SURGEONS

John K K Au, M Carr, Andrew J Duncan, Russell W J Millner, David A C Sharpe, F Sogliani

Bradford Royal Infirmary

Duckworth Lane
Bradford
BD9 6RJ
Tel 01274 542 200

Adult thoracic and paediatric cardiothoracic surgery is performed at this unit.

For information about cardiac surgery services in the local area, please see entry for Leeds General Infirmary (p.168).

WAITING TIMES

Cardiology: outpatient	88%
C/T surgery: outpatient	98%

VOLUMES

Volume data not applicable

SURGEONS

Vladimir A Anikin, Alan J Mearns

Bristol Royal Infirmary

Marlborough Street
Bristol
BS2 8HW
Tel 0117 923 0000

This hospital is the centre for cardio-thoracic services for the northern part of the south west region. The catheter laboratory suite has undergone a major upgrade and refurbishment programme, providing an improved environment and greater privacy for patients. Procedures include cardiac catheterisation, exercise testing and echocardiograms. The hospital has a bi-plane X-ray machine, which provides two-dimensional images of the heart.

WAITING TIMES

Cardiology: outpatient	73%
C/T surgery: outpatient	100%

VOLUMES

Angioplasty	Frequent
Aortic valve replacement	Frequent
Mitral valve replacement	Very high
Pacemaker	Very high

MORTALITY RATES

Aortic valve replacement	101A
Aortic valve replacement	2.0%
CABG	48L
CABG	0.9%

SURGEONS

Gianni Angelini, Alan J Bryan, Franco Ciulli, Jonathan A Hutter, Malcolm J Underwood

Cardiothoracic Centre Liverpool

Thomas Drive
Liverpool
L14 3PE
Tel 0151 228 1616

The Liverpool Cardiothoracic Centre has developed as a 'Centre of Excellence'. It is now one of the largest specialist heart and chest hospitals in the UK and serves a population of over 2.8 million people. A mobile MRI scanner is available every three months.

WAITING TIMES

Cardiology: outpatient	100%
C/T surgery: outpatient	100%

VOLUMES

Angioplasty	-
Aortic valve replacement	-
Mitral valve replacement	-
Pacemaker	-

MORTALITY RATES

Aortic valve replacement	-
Aortic valve replacement	0.8%
CABG	90A
CABG	1.7%

SURGEONS

John A C Chalmers, Walid C Dihmis, Michael J Drakeley, Brian Fabri, Elaine M Griffiths, Neeraj K Mediratta, Richard D Page, David M Pullan, A Rashid-Farrokhi-Fathabadi, Ajaib S Soorae

Castle Hill Hospital

Hull & East Yorkshire Cardiothoracic Centre, Castle Road Cottingham, Hull HU16 5JQ

Tel **01482 875 875**

Cardiac surgery services include valve repair, minimally invasive valve surgery, off-pump coronary artery bypass, revascularisation and general thoracic surgery. The specialist cardiology department provides a regional service for interventional cardiology, electrophysiology, defibrillators and pacing. The department has advanced cardiac ultrasound facilities and cine-magnetic resonance imaging dedicated for cardiac research.

WAITING TIMES

Cardiology: outpatient	79%
C/T surgery: outpatient	100%

VOLUMES

Angioplasty	Frequent
Aortic valve replacement	Frequent
Mitral valve replacement	Frequent
Pacemaker	Frequent

MORTALITY RATES

Aortic valve replacement	84A
Aortic valve replacement	0%
CABG	116A
CABG	2.9%

SURGEONS

Alexander R J Cale, Michael E Cowen, Steven C Griffin, Levent Guvendik

Derriford Hospital

South West Cardiothoracic Centre Derriford Road Plymouth PL6 8DH

Tel **01752 777 111**

The South West Cardiothoracic Centre at Derriford Hospital is now contracted to carry out over 1,100 heart procedures a year, specialising in adult cardiothoracic, thoracic and oesophageal surgery. It also has a new high dependency unit and second catheter laboratory. The unit has undertaken just over 5,000 operations in the five years that it has been open. A substantial rebuild is being planned with the new unit due to open in 2005.

WAITING TIMES

Cardiology: outpatient	41%
C/T surgery: outpatient	98%

VOLUMES

Angioplasty	Frequent
Aortic valve replacement	Frequent
Mitral valve replacement	Frequent
Pacemaker	Very high

MORTALITY RATES

Aortic valve replacement	28A
Aortic valve replacement	0%
CABG	51L
CABG	1.3%

SURGEONS

Simon M Allen, Malcolm J R Dalrymple-Hay, James H U Kuo, Christopher T Lewis, Adrian J Marchbank, Yousif Rahamim, Michael J Unsworth-White

Glenfield Hospital

Groby Road
Leicester
LE3 9QP
Tel 0116 287 1471

The rapid access chest pain clinic
at Glenfield Hospital provides
specialist cardiological assessment
for suspected cardiac pain and has
been awarded 'Beacon Site' status
by the NHS. Procedures routinely
performed range from angiograms,
angioplasty, implantation of pacemakers and automatic cardiac defibrillators, to coronary artery bypass
grafting, heart valve repairs and
valve replacements.

WAITING TIMES

Cardiology: outpatient	96%
C/T surgery: outpatient	100%

VOLUMES

Angioplasty	Very high
Aortic valve replacement	Very high
Mitral valve replacement	Very high
Pacemaker	Very high

MORTALITY RATES

Aortic valve replacement	42A
Aortic valve replacement	2.5%
CABG	102A
CABG	1.7%

SURGEONS

Richard K Firmin, Manuel Galinanes,
Mark St John Hickey, Andrzej
Sosnowski, Tomasz J Spyt, David A
Waller

Guy's and St Thomas' NHS Trust

St Thomas' Hospital
Lambeth Palace Road
London SE1 7EH
Tel 020 7928 9292

Cardiac services are provided at
both sites within the trust – Guy's
and St Thomas' Hospitals – making
this one of the largest units in the
UK. Paediatric surgery takes place at
Guy's Hospital. All interventional cardiological procedures are undertak-
en, supporting a major research initiative. The role of nurses has been
expanded, to nurse case-managers
and nurse consultants. Support for
patients includes cardiac rehabilitation and heart failure clinics.

WAITING TIMES

Cardiology: outpatient	97%
C/T surgery: outpatient	93%

VOLUMES

Angioplasty	Very high
Aortic valve replacement	Very high
Mitral valve replacement	Very high
Pacemaker	Very high

MORTALITY RATES

Aortic valve replacement	92A
Aortic valve replacement	1.4%
CABG	112A
CABG	2.3%

SURGEONS

D R Anderson, C Austin, C I Blauth,
C R Cameron, J E Dussek, J B A
O'Riordan, J C Roxburgh, F P Shabbo,
T Treasure, G E Venn, C P Young

Hammersmith Hospital

Du Cane Road
Shepherds Bush
London W12 0HS
Tel 020 8383 1000

One of two specialist tertiary centres for heart disease and lung services in west London, this unit is known internationally in the field of cardiovascular medicine and is involved in several clinical trials. Its cardiac services are developing rapidly, forging links with primary care in cardiac prevention and re-habilitation, heart failure and rapid access chest pain services. The pulmonary hypertension service has just been awarded NSCAG status.

WAITING TIMES

Cardiology: outpatient	99%
C/T surgery: outpatient	100%

VOLUMES

Angioplasty	Very high
Aortic valve replacement	Frequent
Mitral valve replacement	Frequent
Pacemaker	Frequent

MORTALITY RATES

Aortic valve replacement	87A
Aortic valve replacement	1.5%
CABG	155A
CABG	1.8%

SURGEONS

Jonathan R Anderson, Prakash Punjabi, Peter L C Smith, Kenneth M Taylor

Harefield Hospital

Hill End Road
Harefield
Middlesex UB9 6JH
Tel 01895 823 737

This hospital has very extensive experience in the world of heart and lung transplantation. The unit also has special expertise in aortic root surgery including homografts and the Ross procedure, as well as off-pump coronary artery surgery and mitral valve reconstruction. There is a very busy thoracic surgical programme for all aspects of pulmonary and oesophageal surgery.

WAITING TIMES

Cardiology: outpatient	94%
C/T surgery: outpatient	91%

VOLUMES

Angioplasty	Very high
Aortic valve replacement	Very high
Mitral valve replacement	Very high
Pacemaker	Very high

MORTALITY RATES

Aortic valve replacement	109A
Aortic valve replacement	3.7%
CABG	86A
CABG	2.0%

SURGEONS

Mohamed Amrani, Gilles Dreyfus, Saunders W Fountain, Jullien A R Gaer, Asghar Khaghani, Mohammad O Maiwand, Edward R Townsend

The Heart Hospital (UCLH)

16–18 Westmoreland Street
London
W1M 8PH
Tel **0207 573 8888**

The Heart Hospital became part of
the UCLH Trust in August 2001,
more than doubling the Trust's
cardiac capacity and cutting waiting
times for heart surgery. In its first
year more than 1,100 cardiac operations were carried out. CT and MRI
scanning facilities are based at the
Middlesex Hospital within the Trust.

WAITING TIMES

Cardiology: outpatient	90%
C/T surgery: outpatient	89%

VOLUMES

Angioplasty	Frequent
Aortic valve replacement	Frequent
Mitral valve replacement	Frequent
Pacemaker	Very high

MORTALITY RATES

Aortic valve replacement	234H
Aortic valve replacement	6.9%
CABG	170A
CABG	4.7%

SURGEONS

Carin van Doorn, Martin Hayward,
Shyamsunder K Kolvikar, Robin K
Walesby

James Cook University Hospital

Marton Road
Middlesbrough
TS4 3BW
Tel **01642 850 850**

The heart unit at this hospital serves
a population of 1.5 million, from
Whitehaven in Cumbria to North
Yorkshire, Teesside and Durham.
It offers a full programme of adult
cardiothoracic surgery such as coronary bypass and valve operations.
The cardiology service has facilities
for tests and procedures such as
diagnostic angiography, angioplasty, pacemaker implantation,
electrophysiology studies and
implantable defibrillators.

WAITING TIMES

Cardiology: outpatient	90%
C/T surgery: outpatient	100%

VOLUMES

Angioplasty	Very high
Aortic valve replacement	Frequent
Mitral valve replacement	Frequent
Pacemaker	Very high

MORTALITY RATES

Aortic valve replacement	118A
Aortic valve replacement	3.4%
CABG	107A
CABG	1.9%

SURGEONS

Steven Hunter, Simon W H Kendall,
Graham N Morritt, John Wallis

John Radcliffe Hospital

Oxford Heart Centre
Headley Way, Headington
Oxford OX3 9DU
Tel **01865 741 166**

Surgeons at the Oxford Heart Centre implanted the revolutionary 'Jarvick 2000' mechanical heart, which is about to undergo clinical trials. The centre has an extensive research commitment with Oxford University including the molecular biology of heart failure, vascular endothelial revascularisation and gene therapy. Plans are at an advanced stage for a £23 million development to meet the NSF for coronary heart disease targets.

WAITING TIMES

Cardiology: outpatient	74%
C/T surgery: outpatient	88%

VOLUMES

Angioplasty	Very high
Aortic valve replacement	Frequent
Mitral valve replacement	Very high
Pacemaker	Very high

MORTALITY RATES

Aortic valve replacement	105A
Aortic valve replacement	6.6%
CABG	115A
CABG	2.7%

SURGEONS

Stephen H Armistead, Ravi G Pillai, Chandana P Ratnatunga, David P Taggart, Stephen Westaby

King's College Hospital

Denmark Hill
London
SE5 9RS
Tel **0207 737 4000**

This hospital treats all forms of adult cardiac disease, including coronary artery and valvular heart disease, heart failure, hypertension and conducting system disease. 'Open access' facilities exist for echocardiography, ECG, blood pressure monitoring and exercise testing. Pioneering treatments include intracoronary radiation therapy, percutaneous laser myocardial revascularisation, arterial grafting and beating heart surgery.

WAITING TIMES

Cardiology: outpatient	100%
C/T surgery: outpatient	100%

VOLUMES

Angioplasty	Very high
Aortic valve replacement	Frequent
Mitral valve replacement	Frequent
Pacemaker	Very high

MORTALITY RATES

Aortic valve replacement	31A
Aortic valve replacement	5.0%
CABG	105A
CABG	2.2%

SURGEONS

Jatin B Desai, Ahmed M H M El-Gamel, Lindsay C H John, Michael T Marrinan

Leeds General Infirmary

Yorkshire Heart Centre
Great George Street
Leeds LS1 3EX
Tel 0113 243 2799

This hospital is home to the Yorkshire Heart Centre. It treats both adults and children from across the Yorkshire region, with nearly 7,000 patients admitted each year for surgery or other types of procedure. Another 28,000 are seen every year as outpatients. Diagnostic testing is carried out in the new Jubilee Building at Leeds General Infirmary.

WAITING TIMES

Cardiology: outpatient	80%
C/T surgery: outpatient	100%

VOLUMES

Angioplasty	Very high
Aortic valve replacement	Frequent
Mitral valve replacement	Very high
Pacemaker	Very high

MORTALITY RATES

Aortic valve replacement	81A
Aortic valve replacement	3.3%
CABG	54L
CABG	2.1%

SURGEONS

Pankaj Kaul, Philip H Kay, P Joseph McGoldrick, Christopher M Munsch, R Unni Nair, David J O'Regan, Kostas Papagiannopoulos, J Andrew Thorpe, Kevin G Watterson, Nihal Weerasema

Manchester Royal Infirmary

Manchester Heart Centre
Oxford Road
Manchester M13 9WL
Tel 0161 276 1234

The Manchester Heart Centre is a joint department of cardiology and cardiac surgery. It pioneered the off-pump coronary artery bypass procedure, leading to faster patient recovery. Recently the centre has developed new approaches to bypass grafting, including minimal invasive or MIDCAB grafting which removes the need for a heart and lung machine and allows discharge within three days for some patients.

WAITING TIMES

Cardiology: outpatient	82%
C/T surgery: outpatient	100%

VOLUMES

Angioplasty	Frequent
Aortic valve replacement	Frequent
Mitral valve replacement	Frequent
Pacemaker	Very high

MORTALITY RATES

Aortic valve replacement	101A
Aortic valve replacement	3.2%
CABG	79A
CABG	2.2%

SURGEONS

Geir J Grotte, Ragheb I R Hasan, Daniel J M Keenan, Nicholas J Odom, Brian Prendergast

Newcastle upon Tyne Hospitals NHS Trust

Freeman Hospital
High Heaton
Newcastle upon Tyne NE7 7DN
Tel 0191 284 3111

This unit provides the full range of cardiothoracic surgery and has an active heart and lung transplant programme. Special interests include the treatment of arrhythmias by catheter and surgical techniques. It is one of three units in England providing ECMO for infants with respiratory failure, and has a research programme based at Newcastle University. Adult cardiac surgery also takes place at the Royal Victoria Infirmary in Newcastle.

WAITING TIMES

Cardiology: outpatient	82%
C/T surgery: outpatient	100%

VOLUMES

Angioplasty	Frequent
Aortic valve replacement	Frequent
Mitral valve replacement	Frequent
Pacemaker	Very high

MORTALITY RATES

Aortic valve replacement	109A
Aortic valve replacement	0%
CABG	89A
CABG	2.0%

SURGEONS

Sion Barnard, Stephen C Clark, John H Dark, Jonathan Forty, J R Leslie Hamilton, Asif Hasan, Colin J Hilton, Simon J M Ledingham, Thaseegaran M Pillay, Krys Tocewicz

Northern General Hospital

Herries Road
Sheffield
S5 7AU
Tel 0114 243 4343

The Northern General Hospital is now one of the largest hospitals in the UK and a leading teaching unit. It is a regional centre for cardiothoracic surgery.

WAITING TIMES

Cardiology: outpatient	96%
C/T surgery: outpatient	95%

VOLUMES

Angioplasty	Very high
Aortic valve replacement	Frequent
Mitral valve replacement	Very high
Pacemaker	Very high

MORTALITY RATES

Aortic valve replacement	48A
Aortic valve replacement	1.4%
CABG	88A
CABG	1.7%

SURGEONS

Peter C Braidley, Graham J Cooper, David N Hopkinson, Timothy J Locke, Gaetano Rocco, Roger Vaughan, Glen A L Wilkinson

Nottingham City Hospital

Hucknall Road
Nottingham
NG5 1PB
Tel 0115 969 1169

The cardiology unit provides specialist advice, investigation and treatment of all types of cardiological conditions. The unit undertakes cardiac catheterisation, ablation, angioplasty and implants of pacemakers and cardioverter defibrillators. Three consultants manage the coronary care unit and outpatient clinics, and provide an inpatient referral service, cardiac rehabilitation and nuclear cardiology.

WAITING TIMES

Cardiology: outpatient	76%
C/T surgery: outpatient	100%

VOLUMES

Angioplasty	Frequent
Aortic valve replacement	Frequent
Mitral valve replacement	Frequent
Pacemaker	Frequent

MORTALITY RATES

Aortic valve replacement	96A
Aortic valve replacement	0%
CABG	55A
CABG	1.2%

SURGEONS

Fredericke D Beggs, John P Duffy, Ian M Mitchell, William E Morgan, Surendra K Naik, David Richens

Papworth Hospital

Papworth Everard
Cambridge
CB3 8RE
Tel 01480 830 541

Papworth Hospital is a specialist cardiothoracic hospital and a referral centre for patients from eastern England and the rest of the UK. It provides a full range of adult services including cardiology, cardiac and thoracic surgery, respiratory medicine and heart, lung and heart/lung transplantation.

WAITING TIMES

Cardiology: outpatient	100%
C/T surgery: outpatient	100%

VOLUMES

Angioplasty	-
Aortic valve replacement	-
Mitral valve replacement	-
Pacemaker	-

MORTALITY RATES

Aortic valve replacement	-
Aortic valve replacement	3.2%
CABG	106A
CABG	2.1%

SURGEONS

John J Dunning, David Philip Jenkins, Stephen R Large, Samer A M Nashef, Andrew J Ritchie, Steven S L Tsui, John Wallwork, Francis C Wells

Queen Elizabeth Hospital

Edgbaston
Birmingham
B15 2TH
Tel **0121 472 1311**

© ⊗ ⊕

The unit performs around 26 operations a week including transplants and aortic surgery. There is a new large ITU, and a fast-track facility for patients who do not need to spend more than 24-hours in intensive care.

WAITING TIMES

Cardiology: outpatient	88%
C/T surgery: outpatient	100%

VOLUMES

Angioplasty	Frequent
Aortic valve replacement	Frequent
Mitral valve replacement	Frequent
Pacemaker	Very high

MORTALITY RATES

Aortic valve replacement	114A
Aortic valve replacement	3.8%
CABG	98A
CABG	3.5%

SURGEONS

Robert S Bonser, Timothy R Graham, Bruce E Keogh, Domenico Pagano, Stephen J Rooney, Ian C Wilson

Royal Brompton Hospital

Sydney Street
London
SW3 6NP
Tel **020 7352 8121**

©ᴾᵀ ⊗ ⊕

This hospital is well known for the investigation, care and treatment of people with heart and lung problems. Pioneering work has been carried out in a variety of areas including lung volume reduction surgery, beating heart and robotic surgery, arterial revascularisation and surgery for atrial fibrillation and heart failure.

WAITING TIMES

Cardiology: outpatient	94%
C/T surgery: outpatient	91%

VOLUMES

Angioplasty	Very high
Aortic valve replacement	Very high
Mitral valve replacement	Very high
Pacemaker	Very high

MORTALITY RATES

Aortic valve replacement	109A
Aortic valve replacement	2.8%
CABG	86A
CABG	1.5%

SURGEONS

Anthony C De Souza, Peter Goldstraw, George Ladas, Neil E Moat, John R Pepper, Mario Petru, Babulal Sethia, Darryl F Shore

Royal Sussex County Hospital

Sussex Cardiac Centre
Eastern Road
Brighton BN2 5BE
Tel 01273 696 955

Cardiology services have been
provided here for the past 35 years.
In June 1999, both cardiac intervention and adult cardiac surgical
services were introduced. Over 800
cardiac surgery and 1,000 balloon
angioplasty/stent patients are seen
each year. A large number of arterial
grafts for coronary artery disease,
and selected 'off-pump' coronary
artery bypass grafts are carried out.
Present plans are to double the
unit's output in the next two years.

WAITING TIMES

Cardiology: outpatient	96%
C/T surgery: outpatient	100%

VOLUMES

Angioplasty	Frequent
Aortic valve replacement	Frequent
Mitral valve replacement	Frequent
Pacemaker	Frequent

MORTALITY RATES

Aortic valve replacement	98A
Aortic valve replacement	3.8%
CABG	76A
CABG	3.0%

SURGEONS

Andrew T Forsyth, Jonathon A J Hyde,
Wilfred B Pugsley, Uday H Trivedi

Southampton General Hospital

Wessex Cardiac Unit
Tremona Road
Southampton SO16 6YD
Tel 023 8077 7222

The Wessex Cardiac Unit is one of
the largest such centres in the UK,
serving around 2.8 million people.
Annually it treats over 20,000
patients for all forms of serious heart
problems. Services range from outpatients through to inpatient management and investigation including
angiography, angioplasty and
CABG. It is internationally known for
the treatment of children born with
congenital heart disorders, treating
1,000 children every year.

WAITING TIMES

Cardiology: outpatient	63%
C/T surgery: outpatient	100%

VOLUMES

Angioplasty	Very high
Aortic valve replacement	Very high
Mitral valve replacement	Very high
Pacemaker	Very high

MORTALITY RATES

Aortic valve replacement	50A
Aortic valve replacement	1.0%
CABG	62L
CABG	1.3%

SURGEONS

Clifford W Barlow, Marcus P Haw,
S M Langley, Steven A Livesey, James
L Monro, Sunil K Ohri, G M K Tsang,
David F N Weeden

St George's Hospital

Blackshaw Road
London
SW17 0QT
Tel **020 8672 1255**

This recently expanded cardio-thoracic unit is located in a separate wing to the main hospital and provides services to 1.75 million people in south west London and Surrey. Facilities include four dedicated cardiac theatre suites and two dedicated fast-track beds for cardiac patients. In June 2003 the whole unit will be moving to a new purpose-built centre also on the St George's site, providing greater capacity.

WAITING TIMES

Cardiology: outpatient	79%
C/T surgery: outpatient	100%

VOLUMES

Angioplasty	Very high
Aortic valve replacement	Frequent
Mitral valve replacement	Frequent
Pacemaker	Very high

MORTALITY RATES

Aortic valve replacement	241H
Aortic valve replacement	8.5%
CABG	116A
CABG	3.5%

SURGEONS

Venkatchalam Chandrasekaran, Marjan Jahangiri, Robin Kanagasabay, Mazin Sarsam, Richard Sayer, Edward J Smith

St Mary's Hospital

Praed Street
London
W2 1NY
Tel **020 7886 6666**

The department of cardiology and cardiac surgery takes an integrated, patient-focused approach to care, including cardiovascular disease risk-assessment. There is a coronary care unit with specialist-trained nurses on site, and a mobile catheter lab is used to treat patients who have difficulty getting to the hospital. There is an extensive rehabilitation programme and patient helpline.

WAITING TIMES

Cardiology: outpatient	89%
C/T surgery: outpatient	100%

VOLUMES

Angioplasty	Frequent
Aortic valve replacement	Frequent
Mitral valve replacement	Frequent
Pacemaker	Frequent

MORTALITY RATES

Aortic valve replacement	86A
Aortic valve replacement	2.2%
CABG	103A
CABG	3.3%

SURGEONS

Roberto P Casula, Brian E Glenville, Rex de Lisle Stanbridge

Walsgrave Hospital

Clifford Bridge Road
Walsgrave
Coventry CV2 2DX
Tel 024 7660 2020

Walsgrave Hospital is a regional centre for heart surgery. In recent years the hospital has experienced some difficulties, which are reflected by the relatively high mortality ratios shown. However, a number of steps have recently been taken to address these problems and mortality rates for heart bypass surgery have now fallen to below the national average.

WAITING TIMES

Cardiology: outpatient	59%
C/T surgery: outpatient	100%

VOLUMES

Angioplasty	Very high
Aortic valve replacement	Frequent
Mitral valve replacement	Very high
Pacemaker	Frequent

MORTALITY RATES

Aortic valve replacement	201H
Aortic valve replacement	5.7%
CABG	182H
CABG	3.6%

SURGEONS

Norman P Briffa, Wadih R Dimitri, Robert Norton, Ramesh Patel, Michael D Rosin

Wythenshawe Hospital

Southmoor Road
Wythenshawe
Manchester M23 9LT
Tel 0161 998 7070

This hospital is a renowned centre for the treatment of cardiac and respiratory disease, both of which are particularly prevalent in the Manchester area. It specialises in cardiothoracic surgery, cardiology and thoracic medicine and also houses the fourth UK centre for heart and lung transplants.

WAITING TIMES

Cardiology: outpatient	98%
C/T surgery: outpatient	100%

VOLUMES

Angioplasty	Very high
Aortic valve replacement	Frequent
Mitral valve replacement	Very high
Pacemaker	Very high

MORTALITY RATES

Aortic valve replacement	59A
Aortic valve replacement	1.7%
CABG	172A
CABG	2.2%

SURGEONS

Benjamin J M Bridgewater, Colin S Campbell, John A Carey, Abdulilah H K Deiraniya, Timothy L Hooper, Mark T Jones, Paul D Waterworth, Nizar A A Yonan

Alder Hey Children's Hospital

Eaton Road
Liverpool
L12 2AP
Tel 0151 228 4811

(P) (X)

WAITING TIMES

Cardiology: outpatient   -
C/T surgery: outpatient   -

SURGEONS

Marco Pozzi

Alder Hey is one of the largest paediatric cardiac surgical units in the country. It provides congenital cardiology and paediatric cardiac surgical services for the north west of England. There are close links with the paediatric cardiology service in Manchester – patients from Manchester requiring cardiac surgery are referred to Alder Hey and there are regular joint cardiac clinics to facilitate this.

Diana Princess of Wales Children's Hospital

Steelhouse Lane
Birmingham
B4 6NH
Tel 0121 333 9999

(P) (X) (⊕)

WAITING TIMES

Cardiology: outpatient   -
C/T surgery: outpatient   -

SURGEONS

David J Barron, William J Brawn

This hospital provides a comprehensive range of paediatric cardiothoracic surgery services. It is a specialist referral centre for cardiac, neonatal and transplant surgery through to acute general medical and surgical nursing. Its facilities provide child and family centred care.

Great Ormond Street Hospital for Children

Great Ormond Street
London
WC1N 3JH
Tel 020 7405 9200

The cardiothoracic unit provides fully integrated medical, surgical and intensive care services to children, with special reference to neonates and young infants. It has particular expertise in pulmonary, mediastinal and tracheal surgery and provides antenatal echocardiographic assessment and counselling for fetal congenital heart disease. ECMO is also available here. There is an ongoing programme for heart and heart/lung transplantation.

Royal Hospital for Sick Children

Yorkhill
Glasgow
Scotland G3 8SJ
Tel 0141 201 0000

AVG WAIT

Angiography   20

Angioplasty   -

SURGEONS

Kenneth J D MacArthur, James C S Pollock

The Royal Hospital for Sick Children is the principal children's hospital in the west of Scotland, and one of the three big paediatric centres in the UK. It has around 325 beds, and 30 NICU cots, more than 100 consultants and 25 specialist registrars. It provides hospital care to the children of Glasgow and specialist tertiary care in many subspecialties including cardiology, oncology-haematology, renal disease and neonatal surgery.

Morriston Hospital

Morriston
Swansea
Wales SA6 6NL
Tel 01792 702 222

The Morriston Hospital is the
second cardiac centre in Wales
after University Hospital of Wales.
Interventional cardiology treatments
include percutaneous transluminal
coronary angioplasty, coronary stent
and permanent pacemaker insert-
ion, and defibrillator implantation.

WAITING TIMES

Cardiology: outpatient	76%
C/T surgery: outpatient	-

VOLUMES

Angioplasty	-
Aortic valve replacement	-
Mitral valve replacement	-
Pacemaker	-

MORTALITY RATES

Aortic valve replacement	-
Aortic valve replacement	2.2%
CABG	-
CABG	2.1%

SURGEONS

Vincenzo Argano, Syed S Ashraf,
Aprim Y Youhana

University Hospital of Wales

Heath Park
Cardiff
Wales CF14 4XW
Tel 029 2074 7747

This unit provides cardiac and
thoracic surgery and diagnostic
and interventional cardiology, with
full support facilities. It is expanding
in line with the National Service
Framework for coronary heart disease and there is close collaboration
with the recently opened Welsh
Heart Institute.

WAITING TIMES

Cardiology: outpatient	36%
C/T surgery: outpatient	-

VOLUMES

Angioplasty	-
Aortic valve replacement	-
Mitral valve replacement	-
Pacemaker	-

MORTALITY RATES

Aortic valve replacement	-
Aortic valve replacement	4.5%
CABG	-
CABG	2.7%

SURGEONS

Ahmed A Azzu, Eric G Butchart,
E Nihal P Kulatilake, Peter A O'Keefe,
Ulrich von Oppell

Aberdeen Royal Infirmary

Foresthill
Aberdeen
Scotland AB25 2ZN
Tel 01224 681 818

The clinical cardiology department at Aberdeen Royal Infirmary provides the regional cardiology service for the north east of Scotland. It has a 12-bed CCU equipped with monitoring equipment and an intervention suite with imaging facilities. A coronary triage service is centred at this unit.

AVG WAIT

Angiography	38
Angioplasty	41
CABG	54

VOLUMES

Angiography	1427
Angioplasty	294
CABG	487

MORTALITY RATES

Aortic valve replacement	-
Aortic valve replacement	5.1%
CABG	-
CABG	1.5%

SURGEONS

Keith G Buchan, Hussein M A El-Shafei, Robert R Jeffrey

Glasgow Royal Infirmary

84 Castle Street
Glasgow
Scotland G4 0SF
Tel 0141 211 4000

This hospital is home to the Glasgow University Department of Medical Cardiology, whose work encompasses all aspects of this discipline. Staff work in consultation with colleagues in the University Department of Cardiac Surgery, carrying out clinical studies on patients receiving prosthetic heart valves. The full range of procedures includes interventional techniques and the department has expertise in nuclear cardiology.

AVG WAIT

Angiography	49
Angioplasty	82
CABG	54

VOLUMES

Angiography	1725
Angioplasty	436
CABG	704

MORTALITY RATES

Aortic valve replacement	-
Aortic valve replacement	5.3%
CABG	-
CABG	2.5%

SURGEONS

Ian W Colquhoun, Stewart R Craig, Andrew J Murday, Udim Nkere, James C S Pollock, David J Wheatley

Royal Infirmary of Edinburgh

Lauriston Place
Edinburgh
Scotland EH3 9YW
Tel 0131 536 1000

The cardiothoracic unit is self-contained with its own dedicated theatre suite, ten-bed ICU and a 24-bed post-operative ward. Approximately 850 pump cases are performed annually – two-thirds of these involve coronary artery bypass grafts. Other procedures include aortic surgery, adult congenital heart disease surgery, post-infarct VSD and pericardial and chest wall procedures.

AVG WAIT

Angiography	56
Angioplasty	47
CABG	74

VOLUMES

Angiography	1103
Angioplasty	660
CABG	679

MORTALITY RATES

Aortic valve replacement	-
Aortic valve replacement	3.6%
CABG	-
CABG	2.0%

SURGEONS

Edward T Brackenbury, Ciro Campanella, Pankaj S Mankad, William S Walker, Vipin Y Zamvar

Western Infirmary

Dumbarton Road
Glasgow
Scotland G11 6NT
Tel 0141 211 2000

The Western Infirmary's cardiothoracic department offers services such as coronary care, invasive and non-invasive cardiac investigation and angioplasty.

AVG WAIT

Angiography	13
Angioplasty	50
CABG	25

VOLUMES

Angiography	1976
Angioplasty	107
CABG	837

MORTALITY RATES

Aortic valve replacement	-
Aortic valve replacement	1.1%
CABG	-
CABG	1.5%

SURGEONS

Geoffrey A Berg, John G Butler, Alan Faichney, Alan J B Kirk, Kenneth J D MacArthur, Vivek Pathi

Royal Victoria Hospital

Grosvenor Road
Belfast
Northern Ireland BT12 6BA
Tel 028 9026 3000

The centre for all Northern Ireland's cardiac surgery procedures, the Royal Victoria Hospital has helped develop the use of Xenos multi-wire cameras (designed by NASA for astronauts), portable defibrillators and body surface mapping in ischaemic heart disease. The cardiology centre provides care for approximately 4,000 inpatients per year.

WAITING TIMES

Cardiology: outpatient	-
C/T surgery: outpatient	-

VOLUMES

Angioplasty	-
Aortic valve replacement	
Mitral valve replacement	
Pacemaker	-

MORTALITY RATES

Aortic valve replacement	-
Aortic valve replacement	5.2%
CABG	-
CABG	1.6%

SURGEONS

Gianfranco Campalani, Mark H D Danton, Dennis J Gladstone, Alastair N J Graham, Simon W MacGowan, James A McGuigan, Kieran G McManus

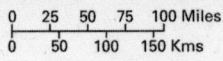

0   25   50   75   100 Miles
0   50   100   150 Kms

Glasgow

Washington

Bingley   Leeds

Cheadle   Sheffield

Nottingham
Leicester

Birmingham

Cambridge

London

Bristol   Cheam

Southampton

© Oxford Cartographers
+44 (0) 1865 882 884
95084

Private hospital index

BMI The Alexandra Hospital

Mill Lane
Cheadle
Cheshire SK8 2PX
Tel 0161 428 3656

(CT) (X) (!) (♥)

VOLUMES

Angiography	>500
Angioplasty	100–200
CABG	300–500
Pacemaker	100–200

This hospital has a dedicated cardiothoracic ward staffed by nurses familiar with all types of cardiac care. Patients include those who require the investigation of undiagnosed chest pain, diagnosed patients recovering from a heart attack or patients who are awaiting a procedure such as angiography, angioplasty or cardiac surgery. Patients will receive lifestyle advice from therapists and dieticians.

BMI London Independent Hospital

1 Beaumont Square
Stepney Green
London E1 4NL
Tel 020 7780 2400

(CT) (X) (!) (♥)

VOLUMES

Angiography	>500
Angioplasty	200–300
CABG	200–300
Pacemaker	<50

The unit has a six-bed intensive care unit and a four-bed high dependency unit. The hospital employs resident experts in intensive care and resident medical officers, available 24 hours a day. The hospital also has a fully equipped cardiac catheterisation laboratory. Diagnostic angiography and angioplasty are performed using the latest drug-eluting stents.

BMI The Park Hospital

Sherwood Lodge Drive
Burntstump Country Park, Arnold
Nottingham NG5 8RX
Tel 0115 967 0670

(CT) (X) (♥)

VOLUMES

Angiography	100–200
Angioplasty	<50
CABG	100–200
Pacemaker	<50

The Park Hospital has a three-bed critical care unit with Level 2 and 3 beds. The hospital has two operating theatres equipped for elective cardiac and valve replacement surgery. The hospital also has a fixed site cardiac catheter laboratory.

BMI The Priory Hospital

Priory Road
Edgbaston
Birmingham B5 7UG
Tel **0121 440 2323**

VOLUMES

Angiography	>500
Angioplasty	50–100
CABG	200–300
Pacemaker	<50

With 15 years' experience, this is the only private hospital in the west Midlands to offer cardiac surgery, a permanent cardiac catheter laboratory and an ITU. Nearly 1,000 private and NHS cardiac operations are carried out each year, most commonly coronary angioplasty, heart bypass surgery and heart valve replacement. This hospital has been chosen by the DoH as part of the Extending Choice Initiative.

BMI Ross Hall Hospital

221 Crookston Road
Glasgow
Scotland G52 3NQ
Tel **0141 810 3151**

VOLUMES

Angiography	300–500
Angioplasty	50–100
CABG	100–200
Pacemaker	<50

This hospital has a dedicated state-of-the-art ITU catering for all types of cardiac and major surgical cases with capacity for five patients including one isolation cubicle. The unit nurses all hold an advanced life support certificate and a recognised intensive care qualification. Patients are cared for by their named consultant and anaesthetist and are further supported by an in-house cardiac registrar available 24 hours.

BMI Thornbury Hospital

312 Fulwood Road
Sheffield
South Yorkshire S10 3BR
Tel **0114 266 1133**

VOLUMES

Angiography	200–300
Angioplasty	Nil
CABG	50–100
Pacemaker	Nil

Thornbury Hospital is a 77-bed acute care hospital. There are three ITU beds and four HDU beds, allowing complex cardiac surgery to be carried out, including CABG and valve replacement. The critical care unit is managed by a team of specialist ITU nurses and an intensivist who is a consultant anaesthetist in ITU at the local NHS Trust hospital. There are resident medical officers on-site 24 hours a day.

BUPA Hospital Bristol

Redland Hill
Durdham Down
Bristol BS6 6UT
Tel 0117 973 2562

VOLUMES

Angiography	300–500
Angioplasty	<50
CABG	200–300
Pacemaker	<50

A cardiology and cardiac surgery programme including coronary artery bypass grafts and valve replacements, has been running here since 1987. There is a fully equipped four-bed ITU and three-bed HDU. Patients are supported by a cardiac rehabilitation programme which includes courses on stress management, relaxation and nutrition leading to an on-going exercise programme

BUPA Cambridge Lea Hospital

30 New Road
Impington
Cambridge CB2 9EL
Tel 01223 266 900

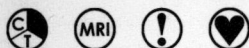

VOLUMES

Angiography	50–100
Angioplasty	<50
CABG	100–200
Pacemaker	Nil

This is the only completely private hospital in East Anglia to undertake cardiac surgery. Facilities include a four-bed ITU, a cardiac catheterisation laboratory and a mobile CT scanner. The laboratory was closed for almost all of 2001 during expansion of the operating theatre suite, which accounts for the relatively low numbers of angiography and angioplasty procedures performed.

BUPA Hospital Leeds

Jackson Avenue
Roundhay
Leeds LS8 1NT
Tel 0113 269 3939

VOLUMES

Angiography	300–500
Angioplasty	50–100
CABG	200–300
Pacemaker	50–100

BUPA Hospital Leeds is the region's leading independent centre for cardiac care and is accredited by BUPA as a cardiac care centre. It also has ISO and HQS quality accreditation. The hospital provides a six-week rehabilitation programme with optional follow-up classes available. There is also a cardiac support group organised by ex-patients.

BUPA Hospital Leicester

Gartree Road
Oadby
Leicester LE2 2FF
Tel **0116 272 0888**

BUPA Hospital Leicester provides an extensive range of services for heart disease patients. It has a cardiac cath lab, two operating theatres and a five-bed intensive care facility. Procedures carried out include CABG and valve replacements. The hospital undertakes cardiac surgery on patients with medical insurance, those under the fixed price surgery scheme and a significant number of NHS waiting list initiative patients.

VOLUMES

Angiography	300–500
Angioplasty	50–100
CABG	100–200
Pacemaker	<50

BUPA Hospital Southampton

Chalybeate Close
Tremona Road
Southampton SO16 6UY
Tel **023 8077 5544**

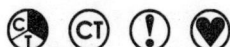

This is one of the largest independent cardiac hospitals in the UK with a dedicated seven-bed critical care unit. Surgeons perform a range of surgery including procedures for congenital heart disease and off-pump coronary heart surgery. 24-hour cover is provided by the team with at least one consultant surgeon available at all times.

VOLUMES

Angiography	300–500
Angioplasty	Nil
CABG	100–200
Pacemaker	<50

BUPA Hospital Washington

Picktree Lane, Rickleton
Washington
Tyne & Wear NE38 9JZ
Tel **0191 415 1272**

This is the only private hospital in the north east of England undertaking cardiothoracic surgery, alongside treatment for a wide range of different specialties. Facilities include three operating theatres, a dedicated day care unit and a fully equipped ITU.

VOLUMES

Angiography	N/A
Angioplasty	N/A
CABG	100–200
Pacemaker	N/A

Cromwell Hospital

Cromwell Road
London
SW5 0TU
Tel 020 7460 2000

VOLUMES

Angiography	200–300
Angioplasty	50–100
CABG	100–200
Pacemaker	50–100

A comprehensive range of cardiac investigations is provided as well as acute monitoring for all cardiac catheter cases. The angiography suite uses digital technology to enable high-speed operation. Cardiac surgery is supported by full-time resident surgical officers and intensive care medical officers, cardiac trained nurses in ITU and HDU, perfusionists and technicians. 24-hour emergency cover is in place.

Harley Street Clinic

35 Weymouth Street
London
W1G 8BJ
Tel 020 7935 7700

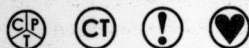

VOLUMES

Angiography	>500
Angioplasty	50–100
CABG	300–500
Pacemaker	50–100

This clinic offers a comprehensive cardiac facility for adults and children, with outpatient facilities, newly refurbished cardiac catheterisation labs and a critical care department. The hospital undertakes adult surgery including CABG and mitral valve, and both open and closed paediatric heart surgery.

Leicester Nuffield Hospital

Scraptoft Lane
Leicester
LE5 1HY
Tel 0116 276 9401

VOLUMES

Angiography	Nil
Angioplasty	Nil
CABG	100–200
Pacemaker	Nil

This is a modern well-equipped hospital with 46 private rooms with over 130 staff. Together with cardiothoracic surgery, a number of non-invasive investigations into heart disease are available, including 24-hour ambulatory electrocardiograph (ECG) monitoring, 24-hour mini-ECG monitoring, 24-hour blood pressure monitoring and two-dimensional echocardiography.

London Bridge Hospital

27 Tooley Street
London
SE1 2PR
Tel **020 7407 3100**

VOLUMES

Angiography	>500
Angioplasty	100–200
CABG	300–500
Pacemaker	100–200

This 31-bed cardiac unit includes a progressive care unit with ventilation facilities and HDU beds. Stents, angioplasties, valvuloplasties and cardiac surgery are available. The multi-disciplinary team includes specialist nurses, physiotherapists, cardiology technicians and a dietician. This is the only private unit in the country to publish its outcome data in the SCTS National Adult Surgical Cardiac Database

Nuffield Hospital Leeds

2 Leighton Street
Leeds
LS1 3EB
Tel **0113 388 2000**

VOLUMES

Angiography	-
Angioplasty	-
CABG	-
Pacemaker	-

This Hospital opened in September 2002. Its main services are cardiology and cardiac surgery. Facilities include a dedicated cardiac theatre, angiography suite and cardiac ward beds. A framework of minimum standards for angioplasty, angiography and cardiac surgery, referencing the NSF, National Care Standards, BCIS and the British Cardiac Society, has been implemented and adhered to.

St Anthony's Hospital

London Road
North Cheam, Sutton
Surrey SM3 9DW
Tel **020 8337 6691**

VOLUMES

Angiography	>500
Angioplasty	300–500
CABG	200–300
Pacemaker	50–100

This hospital has specialised in cardiac surgery since 1975, carrying out around 300 bypass graft and valve replacement procedures each year. Services include four fully equipped operating theatres, an eight-bed ITU, a four-bed HDU, telemetry with central cardiac monitoring station and two cardiac catheterisation laboratories. The hospital also has on-site accommodation for patients' relatives.

Wellington Hospital

8a Wellington Place
London
NW8 9LE
Tel 020 7586 5959

The Wellington Hospital has one of the largest cardiac surgical programmes in Europe and has been given a Centre of Excellence award. The cardiac unit offers both intensive care and progressive care beds, a dedicated theatre and two cardiac catheterisation laboratories.

VOLUMES

Angiography	>500
Angioplasty	50–100
CABG	300–500
Pacemaker	100–200

The Yorkshire Clinic

Bradford Road
Bingley
West Yorkshire BD16 1TW
Tel 01274 560 311

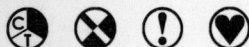

The Yorkshire Clinic has a dedicated cardiac theatre, ITU facilities and a cardiac investigation and catheterisation suite. The six-week rehabilitation programme is co-ordinated by two cardiothoracic trained staff nurses and a trained physiotherapy assistant. A cardiac care booklet outlining the services on offer is available.

VOLUMES

Angiography	300–500
Angioplasty	100–200
CABG	300–500
Pacemaker	<50

Ascot • **Heatherwood Hospital**

London Road
Ascot
Berkshire SL5 8AA
Tel **01753 633 000**

CCU

Cardiology: outpatient wait   95%
Angiography available on site   No

Ashford • **Ashford Hospital**

London Road
Ashford
Middlesex TW15 3AA
Tel **01784 884 488**

CCU

Cardiology: outpatient wait   -
Angiography available on site   Yes

Ashington • **Wansbeck General Hospital**

Woodhorn Lane
Ashington
Northumberland NE63 9JJ
Tel **01670 521 212**

CCU

Cardiology: outpatient wait   -
Angiography available on site   No

Ashton-under-Lyne • **Tameside General Hospital**

Fountain Street
Ashton-under-Lyne
Lancashire OL6 9RW
Tel **0161 331 6000**

CCU

Cardiology: outpatient wait   -
Angiography available on site   No

Aylesbury • **Stoke Mandeville Hospital**

Mandeville Road
Aylesbury
Buckinghamshire HP21 8AL
Tel **01296 315 000**

30 CCU

Cardiology: outpatient wait   100%
Angiography available on site   No

Banbury • **Horton Hospital**

Oxford Road
Banbury
Oxfordshire OX16 9AL
Tel **01295 275 500**

CCU

Cardiology: outpatient wait   74%
Angiography available on site   No

Barnsley • **Barnsley DGH**

Gawber Road
Barnsley
South Yorkshire S75 2EP
Tel **01226 730 000**

Cardiology: outpatient wait -
Angiography available on site No

Barnstaple • **North Devon District Hospital**

Raleigh Park
Barnstaple
Devon EX31 4JB
Tel **01271 322 577**

Cardiology: outpatient wait 78%
Angiography available on site No

Barrow-in-Furness • **Furness General Hospital**

Dalton Lane
Barrow-in-Furness
Cumbria LA14 4LF
Tel **01229 870 870**

Cardiology: outpatient wait 100%
Angiography available on site No

Basildon • **Basildon Hospital**

Nethermayne
Basildon
Essex SS16 5NL
Tel **01268 533 911**

Cardiology: outpatient wait 49%
Angiography available on site No

Basingstoke • **North Hampshire Hospital**

Aldermaston Road
Basingstoke
Hampshire RG24 9NA
Tel **01256 473202**

Cardiology: outpatient wait 79%
Angiography available on site Yes

Bath • **Royal United Hospital**

Combe Park
Bath
Somerset BA1 3NG
Tel **01225 428 331**

Cardiology: outpatient wait 67%
Angiography available on site Yes

Bedford • **Bedford Hospital**

Kempston Road
Bedford
Bedfordshire MK42 9DJ
Tel **01234 355122**

Cardiology: outpatient wait   67%
Angiography available on site   No

Birmingham • **Selly Oak Hospital**

Raddlebarn Road
Birmingham
B29 6JD
Tel **0121 627 1627**

Cardiology: outpatient wait   88%
Angiography available on site   Yes

Bishop Auckland • **Bishop Auckland General Hospital**

Cockton Hill Road
Bishop Auckland
County Durham DL14 6AD
Tel **01388 454 000**

Cardiology: outpatient wait   -
Angiography available on site   No

Blackburn • **Blackburn Royal Infirmary**

Bolton Road
Blackburn
Lancashire BB2 3LR
Tel **01254 263 555**

Cardiology: outpatient wait   100%
Angiography available on site   No

Bolton • **Royal Bolton Hospital**

Farnworth
Bolton
Lancashire BL4 0JR
Tel **01204 390 390**

Cardiology: outpatient wait   -
Angiography available on site   No

Boston • **Pilgrim Hospital**

Sibsey Road
Boston
Lincolnshire PE21 9QS
Tel **01205 364 801**

Cardiology: outpatient wait   76%
Angiography available on site   No

Bournemouth • **Royal Bournemouth Hospital**

Castle Lane East
Bournemouth
Dorset BH7 7DW
Tel **01202 303 626**

Cardiology: outpatient wait   89%
Angiography available on site   Yes

Bradford • **St Luke's Hospital**

Little Horton Lane
Bradford
West Yorkshire BD5 0NA
Tel **01274 734 744**

Cardiology: outpatient wait   88%
Angiography available on site   No

Bristol • **Frenchay Hospital**

Beckspool Road
Bristol
BS16 1JE
Tel **0117 970 1070**

Cardiology: outpatient wait   59%
Angiography available on site   Yes

Bristol • **Southmead Hospital**

Westbury-on-Trym
Bristol
BS10 5NB
Tel **0117 950 5050**

Cardiology: outpatient wait   59%
Angiography available on site   Yes

Burnley • **Burnley General Hospital**

Casterton Avenue
Burnley
Lancashire BB10 2PQ
Tel **01282 425 071**

Cardiology: outpatient wait   76%
Angiography available on site   No

Burton upon Trent • **Queen's Hospital**

Belvedere Road
Burton upon Trent
Staffordshire DE13 0RB
Tel **01283 566 333**

Cardiology: outpatient wait   49%
Angiography available on site   No

Bury • **Fairfield General Hospital**

Rochdale Old Road
Bury
Lancashire BL9 7TD
Tel **0161 764 6081**

Cardiology: outpatient wait 70%
Angiography available on site No

Bury St Edmunds • **West Suffolk Hospital**

Hardwick Lane
Bury St Edmunds
Suffolk IP33 2QZ
Tel **01284 713 000**

Cardiology: outpatient wait 56%
Angiography available on site No

Cambridge • **Addenbrooke's Hospital**

Hills Road
Cambridge
Cambridgeshire CB2 2QQ
Tel **01223 245 151**

Cardiology: outpatient wait 85%
Angiography available on site No

Canterbury • **Kent & Canterbury Hospital**

Ethelbert Road
Canterbury
Kent CT1 3NG
Tel **01227 766 877**

Cardiology: outpatient wait 66%
Angiography available on site No

Carlisle • **Cumberland Infirmary**

Newtown Road
Carlisle
Cumbria CA2 7HY
Tel **01228 523 444**

Cardiology: outpatient wait 65%
Angiography available on site Yes

Chelmsford • **Broomfield Hospital**

Court Road
Chelmsford
Essex CM1 7ET
Tel **01245 440 761**

Cardiology: outpatient wait 94%
Angiography available on site No

Cheltenham • **Cheltenham General Hospital**

Sandford Road
Cheltenham
Gloucestershire GL53 7AN
Tel **01242 222 222**

Cardiology: outpatient wait 65%
Angiography available on site Yes

Chertsey • **St Peter's Hospital**

Guildford Road
Chertsey
Surrey KT16 0PZ
Tel **01932 872 000**

Cardiology: outpatient wait -
Angiography available on site Yes

Chester • **Countess of Chester Hospital**

Liverpool Road
Chester
Cheshire CH2 1UL
Tel **01244 365 000**

Cardiology: outpatient wait 77%
Angiography available on site No

Chesterfield • **Chesterfield & N. Derbyshire Royal Hospital**

Calow
Chesterfield
Derbyshire S44 5BL
Tel **01246 277 271**

Cardiology: outpatient wait -
Angiography available on site No

Chichester • **St Richard's Hospital**

Chichester
West Sussex
PO19 4SE
Tel **01243 788 122**

Cardiology: outpatient wait 88%
Angiography available on site No

Chorley • **Chorley & South Ribble DGH**

Preston Road
Chorley
Lancashire PR7 1PP
Tel **01257 261 222**

Cardiology: outpatient wait
Angiography available on site No

Colchester • **Colchester General Hospital**

Turner Road
Colchester
Essex CO4 5JL
Tel **01206 747 474**

Cardiology: outpatient wait   77%
Angiography available on site   Yes

Crewe • **Leighton Hospital**

Middlewich Road
Crewe
Cheshire CW1 4QJ
Tel **01270 255 141**

Cardiology: outpatient wait   -
Angiography available on site   No

Darlington • **Darlington Memorial Hospital**

Hollyhurst Road
Darlington
County Durham DL3 6HW
Tel **01325 380100**

Cardiology: outpatient wait   -
Angiography available on site   No

Dartford • **Darent Valley Hospital**

Darenth Wood Road
Dartford
Kent DA2 8DA
Tel **01322 428 100**

Cardiology: outpatient wait   83%
Angiography available on site   No

Derby • **Derby City General Hospital**

Uttoxeter Road
Derby
Derbyshire DE22 3NE
Tel **01332 340 131**

Cardiology: outpatient wait   79%
Angiography available on site   No

Derby • **Derbyshire Royal Infirmary**

London Road
Derby
Derbyshire DE1 2QY
Tel **01332 347 141**

Cardiology: outpatient wait   79%
Angiography available on site   Yes

Dewsbury • **Dewsbury & District Hospital**

Halifax Road
Dewsbury
West Yorkshire WF13 4HS
Tel **01924 512 000**

Cardiology: outpatient wait 62%
Angiography available on site Yes

Doncaster • **Doncaster Royal Infirmary & Montagu Hospital**

Armthorpe Road
Doncaster
South Yorkshire DN2 5LT
Tel **01302 366 666**

Cardiology: outpatient wait -
Angiography available on site Yes

Dorchester • **Dorset County Hospital**

Williams Avenue
Dorchester
Dorset DT1 2JY
Tel **01305 251 150**

Cardiology: outpatient wait 50%
Angiography available on site Yes

Dryburn • **University Hospital of North Durham**

North Road
Dryburn
County Durham DH1 5TW
Tel **0191 333 2333**

Cardiology: outpatient wait 70%
Angiography available on site No

Eastbourne • **Eastbourne DGH**

Kings Drive
Eastbourne
East Sussex BN21 2UD
Tel **01323 417400**

Cardiology: outpatient wait 73%
Angiography available on site Yes

Exeter • **Royal Devon & Exeter Hospital**

Barrack Road
Exeter
Devon EX2 5DW
Tel **01392 411 611**

Cardiology: outpatient wait -
Angiography available on site Yes

Frimley • **Frimley Park Hospital**

Portsmouth Road
Frimley
Surrey GU16 7UJ
Tel **01276 604 604**

Cardiology: outpatient wait   -
Angiography available on site   No

Gateshead • **Queen Elizabeth Hospital**

Queen Elizabeth Avenue
Gateshead
Tyne & Wear NE9 6SX
Tel **0191 482 0000**

Cardiology: outpatient wait   57%
Angiography available on site   Yes

Gillingham • **Medway Maritime Hospital**

Windmill Road
Gillingham
Kent ME7 5NY
Tel **01634 830 000**

Cardiology: outpatient wait   77%
Angiography available on site   No

Gloucester • **Gloucestershire Royal Hospital**

Great Western Road
Gloucester
Gloucestershire GL1 3NN
Tel **01452 528 555**

Cardiology: outpatient wait   87%
Angiography available on site   No

Grantham • **Grantham & District Hospital**

101 Manthorpe Road
Grantham
Lincolnshire NG31 8DG
Tel **01476 565 232**

Cardiology: outpatient wait   76%
Angiography available on site   No

Great Yarmouth • **James Paget Hospital**

Lowestoft Road
Great Yarmouth
Norfolk NR31 6LA
Tel **01493 452 452**

Cardiology: outpatient wait   -
Angiography available on site   No

Grimsby • **Diana, Princess of Wales Hospital**

Scartho Road
Grimsby
North East Lincolnshire DN33 2BA
Tel **01472 874 111**

Cardiology: outpatient wait   87%
Angiography available on site   Yes

Guildford • **Royal Surrey County Hospital**

Egerton Road
Guildford
Surrey GU2 7XX
Tel **01483 571 122**

Cardiology: outpatient wait   85%
Angiography available on site   Yes

Halifax • **Calderdale Royal Hospital**

Salterhebble
Halifax
West Yorkshire HX3 0PW
Tel **01422 357 171**

Cardiology: outpatient wait   61%
Angiography available on site   Yes

Harlow • **Princess Alexandra Hospital**

Hamstel Road
Harlow
Essex CM20 1QX
Tel **01279 444 455**

Cardiology: outpatient wait   -
Angiography available on site   No

Harrogate • **Harrogate District Hospital**

Lancaster Park Road
Harrogate
North Yorkshire HG2 7SX
Tel **01423 885 959**

Cardiology: outpatient wait   -
Angiography available on site   No

Hartlepool • **University Hospital of Hartlepool**

Holdforth Road
Hartlepool
Cleveland TS24 9AH
Tel **01429 266 654**

Cardiology: outpatient wait   -
Angiography available on site   No

Haywards Heath • **Princess Royal Hospital**

Lewes Road
Haywards Heath
West Sussex RH16 4EX
Tel **01444 441 881**

Cardiology: outpatient wait   98%
Angiography available on site   No

Hemel Hempstead • **Hemel Hempstead General Hospital**

Hillfield Road
Hemel Hempstead
Hertfordshire HP2 4AD
Tel **01442 213 141**

Cardiology: outpatient wait   39%
Angiography available on site   No

Hereford • **County Hospital**

Hereford
Herefordshire
HR1 2ER
Tel **01432 355 444**

Cardiology: outpatient wait   36%
Angiography available on site   Yes

Hexham • **Hexham General Hospital**

Corbridge Road
Hexham
Northumberland NE46 1QJ
Tel **01434 655 655**

Cardiology: outpatient wait   -
Angiography available on site   No

High Wycombe • **Wycombe Hospital**

Queen Alexandra Road
High Wycombe
Buckinghamshire HP11 2TT
Tel **01494 526 161**

Cardiology: outpatient wait   -
Angiography available on site   No

Huddersfield • **Huddersfield Royal Infirmary**

Acre Street, Lindley
Huddersfield
West Yorkshire HD3 3EA
Tel **01484 342 000**

Cardiology: outpatient wait   61%
Angiography available on site   No

Hull • **Hull Royal Infirmary**

Anlaby Road
Hull
East Yorkshire HU3 2JZ

Cardiology: outpatient wait   79%

Tel **01482 328 541**

Angiography available on site Yes

Huntingdon • **Hinchingbrooke Hospital**

Hinchingbrooke Park
Huntingdon
Cambridgeshire PE29 6NT

Cardiology: outpatient wait   82%

Tel **01480 416 416**

Angiography available on site No

Ipswich • **Ipswich Hospital**

Heath Road
Ipswich
Suffolk IP4 5PD

Cardiology: outpatient wait   71%

Tel **01473 712 233**

Angiography available on site No

Keighley • **Airedale General Hospital**

Skipton Road, Steeton
Keighley
West Yorkshire BD20 6TD

Cardiology: outpatient wait   75%

Tel **01535 652 511**

Angiography available on site Yes

Kettering • **Kettering General Hospital**

Rothwell Road
Kettering
Northamptonshire NN16 8UZ

Cardiology: outpatient wait   90%

Tel **01536 492 000**

Angiography available on site No

King's Lynn • **Queen Elizabeth Hospital**

Gayton Road
King's Lynn
Norfolk PE30 4ET

Cardiology: outpatient wait   47%

Tel **01553 613 613**

Angiography available on site No

Lancaster • **Royal Lancaster Infirmary**

Ashton Road
Lancaster
Lancashire LA1 4RP
Tel **01524 659 444**

Cardiology: outpatient wait 100%
Angiography available on site No

Leeds • **St James's University Hospital**

Beckett Street
Leeds
West Yorkshire LS9 7TF
Tel **0113 243 3144**

Cardiology: outpatient wait 80%
Angiography available on site No

Leicester • **Leicester General Hospital**

Gwendolen Road
Leicester
LE5 4PW
Tel **0116 249 0490**

Cardiology: outpatient wait 96%
Angiography available on site No

Leicester • **Leicester Royal Infirmary**

Infirmary Square
Leicester
LE1 5WW
Tel **0116 254 1414**

Cardiology: outpatient wait 96%
Angiography available on site No

Lincoln • **Lincoln County Hospital**

Greetwell Road
Lincoln
Lincolnshire LN2 5QY
Tel **01522 512 512**

Cardiology: outpatient wait 76%
Angiography available on site Yes

Liverpool • **Royal Liverpool University Hospital**

Prescot Street
Liverpool
L7 8XP
Tel **0151 706 2000**

Cardiology: outpatient wait 85%
Angiography available on site Yes

Liverpool • **University Hospital Aintree**

Longmoor Lane
Liverpool
L9 7AL
Tel **0151 525 5980**

Cardiology: outpatient wait	69%
Angiography available on site	No

London • **Barnet Hospital**

Wellhouse Lane
Barnet
Hertfordshire EN5 3DH
Tel **020 8216 4000**

Cardiology: outpatient wait	20%
Angiography available on site	No

London • **Bromley Hospital**

Cromwell Avenue
Bromley
Kent BR2 9AJ
Tel **020 8289 7000**

Cardiology: outpatient wait	76%
Angiography available on site	No

London • **Central Middlesex Hospital**

Acton Lane
Park Royal
London NW10 7NS
Tel **020 8965 5733**

Cardiology: outpatient wait	71%
Angiography available on site	No

London • **Charing Cross Hospital**

Fulham Palace Road
Hammersmith
London W6 8RF
Tel **020 8383 0000**

Cardiology: outpatient wait	99%
Angiography available on site	No

London • **Chase Farm Hospital**

The Ridgeway
Enfield
Middlesex EN2 8JL
Tel **020 8366 6600**

Cardiology: outpatient wait	20%
Angiography available on site	No

London • **Chelsea & Westminster Hospital**

369 Fulham Road
London
SW10 9NH
Tel **020 8746 8000**

(CCU) (ECG)

Cardiology: outpatient wait   82%
Angiography available on site   No

London • **Ealing Hospital**

Uxbridge Road
Southall
Middlesex UB1 3HW
Tel **020 8967 5000**

(30) (CCU) (ECG)

Cardiology: outpatient wait   34%
Angiography available on site   No

London • **Epsom General Hospital**

Dorking Road
Epsom
Surrey KT18 7EG
Tel **01372 735 735**

(CCU) (ECG)

Cardiology: outpatient wait   79%
Angiography available on site   No

London • **Harold Wood Hospital**

Gubbins Lane
Romford
Essex RM3 0BE
Tel **01708 345 533**

(CCU)

Cardiology: outpatient wait   90%
Angiography available on site   No

London • **Hillingdon Hospital**

Pield Heath Road
Uxbridge
Middlesex UB8 3NN
Tel **01895 238 282**

(30) (CCU) (ECG)

Cardiology: outpatient wait   96%
Angiography available on site   No

London • **Homerton University Hospital**

Homerton Row
Hackney
London E9 6SR
Tel **020 8510 5555**

(CCU) (ECG)

Cardiology: outpatient wait   85%
Angiography available on site   No

London • **King George Hospital**

Barley Lane
Goodmayes, Ilford
Essex IG3 8YB
Tel **020 8983 8000**

Cardiology: outpatient wait   90%
Angiography available on site   No

London • **Kingston Hospital**

Galsworthy Road
Kingston upon Thames
Surrey KT2 7QB
Tel **020 8546 7711**

Cardiology: outpatient wait   96%
Angiography available on site   No

London • **Mayday Hospital**

London Road
Croydon
London CR7 7YE
Tel **0208 401 3000**

Cardiology: outpatient wait   85%
Angiography available on site   Yes

London • **Middlesex & University College Hospitals**

Mortimer Street
London
W1T 3AA
Tel **020 7636 8333**

Cardiology: outpatient wait   90%
Angiography available on site   Yes

London • **Newham General Hospital**

Glen Road
Plaistow
London E13 8SL
Tel **020 7476 4000**

Cardiology: outpatient wait   81%
Angiography available on site   No

London • **North Middlesex University Hospital**

Sterling Way
Edmonton
London N18 1QX
Tel **020 8887 2000**

Cardiology: outpatient wait   85%
Angiography available on site   Yes

London • **Northwick Park Hospital**

Watford Road
Harrow
Middlesex HA1 3UJ
Tel **020 8864 3232**

Cardiology: outpatient wait 71%
Angiography available on site Yes

London • **Oldchurch Hospital**

Waterloo Road
Romford
Essex RM7 0BE
Tel **01708 345 533**

Cardiology: outpatient wait 90%
Angiography available on site No

London • **Queen Elizabeth Hospital**

Stadium Road
Woolwich
London SE18 4QH
Tel **020 8858 8141**

Cardiology: outpatient wait 50%
Angiography available on site Yes

London • **Queen Mary's Hospital**

Frognal Avenue
Sidcup
Kent DA14 6LT
Tel **020 8302 2678**

Cardiology: outpatient wait 98%
Angiography available on site No

London • **Royal Free Hospital**

Pond Street
Hampstead
London NW3 2QG
Tel **020 7794 0500**

Cardiology: outpatient wait 64%
Angiography available on site Yes

London • **Royal London Hospital**

Whitechapel Road
London
E1 1BB
Tel **020 7377 7000**

Cardiology: outpatient wait 98%
Angiography available on site No

London • **St Helier Hospital**

Wrythe Lane
Carshalton
Surrey SM5 1AA
Tel **020 8296 2000**

Cardiology: outpatient wait 79%
Angiography available on site No

London • **University Hospital Lewisham**

High Street
Lewisham
London SE13 6LH
Tel **020 8333 3000**

Cardiology: outpatient wait 49%
Angiography available on site No

London • **West Middlesex University Hospital**

Twickenham Road
Isleworth
Middlesex TW7 6AF
Tel **020 8560 2121**

Cardiology: outpatient wait 80%
Angiography available on site No

London • **Whipps Cross University Hospital**

Whipps Cross Road
Leytonstone
London E11 1NR
Tel **020 8539 5522**

Cardiology: outpatient wait 89%
Angiography available on site No

London • **Whittington Hospital**

Highgate Hill
Archway
London N19 5NF
Tel **020 7272 3070**

Cardiology: outpatient wait 92%
Angiography available on site No

Luton • **Luton & Dunstable Hospital**

Lewsey Road
Luton
Bedfordshire LU4 0DZ
Tel **01582 491122**

Cardiology: outpatient wait 93%
Angiography available on site No

Macclesfield • **Macclesfield DGH**

Victoria Road
Macclesfield
Cheshire SK10 3BL
Tel **01625 421 000**

Cardiology: outpatient wait   46%
Angiography available on site   No

Maidstone • **Maidstone Hospital**

Hermitage Lane
Maidstone
Kent ME16 9QQ
Tel **01622 729 000**

Cardiology: outpatient wait   70%
Angiography available on site   No

Manchester • **North Manchester General Hospital**

Delaunays Road
Crumpsall
Manchester M8 5RL
Tel **0161 795 4567**

Cardiology: outpatient wait   51%
Angiography available on site   No

Manchester • **Trafford General Hospital**

Moorside Road, Davyhulme
Manchester
M41 5SL
Tel **0161 748 4022**

Cardiology: outpatient wait   99%
Angiography available on site   No

Margate • **Queen Elizabeth The Queen Mother Hospital**

St Peters Road
Margate
Kent CT9 4AN
Tel **01843 225 544**

Cardiology: outpatient wait   66%
Angiography available on site   No

Middlesbrough • **Middlesbrough General Hospital**

Ayresome Green Lane
Middlesbrough
Cleveland TS5 5AZ
Tel **01642 850 850**

Cardiology: outpatient wait   90%
Angiography available on site   No

Milton Keynes • **Milton Keynes General Hospital**

Standing Way, Eaglestone
Milton Keynes
Buckinghamshire MK6 5LD
Tel **01908 660 033**

Cardiology: outpatient wait   94%
Angiography available on site No

Newport (IoW) • **St Mary's Hospital**

Parkhurst Road
Newport
Isle of Wight PO30 5TG
Tel **01983 524 081**

Cardiology: outpatient wait   49%
Angiography available on site No

North Shields • **North Tyneside General Hospital**

Rake Lane
North Shields
Tyne & Wear NE29 8NH
Tel **0191 259 6660**

Cardiology: outpatient wait   -
Angiography available on site No

Northallerton • **Friarage Hospital**

Northallerton
North Yorkshire
DL6 1JG
Tel **01609 779 911**

Cardiology: outpatient wait   -
Angiography available on site No

Northampton • **Northampton General Hospital**

Cliftonville
Northampton
Northamptonshire NN1 5BD
Tel **01604 634 700**

Cardiology: outpatient wait   -
Angiography available on site Yes

Norwich • **Norfolk & Norwich University Hospital**

Colney Lane
Norwich
Norfolk NR4 7UY
Tel **01603 286 286**

Cardiology: outpatient wait   76%
Angiography available on site Yes

Nottingham • **Queen's Medical Centre**

Derby Road
Nottingham
NG7 2UH
Tel **0115 924 9924**

Cardiology: outpatient wait   96%
Angiography available on site   Yes

Nuneaton • **George Eliot Hospital**

College Street
Nuneaton
Warwickshire CV10 7DJ
Tel **02476 351 351**

Cardiology: outpatient wait   -
Angiography available on site   No

Oldham • **Royal Oldham Hospital**

Rochdale Road
Oldham
Lancashire OL1 2JH
Tel **0161 624 0420**

Cardiology: outpatient wait   68%
Angiography available on site   No

Ormskirk • **Ormskirk & District General Hospital**

Wigan Road
Ormskirk
Lancashire L39 2AZ
Tel **01695 577 111**

Cardiology: outpatient wait   -
Angiography available on site   No

Oxford • **Radcliffe Infirmary**

Woodstock Road
Oxford
OX2 6HE
Tel **01865 311 188**

Cardiology: outpatient wait   74%
Angiography available on site   No

Peterborough • **Peterborough District Hospital**

Thorpe Road
Peterborough
Cambridgeshire PE3 6DA
Tel **01733 874 000**

Cardiology: outpatient wait   51%
Angiography available on site   No

Pontefract • **Pontefract General Infirmary**

Friarwood Lane
Pontefract
West Yorkshire WF8 1PL

Cardiology: outpatient wait   62%

Tel **01977 600 600**

Angiography available on site Yes

Poole • **Poole Hospital**

Longfleet Road
Poole
Dorset BH15 2JB

Cardiology: outpatient wait   85%

Tel **01202 665 511**

Angiography available on site No

Portsmouth • **Queen Alexandra Hospital**

Southwick Hill Road
Portsmouth
Hampshire PO6 3LY

Cardiology: outpatient wait   88%

Tel **02392 286 000**

Angiography available on site No

Portsmouth • **St Mary's Hospital**

Milton Road
Portsmouth
Hampshire PO3 6AD

Cardiology: outpatient wait   88%

Tel **02392 286 000**

Angiography available on site Yes

Prescot • **Whiston Hospital**

Whiston
Prescot
Merseyside L35 5DR

Cardiology: outpatient wait   45%

Tel **0151 426 1600**

Angiography available on site No

Preston • **Royal Preston Hospital**

Sharoe Green Lane North
Preston
Lancashire PR2 9HT

Cardiology: outpatient wait   70%

Tel **01772 716 565**

Angiography available on site No

Reading • **Royal Berkshire & Battle Hospitals**

London Road
Reading
Berkshire RG1 5AN
Tel **0118 987 5111**

Cardiology: outpatient wait 97%
Angiography available on site Yes

Redditch • **Alexandra Hospital**

Woodrow Drive
Redditch
Worcestershire B98 7UB
Tel **01527 503 030**

Cardiology: outpatient wait 73%
Angiography available on site Yes

Redhill • **East Surrey & Crawley Hospitals**

Canada Avenue
Redhill
Surrey RH1 5RH
Tel **01737 768511**

Cardiology: outpatient wait 67%
Angiography available on site No

Rochdale • **Rochdale Infirmary**

Whitehall Street
Rochdale
Lancashire OL12 0NB
Tel **01706 377 777**

Cardiology: outpatient wait 74%
Angiography available on site Yes

Rotherham • **Rotherham DGH**

Moorgate Road, Oakwood
Rotherham
South Yorkshire S60 2UD
Tel **01709 820 000**

Cardiology: outpatient wait 99%
Angiography available on site No

Runcorn • **Halton General Hospital**

Hospital Way
Runcorn
Cheshire WA7 2DA
Tel **01928 714 567**

Cardiology: outpatient wait 85%
Angiography available on site No

Salford • **Hope Hospital**

Stott Lane
Salford
Lancashire M6 8WH
Tel **0161 789 7373**

Cardiology: outpatient wait   99%
Angiography available on site   No

Salisbury • **Salisbury District Hospital**

Odstock Road
Salisbury
Wiltshire SP2 8BJ
Tel **01722 336 262**

Cardiology: outpatient wait   100%
Angiography available on site   No

Scarborough • **Scarborough General Hospital**

Woodlands Drive
Scarborough
North Yorkshire YO12 6QL
Tel **01723 368 111**

Cardiology: outpatient wait   -
Angiography available on site   No

Scunthorpe • **Scunthorpe General Hospital**

Cliff Gardens
Scunthorpe
North Lincolnshire DN15 7BH
Tel **01724 282 282**

Cardiology: outpatient wait   87%
Angiography available on site   No

Sheffield • **Royal Hallamshire Hospital**

Glossop Road
Sheffield
South Yorkshire S10 2JF
Tel **0114 271 1900**

Cardiology: outpatient wait   96%
Angiography available on site   No

Shrewsbury • **Royal Shrewsbury Hospital**

Mytton Oak Road
Shrewsbury
Shropshire SY3 8XQ
Tel **01743 261 000**

Cardiology: outpatient wait   60%
Angiography available on site   Yes

Slough • **Wexham Park Hospital**

Wexham Street
Slough
Berkshire SL2 4HL
Tel **01753 633 000**

Cardiology: outpatient wait	95%
Angiography available on site	No

Solihull • **Solihull Hospital**

Lode Lane
Solihull
West Midlands B91 2JL
Tel **0121 424 2000**

Cardiology: outpatient wait	85%
Angiography available on site	No

South Shields • **South Tyneside District Hospital**

Harton Lane
South Shields
Tyne & Wear NE34 0PL
Tel **0191 454 8888**

Cardiology: outpatient wait	57%
Angiography available on site	No

Southport • **Southport & Formby DGH**

Town Lane, Kew
Southport
Merseyside PR8 6PN
Tel **01704 547 471**

Cardiology: outpatient wait	-
Angiography available on site	No

St Leonards on Sea • **Conquest Hospital**

The Ridge
St Leonards on Sea
East Sussex TN37 7RD
Tel **01424 755 255**

Cardiology: outpatient wait	44%
Angiography available on site	Yes

Stafford • **Staffordshire General Hospital**

Weston Road
Stafford
ST16 3SA
Tel **01785 257 731**

Cardiology: outpatient wait	-
Angiography available on site	No

Stevenage • **Lister Hospital**

Coreys Mill Lane
Stevenage
Hertfordshire SG1 4AB
Tel **01438 314 333**

Cardiology: outpatient wait   85%
Angiography available on site   Yes

Stockport • **Stepping Hill Hospital**

Poplar Grove
Stockport
Cheshire SK2 7JE
Tel **0161 483 1010**

Cardiology: outpatient wait   -
Angiography available on site   No

Stockton on Tees • **University Hospital of North Tees**

Hardwick
Stockton on Tees
Cleveland TS19 8PE
Tel **01642 617 617**

Cardiology: outpatient wait   -
Angiography available on site   No

Stoke-on-Trent • **North Staffordshire Hospital**

Princes Road, Hartshill
Stoke-on-Trent
Staffordshire ST4 7LN
Tel **01782 715 444**

Cardiology: outpatient wait   51%
Angiography available on site   Yes

Stourbridge • **Russells Hall, Wordsley, Corbett & Guest Hospitals**

Wordsley Hospital, Stream Road
Wordsley, Stourbridge
West Midlands DY8 5QX
Tel **01384 456 111**

Cardiology: outpatient wait   -
Angiography available on site   Yes

Sunderland • **Sunderland Royal Hospital**

Kayll Road
Sunderland
Tyne & Wear SR4 7TP
Tel **0191 565 6256**

Cardiology: outpatient wait   68%
Angiography available on site   Yes

Sutton Coldfield • **Good Hope DGH**

Rectory Road
Sutton Coldfield
West Midlands B75 7RR
Tel **0121 378 2211**

Cardiology: outpatient wait   -
Angiography available on site   Yes

Sutton in Ashfield • **King's Mill Hospital**

Mansfield Road
Sutton in Ashfield
Nottinghamshire NG17 4JL
Tel **01623 622 515**

Cardiology: outpatient wait   88%
Angiography available on site   No

Swindon • **Princess Margaret Hospital**

Okus Road
Swindon
Wiltshire SN1 4JU
Tel **01793 536 231**

Cardiology: outpatient wait   92%
Angiography available on site   Yes

Taunton • **Taunton & Somerset Hospital**

Musgrove Park
Taunton
Somerset TA1 5DA
Tel **01823 333 444**

Cardiology: outpatient wait   79%
Angiography available on site   Yes

Telford • **Princess Royal Hospital**

Apley Castle
Telford
Shropshire TF1 6TF
Tel **01952 641 222**

Cardiology: outpatient wait   62%
Angiography available on site   Yes

Torquay • **Torbay DGH**

Lawes Bridge
Torquay
Devon TQ2 7AA
Tel **01803 614 567**

Cardiology: outpatient wait   84%
Angiography available on site   Yes

Truro • **Royal Cornwall Hospital**

Treliske
Truro
Cornwall TR1 3LJ
Tel **01872 250 000**

Cardiology: outpatient wait   68%
Angiography available on site   Yes

Tunbridge Wells • **Kent & Sussex Hospital**

Mount Ephraim
Tunbridge Wells
Kent TN2 4AT
Tel **01892 526 111**

Cardiology: outpatient wait   70%
Angiography available on site   No

Wakefield • **Pinderfields General Hospital**

Aberford Road
Wakefield
West Yorkshire WF1 4DG
Tel **01924 201 688**

Cardiology: outpatient wait   62%
Angiography available on site   Yes

Walsall • **Manor Hospital**

Moat Road
Walsall
West Midlands WS2 9PS
Tel **01922 721 172**

Cardiology: outpatient wait   -
Angiography available on site   Yes

Warrington • **Warrington Hospital**

Lovely Lane
Warrington
Cheshire WA5 1QG
Tel **01925 635 911**

Cardiology: outpatient wait   85%
Angiography available on site   No

Warwick • **Warwick Hospital**

Lakin Road
Warwick
Warwickshire CV34 5BW
Tel **01926 495 321**

Cardiology: outpatient wait   44%
Angiography available on site   No

Watford • **Watford General Hospital**

60 Vicarage Road
Watford
Hertfordshire WD1 80HB
Tel **01923 244 366**

Cardiology: outpatient wait   39%
Angiography available on site   No

Welwyn Garden City • **Queen Elizabeth II Hospital**

Howlands
Welwyn Garden City
Hertfordshire AL7 4HQ
Tel **01707 328 111**

Cardiology: outpatient wait   85%
Angiography available on site   No

West Bromwich • **Sandwell General Hospital**

Lyndon
West Bromwich
West Midlands B71 4HU
Tel **0121 553 1831**

Cardiology: outpatient wait   71%
Angiography available on site   Yes

Westcliff-on-Sea • **Southend Hospital**

Prittlewell Chase
Westcliff-on-Sea
Essex SS0 0RT
Tel **01702 435 555**

Cardiology: outpatient wait   99%
Angiography available on site   Yes

Weston-super-Mare • **Weston General Hospital**

Grange Road, Uphill
Weston-super-Mare
Somerset BS23 4TQ
Tel **01934 636 363**

Cardiology: outpatient wait   4%
Angiography available on site   No

Whitehaven • **West Cumberland Hospital**

Hensingham
Whitehaven
Cumbria CA28 8JG
Tel **01946 693 181**

Cardiology: outpatient wait   65%
Angiography available on site   Yes

Wigan • **Royal Albert Edward Infirmary**

Wigan Lane
Wigan
Lancashire WN1 2NN   Cardiology: outpatient wait   -
Tel **01942 244 000**   Angiography available on site   No

Willsborough • **William Harvey Hospital**

Kennington Road
Willsborough
Berkshire SL5 8AA   Cardiology: outpatient wait   66%
Tel **01233 633 331**   Angiography available on site   No

Winchester • **Royal Hampshire County Hospital**

Romsey Road
Winchester
Hampshire SO22 5DG   Cardiology: outpatient wait   100%
Tel **01962 863 535**   Angiography available on site   No

Winton Green • **City Hospital**

Dudley Road
Winton Green
Birmingham B18 7QH   Cardiology: outpatient wait   73%
Tel **0121 554 3801**   Angiography available on site   Yes

Wirral • **Wirral Hospital (Arrowe Park & Clatterbridge)**

Arrowe Park Road
Upton, Wirral
Merseyside CH49 5PE   Cardiology: outpatient wait   72%
Tel **0151 678 5111**   Angiography available on site   Yes

Wolverhampton • **New Cross Hospital**

Wednesfield Road
Wolverhampton
West Midlands WV10 0QP   Cardiology: outpatient wait   85%
Tel **01902 307 999**   Angiography available on site   No

Worcester • **Worcester Royal Hospital**

Ronkswood Branch
Newtown Road
Worcester WR5 1HN
Tel **01905 763 333**

Cardiology: outpatient wait   73%
Angiography available on site   Yes

Worksop • **Bassetlaw DGH**

Kilton Hill
Worksop
Nottinghamshire S81 0BD
Tel **01909 500 990**

Cardiology: outpatient wait   -
Angiography available on site   No

Worthing • **Worthing Hospital**

Lyndhurst Road
Worthing
West Sussex BN43 6TQ
Tel **01903 205 111**

Cardiology: outpatient wait   83%
Angiography available on site   No

Yeovil • **Yeovil District Hospital**

Higher Kingston
Yeovil
Somerset BA21 4AT
Tel **01935 475 122**

Cardiology: outpatient wait   66%
Angiography available on site   No

York • **York District Hospital**

Wigginton Road
York
North Yorkshire YO31 8HE
Tel **01904 631 313**

Cardiology: outpatient wait   -
Angiography available on site   Yes

Abergavenny • **Nevill Hall Hospital**

Brecon Road, Abergavenny
Monmouthshire
Wales NP7 7EG
Tel **01873 732 732**

Cardiology: outpatient wait   -
Angiography available on site   Yes

Aberystwyth • **Bronglais General Hospital**

Caradog Road
Aberystwyth, Ceredigion
Wales SY23 1ER
Tel **01970 623 131**

Cardiology: outpatient wait   50%
Angiography available on site   No

Bangor • **Ysbyty Gwynedd**

Penrhosgarnedd
Bangor, Gwynedd
Wales LL57 2PW
Tel **01248 384 384**

Cardiology: outpatient wait   69%
Angiography available on site   No

Bridgend • **Princess of Wales Hospital**

Coity Road
Bridgend, Mid-Glamorgan
Wales CF31 1RQ
Tel **01656 752 752**

Cardiology: outpatient wait   25%
Angiography available on site   Yes

Carmarthen • **West Wales General Hospital**

Glangwili
Carmarthen
Wales SA31 2AF
Tel **01267 235 151**

Cardiology: outpatient wait   33%
Angiography available on site   No

Haverfordwest • **Withybush General Hospital**

Fishguard Road, Haverfordwest
Pembrokeshire
Wales SA61 2PZ
Tel **01437 764 545**

Cardiology: outpatient wait   -
Angiography available on site   No

Llanelli • **Prince Philip Hospital**

Bryngwynmawr
Llanelli, Carmarthenshire
Wales SA14 8QF
Tel **01554 756 567**

Cardiology: outpatient wait   33%
Angiography available on site   No

Llantrisant • **Royal Glamorgan Hospital**

Ynys Maerdy, Llantrisant
Mid-Glamorgan
Wales CF72 8XR
Tel **01443 443 443**

Cardiology: outpatient wait   -
Angiography available on site   No

Merthyr Tydfil • **Prince Charles Hospital**

Merthyr Tydfil
Mid-Glamorgan
Wales CF47 9DT
Tel **01685 721 721**

Cardiology: outpatient wait   -
Angiography available on site   No

Newport • **Royal Gwent Hospital**

Cardiff Road, Newport
Monmouthshire
Wales NP20 2UB
Tel **01633 234 234**

Cardiology: outpatient wait   -
Angiography available on site   Yes

Penarth • **Llandough Hospital**

Penlan Road, Penarth
Vale of Glamorgan
Wales CF64 2XX
Tel **029 2071 1711**

Cardiology: outpatient wait   36%
Angiography available on site   No

Rhyl • **Glan Clwyd DGH**

Bodelwyddan
Rhyl, Conwy
Wales LL18 5UJ
Tel **01745 583 910**

Cardiology: outpatient wait   83%
Angiography available on site   No

Swansea • **Singleton Hospital**

Sketty Road
Swansea
Wales SA2 8QA
Tel **01792 205 666**

CCU

Cardiology: outpatient wait   76%
Angiography available on site   No

Wrexham • **Wrexham Maelor Hospital**

Croesnewydd Road
Wrexham
Wales LL13 7TD
Tel **01978 291 100**

Cardiology: outpatient wait   62%
Angiography available on site   No

Antrim • **Antrim Hospital**

45 Bush Road
Antrim, Co Antrim
Northern Ireland BT41 2RL
Tel **028 9442 4000**

Angiography available on site   No

Belfast • **Belfast City Hospital**

Lisburn Road
Belfast
Northern Ireland BT9 7AB
Tel **028 9032 9241**

Angiography available on site   Yes

Belfast • **Mater Hospital**

47–51 Crumlin Road
Belfast
Northern Ireland BT14 6AB
Tel **028 9074 1211**

Angiography available on site   No

Belfast • **The Royal Hospitals**

Grosvenor Road
Belfast
Northern Ireland BT12 6BA
Tel **028 9024 0503**

Angiography available on site   Yes

Coleraine • **Causeway Hospital**

Newbridge Road
Coleraine, Co Londonderry
Northern Ireland BT52 1TT
Tel **028 7032 7032**

Angiography available on site   No

Craigavon • **Craigavon Area Hospital**

68 Lurgan Road
Craigavon, Co Down
Northern Ireland BT63 5QQ
Tel **028 3833 4444**

Angiography available on site   Yes

Downpatrick • **Downe Hospital**

9a Pound Lane
Downpatrick, Co Down
Northern Ireland BT30 6JA
Tel **028 4461 3311**

Angiography available on site   No

Dundonald • **Ulster Hospital**

Upper Newtownards Road
Dundonald, Co Down
Northern Ireland BT16 0RH
Tel **028 9048 4511**

Angiography available on site   Yes

Londonderry • **Altnagelvin Area Hospital**

Glenshane Road
Londonderry, Co Londonderry
Northern Ireland BT47 6SB
Tel **028 7134 5171**

Angiography available on site   Yes

Newry • **Daisy Hill Hospital**

5 Hospital Road
Newry, Co Down
Northern Ireland BT35 8DR
Tel **02830 835 000**

Angiography available on site   No

Airdrie • **Monklands Hospital**

Monkscourt Avenue
Airdrie, Lanarkshire
Scotland ML6 0JS
Tel **01236 748 748**

VOLUMES	Angiography	n/a
	Angioplasty	-
AVG WAIT	Angiography	n/a
	Angioplasty	-

Alexandria • **Vale of Leven DGH**

Main Street
Alexandria, Dunbartonshire
Scotland G83 0UA
Tel **01389 754 121**

VOLUMES	Angiography	-
	Angioplasty	-
AVG WAIT	Angiography	-
	Angioplasty	-

Ayr • **Ayr Hospital**

Dalmellington Road
Ayr, Ayrshire
Scotland KA6 6DX
Tel **01292 610 555**

VOLUMES	Angiography	600
	Angioplasty	-
AVG WAIT	Angiography	36
	Angioplasty	-

Dumfries • **Dumfries & Galloway Royal Infirmary**

Bankend Road
Dumfries
Scotland DG1 4AP
Tel **01387 246 246**

VOLUMES	Angiography	281
	Angioplasty	-
AVG WAIT	Angiography	55
	Angioplasty	-

Dundee • **Ninewells Hospital**

Dundee
Scotland
DD1 9SY
Tel **01382 660 111**

VOLUMES	Angiography	675
	Angioplasty	n/a
AVG WAIT	Angiography	27
	Angioplasty	n/a

Dunfermline • **Queen Margaret Hospital**

Whitefield Road	VOLUMES	Angiography	n/a
Dunfermline, Fife		Angioplasty	n/a
Scotland KY12 0SU			
Tel **01383 623 623**			
	AVG WAIT	Angiography	n/a
		Angioplasty	n/a

Edinburgh • **Western General Hospital**

Crewe Road	VOLUMES	Angiography	1483
Edinburgh		Angioplasty	628
Scotland EH3 9EF			
Tel **0131 537 1000**			
	AVG WAIT	Angiography	17
		Angioplasty	37

Elgin • **Dr Gray's Hospital**

Elgin	VOLUMES	Angiography	-
Moray		Angioplasty	-
Scotland IV30 1SN			
Tel **01343 543 131**			
	AVG WAIT	Angiography	-
		Angioplasty	-

Falkirk • **Falkirk Royal Infirmary**

Majors Loan	VOLUMES	Angiography	-
Falkirk		Angioplasty	-
Scotland FK1 5QE			
Tel **01324 624 000**			
	AVG WAIT	Angiography	-
		Angioplasty	-

Glasgow • **Hairmyres Hospital**

Eaglesham Road	VOLUMES	Angiography	1190
East Kilbride, Glasgow		Angioplasty	497
Scotland G75 8RG			
Tel **01355 220 292**			
	AVG WAIT	Angiography	55
		Angioplasty	43

Glasgow • **Southern General Hospital**

1345 Govan Road Glasgow Scotland G51 4TF Tel **0141 201 1100**	VOLUMES	Angiography Angioplasty	- -
	AVG WAIT	Angiography Angioplasty	- -

Glasgow • **Stobhill Hospital**

Balornock Road Glasgow Scotland G21 3UW Tel **0141 201 3907**	VOLUMES	Angiography Angioplasty	21 -
	AVG WAIT	Angiography Angioplasty	3 -

Glasgow • **Victoria Infirmary**

Langside Glasgow Scotland G42 9TT Tel **0141 201 6000**	VOLUMES	Angiography Angioplasty	- -
	AVG WAIT	Angiography Angioplasty	- -

Greenock • **Inverclyde Royal Hospital**

Larkfield Road Greenock, Renfrewshire Scotland PA16 0XN Tel **01475 633 777**	VOLUMES	Angiography Angioplasty	238 -
	AVG WAIT	Angiography Angioplasty	126 -

Inverness • **Raigmore Hospital**

Old Perth Road Inverness, Highland Scotland IV2 3UJ Tel **01463 704 000**	VOLUMES	Angiography Angioplasty	296 -
	AVG WAIT	Angiography Angioplasty	23 -

Kilmarnock • **Crosshouse Hospital**

Crosshouse
Kilmarnock, East Ayrshire
Scotland KA2 0BE
Tel **01563 521 133**

	VOLUMES		
	VOLUMES	Angiography	n/a
		Angioplasty	n/a
	AVG WAIT	Angiography	n/a
		Angioplasty	n/a

Kirkcaldy • **Victoria Hospital**

Hayfield Road
Kirkcaldy, Fife
Scotland KY2 5AH
Tel **01592 643 355**

	VOLUMES	Angiography	-
		Angioplasty	-
	AVG WAIT	Angiography	-
		Angioplasty	-

Livingston • **St John's Hospital at Howden**

Howden Road West
Livingston, West Lothian
Scotland EH54 6PP
Tel **01506 419 666**

	VOLUMES	Angiography	-
		Angioplasty	-
	AVG WAIT	Angiography	-
		Angioplasty	-

Melrose • **Borders General Hospital**

Melrose
Roxburghshire
Scotland TD6 9BS
Tel **01896 826 000**

	VOLUMES	Angiography	-
		Angioplasty	-
	AVG WAIT	Angiography	-
		Angioplasty	-

Paisley • **Royal Alexandra Hospital**

Corsebar Road, Paisley
Renfrewshire
Scotland PA2 9PN
Tel **0141 887 9111**

	VOLUMES	Angiography	-
		Angioplasty	-
	AVG WAIT	Angiography	-
		Angioplasty	-

Perth • **Perth Royal Infirmary**

Taymount Terrace
Perth and Kinross
Scotland PH1 1NX
Tel **01738 623 311**

VOLUMES	Angiography	-
	Angioplasty	-
AVG WAIT	Angiography	-
	Angioplasty	-

Stirling • **Stirling Royal Infirmary**

Livilands
Stirling
Scotland FK8 2AU
Tel **01786 434 000**

VOLUMES	Angiography	n/a
	Angioplasty	-
AVG WAIT	Angiography	n/a
	Angioplasty	-

Cardiothoracic surgeon index

Year shown relates to date of primary qualification.

■ Sub specialties

● Special interests

♦ Research interests

Allen, Simon M 1981 ●Coronary artery bypass grafting

Amrani, Mohamed 1987 ■Adult cardiac surgery, coronary artery bypass grafting, aortic valve surgery, thoracic organ transplantation ●Minimally invasive cardiac surgery, aortic root surgery, arterial coronary artery bypass grafts, off-pump surgery ♦Beating heart and aortic root surgery, myocardial protection, arterial conduits for CABG

Anderson, David R 1979 ■Paediatric cardiothoracic surgery

Anderson, Jonathan R 1987 ●Adult cardiac surgery

Angelini, Gianni 1979 ■Adult cardiac surgery, coronary artery bypass grafting, mitral valve surgery ●Off-pump coronary artery bypass, mitral valve surgery, heart failure surgery

Anikin, Vladimir A 1979 ■Thoracic surgery, oesophageal surgery ●Oesophageal cancer surgery, thoracic surgical oncology, video-assisted thoracoscopic surgery ♦Research related to thoracic surgical oncology

Argano, Vincenzo 1982 ●Arterial coronary artery bypass grafts, aortic surgery (thoracic), valvular surgery

Armistead, Stephen H 1974 ●Valvular surgery, coronary artery bypass grafting

Ascione, Raimondo *No further information available*

Ashraf, Syed S 1981

Au, John K K 1980 ■Adult cardiothoracic surgery

Austin, Conal 1986 ■Paediatric cardiac surgery ●Adult cardiac surgery

Azzu, Ahmed A MD 1977 ■Adult cardiac surgery, adult thoracic surgery ●Coronary artery bypass grafting, valvular surgery, lung cancer surgery, video-assisted thoracoscopic surgery

Barlow, Clifford W 1985 ●Coronary artery bypass grafting, mitral valve surgery

Barnard, Sion *No further information available*

Barron, David J *No further information available*

Beggs, Fredericke D 1973 ■Adult thoracic surgery, oesophageal surgery ♦Surgery of oesophageal cancer, lung cancer and oesophageal benign conditions

Berg, Geoffrey A 1980 ■Adult cardiac surgery ●Aortic valve surgery, coronary artery bypass grafting

Bhatnagar, Narendra K *No further information available*

Blauth, Christopher I 1978 ■Adult cardiac surgery ●Off-pump CABG

Bonser, Robert S 1977 ●Aortic surgery (thoracic)

Brackenbury, Edward T 1984 ■Adult cardiac surgery, adult thoracic surgery, mitral valve surgery, coronary artery bypass grafting ●Arterial coronary artery bypass grafts, mitral valve surgery, aortic root surgery, lung cancer surgery

Braidley, Peter C 1988 ●Mitral valve surgery

Brawn, William J 1970 ■Congenital cardiothoracic surgery

Bridgewater, Benjamin J M 1986 ■Adult cardiac surgery ●Mitral valve surgery

Briffa, Norman P 1983 ■Adult cardiac surgery, adult thoracic surgery ●Off-pump coronary artery bypass, arterial coronary artery bypass grafts, aortic valve surgery, video-assisted thoracoscopic surgery ♦Myocardial protection, ischaemic pre-conditioning and the long-term effects of sequential left internal mammary artery grafts

Bryan, Alan J 1982 ■Adult cardiac surgery ●Coronary artery bypass grafting, aortic surgery (thoracic)

Buchan, Keith G 1986 ■Adult cardiothoracic surgery ♦Intracardiac mechanics and the study of the influence of three-dimensional geometric changes on the function of the porcine mitral valve

Butchart, Eric G 1965

Butler, John G 1983

Cale, Alexander R J 1985 ■Coronary artery bypass grafting, mitral valve surgery, aortic valve surgery, thoracic surgery ●Arterial coronary artery bypass grafts, aortic surgery (thoracic), redo cardiac surgery, lung cancer surgery ♦Clinical trials involving the role of bypass surgery in heart failure, complete arterial revascularisation, comparing stented and stentless valves and the treatment of mesothelioma (performs extrapleural pneumonectomy for these patients)

Cameron, Charles R 1970 ■Thoracic surgery ●Lung cancer surgery

Campalani, Gianfranco 1975 ■Adult cardiothoracic surgery ●Off-pump coronary artery bypass, valvular surgery ♦Evaluation of stentless valves, off-pump coronary surgery and single tilting disk heart valve prosthesis versus bi-leaflet heart valve prosthesis

Campanella, Ciro 1974

Campbell, Colin S 1970 ■Adult cardiac surgery, thoracic organ transplantation ●Off-pump surgery

Carey, John A 1984 ■Adult cardiac surgery, coronary artery bypass grafting, mitral valve surgery, aortic valve surgery

Carr, M *No further information available*

Casula, Roberto P 1989 ■Cardiac surgery, thoracic surgery ●Minimally invasive cardiac surgery, off-pump coronary artery bypass, arterial coronary artery bypass grafts

Chalmers, John A C 1977

Chandrasekaran, Venkatchalam 1978 ●Off-pump surgery, valvular surgery, arterial coronary artery bypass grafts

Ciulli, Franco 1986 ■Adult cardiothoracic surgery, coronary artery bypass grafting, mitral valve surgery, aortic valve surgery ●Heart failure surgery, off-pump coronary artery bypass, redo coronary artery bypass grafting, arterial coronary artery bypass grafts ♦Physiology of beating heart coronary artery surgery, evaluation of modern mechanical valve prostheses using dobutamine echocardiography and the use of cell saver technology in off-pump coronary artery surgery

Clark, Stephen C 1989 ■Adult cardiac surgery, adult thoracic surgery, thoracic organ transplantation ●Valvular surgery, coronary artery bypass grafting, lung cancer surgery

Cohen, Andrew S 1989

Collins, Francis J 1969 ■Thoracic surgery, oesophageal surgery ●Oesophageal surgery, lung cancer surgery ♦Treatment of chest wall tumours, lung cancer treatment and major airways surgery

Colquhoun, Ian W 1982

Cooper, Graham J 1984 ●Aortic surgery (thoracic)

Cowen, Michael E 1982 ●Lung cancer surgery, oesophageal cancer surgery

Craig, Stewart R 1985 ■Adult cardiac surgery, adult thoracic surgery ●Adult cardiothoracic surgery

Dalrymple-Hay, Malcolm J R 1990

Danton, Mark H D 1987

Dark, John H 1976 ■Thoracic organ transplantation

De Souza, Anthony C 1985

Deiraniya, Abdulilah H K 1962 ■Thoracic organ transplantation ●Adult cardiac surgery, redo coronary artery bypass grafting, lung cancer surgery, oesophageal cancer surgery

Desai, Jatin B 1975 ●Arterial coronary artery bypass grafts, mitral valve surgery

Dihmis, Walid C 1985 ■Adult cardiac surgery, coronary artery bybass grafting, aortic valve surgery, mitral valve surgery ●Off-pump surgery, arterial coronary artery bypass grafts, aortic root surgery, aortic valve surgery ♦The radial artery

Dimitri, Wadih R 1968

van Doorn, Carin A M 1984 ■Paediatric cardiothoracic surgery, adult cardiothoracic surgery ♦Heart failure and mechanical cardiac assistance, congenital heart disease

Drakeley, Michael J 1964

Dreyfus, Gilles 1982 ■Cardiac surgery

Duffy, John P 1982 ■Thoracic surgery

Duncan, Andrew J 1983

Dunning, John J 1984 ●Aortic surgery (thoracic)

Dussek, Julian E 1966 ■Thoracic surgery

Edmondson, Stephen J 1974 ●Valvular surgery, aortic surgery (thoracic)

El Shafei, Hussein M A 1978

El-Gamel, Ahmed M H M 1980 ■Adult cardiothoracic surgery, mitral valve surgery, aortic valve surgery, coronary artery bypass grafting ●Off-pump surgery, redo cardiac surgery, aortic root surgery, arterial coronary artery bypass grafts ◆Surgical stress response in senior patients, interaction between surgical stress, inflammation and coagulation to reduce thrombotic and embolic complications in cardiac surgery, evaluating new surgical ablation for atrial fibrillation, development of new automatic anastomotic devices to simplify minimally invasive cardiac surgery and new retractor system for mitral valve surgery, new applications for beating heart surgery, implementing new circulatory assist devices (artificial heart) for acute and chronic circulatory support.

Elliott, Martin J 1973 ■Paediatric cardiac surgery, paediatric thoracic surgery, thoracic organ transplantation, congenital cardiothoracic surgery ●Cardiac transplantation, chest wall deformity

Fabri, Brian 1975 ■Cardiac surgery ●Off-pump coronary artery bypass, arterial coronary artery bypass grafts, mitral valve surgery

Faichney, Alan 1973

Firmin, Richard K 1973 ■Paediatric cardiac surgery, adult cardiac surgery

Forrester-Wood, Christopher P 1969

Forsyth, Andrew T 1970 ■Adult cardiac surgery, adult thoracic surgery ●Arterial coronary artery bypass grafts, redo coronary artery bypass grafting ◆Long-term follow-up of patients with total arterial grafting for coronary artery disease

Forty, Jonathan 1980 ●Cardiac transplantation, heart failure surgery

Fountain, Saunders W 1970 ■Thoracic surgery

Gaer, Jullien A R 1983 ■Adult cardiac surgery, thoracic organ transplantation ●Arterial coronary artery bypass grafts, off-pump coronary artery bypass, valvular surgery, aortic root surgery

Galinanes, Manuel 1976 ■Cardiac surgery ●Aortic valve surgery

Gladstone, Dennis J 1971 ■Adult cardiac surgery, paediatric cardiac surgery

Glenville, Brian E 1978 ■Adult cardiothoracic surgery, coronary artery bypass grafting, aortic valve surgery, mitral valve surgery ●Off-pump coronary artery bypass, minimally invasive cardiac surgery, aortic valve surgery, mitral valve surgery ◆All areas of beating heart surgery for coronary artery bypass grafts

Goldstraw, Peter 1968 ■Thoracic surgery, adult thoracic surgery, paediatric thoracic surgery, pleural surgery ●Lung cancer surgery, thoracic surgical oncology, chest wall deformity, video-assisted thoracoscopic surgery ◆Chairman of the International Association for the Study of Lung Cancer Staging Committee which is preparing recommendations for the next revision of the TNM Staging Classification for lung cancer

Graham, Alastair N J 1986

Graham, Timothy R 1979 ■Adult cardiothoracic surgery

Griffin, Steven C 1981 ■Cardiac surgery, thoracic surgery

Griffiths, Elaine M 1979 ■Adult cardiac surgery, mitral valve surgery, aortic valve surgery, general cardiothoracic surgery ●Valvular surgery, arterial coronary artery bypass grafts, redo coronary artery bypass grafting, off-pump coronary artery bypass

Grotte, Geir J 1969 ■Coronary artery bypass grafting ●Redo coronary artery bypass grafting, aortic valve surgery

Guvendik, Levent 1969 ●Mitral valve surgery, arterial coronary artery bypass grafts

Hadjinikolaou, Leon 1985

Hamilton, J R Leslie 1977 ■Paediatric cardiothoracic surgery, adult cardiac surgery ●Cardiac transplantation

Hasan, Asif 1979 ●Aortic root surgery

Hasan, Ragheb I R 1980 ■Adult cardiothoracic surgery, coronary artery bypass grafting, aortic valve surgery, mitral valve surgery ●Off-pump surgery

Haw, Marcus P 1982 ■Adult cardiac surgery, paediatric cardiac surgery

Hayward, Martin *No further information available*

Hickey, Mark St John 1976

Hilton, Colin J 1968

Hooper, Timothy L 1979 ●Mitral valve surgery, aortic root surgery

Hopkinson, David N 1988

Hunter, Steven 1986 ■Adult cardiothoracic surgery ●Mitral valve surgery, aortic valve surgery, aortic root surgery ♦Stentless aortic valve bioprostheses

Hutter, Jonathan A 1976 ■Adult cardiac surgery, coronary artery bypass grafting ●Coronary artery bypass grafting

Hyde, Jonathon A J *No further information available*

Jahangiri, Marjan 1988 ■Adult congenital aortic surgery, off-pump coronary surgery

Jeffrey, Robert R 1978

Jenkins, David P 1986 ■Adult cardiothoracic surgery, coronary artery bypass grafting, thoracic organ transplantation ●Adult cardiac surgery, coronary artery bypass grafting, cardiac transplantation ♦Myocardial protection, risk stratification and training in cardiac surgery

John, Lindsay C H 1981 ■Adult cardiac surgery

Jones, Mark T 1977 ■Cardiac surgery, thoracic surgery ●Adult thoracic surgery

Kanagasabay, Robin 1990 ●Off-pump surgery

Kaul, Pankaj 1982 ■Adult cardiac surgery, coronary artery bypass grafting, mitral valve surgery, aortic valve surgery ●Redo cardiac surgery, redo coronary artery bypass grafting, arterial coronary artery bypass grafts, valvular surgery

Kay, Philip H 1974 ●Coronary artery bypass grafting, valvular surgery

Keenan, Daniel J M 1975 ■Adult cardiothoracic surgery ●Arterial coronary artery bypass grafts

Kendall, Simon W H 1984 ■Adult cardiothoracic surgery, coronary artery bypass grafting, aortic valve surgery ●Coronary artery bypass grafting, mitral valve surgery, adult thoracic surgery ◆Surgical treatment for atrial fibrillation

Keogh, Bruce E 1980 ■Adult cardiac surgery ●Coronary artery bypass grafting, mitral valve surgery

Khaghani, Asghar 1972 ■Adult cardiac surgery, transplant surgery, cardiac transplantation surgery, pulmonary transplantation surgery

Khalil-Marzouk, Youssef F 1976 ■Thoracic surgery, oesophageal surgery ●Thoracic surgical oncology, video-assisted thoracoscopic surgery, oesophageal cancer surgery ◆Value of muscle-sparing thoracotomy for pulmonary and oesophageal surgery, long-term risks of tracheal stenosis in percutaneous tracheostomy, pneumonectomy and pulmonary water impact on the development of ARDS, the 'Cuirass' ventilator in the post-operative performance in thoracic surgery and MRC trials in oesophageal and lung cancer surgery

Kirk, Alan J B 1979

Kolvikar, Shyamsunder K 1983 ●Off-pump surgery, video-assisted thoracoscopic surgery

Kulatilake, E Nihal P 1974 ●Valvular surgery

Kuo, James H U 1984 ●Aortic surgery (thoracic), coronary artery bypass grafting

Ladas, George 1980 ■Adult thoracic surgery ●Lung cancer surgery, endoscopic laser surgery, chest wall deformity

Langley, S M *No further information available*

Large, Stephen R 1976 ■Adult cardiac surgery, thoracic organ transplantation ◆Cadaveric donor heart physiology, training tomorrow's surgeons, effective teaching methods

Lawson, Robert A M *No further information available*

Ledingham, Simon J M 1977

de Leval, Marc 1966

Leverment, Joseph N 1963

Levine, Adrian J *No further information available*

Lewis, Christopher T 1968 ■Adult cardiothoracic surgery ●Valvular surgery

Livesey, Steven A 1979

Locke, Timothy J 1978 ◆Ethics

MacArthur, Kenneth J D 1976

MacGowan, Simon W 1983

Magee, Patrick G 1971 ■Adult cardiac surgery, adult thoracic surgery ●Adult cardiac surgery, coronary artery bypass grafting, redo coronary artery bypass grafting, thoracic surgical oncology ◆Assessment of the appropriateness of revascularisation (ACRE study)

Maiwand, Mohammad O 1965 ■Thoracic surgery

Mankad, Pankaj S 1977 ●Off-pump coronary artery bypass, mitral valve surgery

Marchbank, Adrian J 1988 ■Adult cardiothoracic surgery ●Arterial coronary artery bypass grafts, off-pump coronary artery bypass

Marrinan, Michael T 1981

McGoldrick, P Joseph 1981

McGuigan, James A 1976

McManus, Kieran G 1980 ●Oesophageal cancer surgery

Mearns, Alan J 1963

Mediratta, Neeraj K 1984

Millner, Russell W J 1983 ■Coronary artery bypass grafting, adult cardiac surgery, aortic valve surgery ●Coronary artery bypass grafting, valvular surgery

Mitchell, Ian M 1981 ■Adult cardiac surgery ●Aortic surgery (thoracic), off-pump coronary artery bypass

Moat, Neil E 1981 ●Mitral valve surgery

Monro, James L 1964 ■Paediatric cardiac surgery

Morgan, John A *No further information available*

Morgan, William E 1969 ■Thoracic surgery, oesophageal surgery ●Adult thoracic surgery, lung cancer surgery, oesophageal surgery, video-assisted thoracoscopic surgery ♦Clinical research into the surgery of lung and oesophageal cancers

Morritt, Graham N 1969 ●Coronary artery bypass grafting, lung cancer surgery

Munsch, Christopher M 1978 ●Mitral valve surgery, coronary artery bypass grafting

Murday, Andrew J 1977

Naik, Surendra K 1975

Nair, R Unni 1970 ■Adult cardiothoracic surgery ●Mitral valve surgery, minimally invasive cardiac surgery, heart failure surgery

Nashef, Samer A M 1980 ■Cardiac surgery, thoracic organ transplantation, congenital cardiothoracic surgery ●Coronary artery bypass grafting, aortic root surgery, minimally invasive cardiac surgery ♦Research into risk management and quality monitoring in cardiac surgery

Nkere, Udim 1981

Norton, Robert 1966 ●Oesophageal surgery

Odom, Nicholas J 1974 ■Adult cardiac surgery, adult thoracic surgery ●Aortic valve surgery, aortic root surgery, chest wall deformity, arterial coronary artery bypass grafts

Ohri, Sunil K 1985 ■Adult cardiac surgery ●Arterial coronary artery bypass grafts, off-pump surgery

O'Keefe, Peter A 1987 ■Adult cardiac surgery, coronary artery bypass grafting, aortic valve surgery, mitral valve surgery ●Arterial coronary artery bypass grafts, mitral valve surgery, aortic root surgery ♦Electro-surgical devices in cardiothoracic surgery, vascular biology of arterial conduits and management of sternal wound infection and dehiscence

von Oppell, Ulrich *No further information available*

O'Regan, David J 1985 ■Adult cardiac surgery, coronary artery bypass grafting, aortic valve surgery, mitral valve surgery ●Adult cardiac surgery, coronary artery bypass grafting, arterial coronary artery bypass grafts ♦Endothelial and smooth muscle cell responses to injury in the setting of angioplasty and cardiopulmonary bypass and investigating vascular biology effects of statins

O'Riordan, John 1965 ■Adult cardiac surgery ●Coronary artery bypass grafting

Owens, Andrew W 1990

Pagano, Domenico 1988

Page, Richard D 1982 ●Oesophageal cancer surgery, lung cancer surgery

Papagiannopoulos, Kostas 1990 ■Thoracic surgery, oesophageal surgery ●Thoracic surgical oncology, video-assisted thoracoscopic surgery, oesophageal cancer surgery

Parmar, Jitendra M *No further information available*

Patel, Ramesh 1980 ●Mitral valve surgery, arterial coronary artery bypass grafts

Pathi, Vivek 1985

Pepper, John R 1971

Peters, Paul 1987 ●Aortic root surgery, redo cardiac surgery

Petros, Andy *No further information available*

Petru, Mario *No further information available*

Pillai, Ravi G 1974 ■Adult cardiothoracic surgery, congenital cardiothoracic surgery, coronary artery bypass grafting, aortic valve surgery ●Valvular surgery, coronary artery bypass grafting, aortic root surgery, arterial coronary artery bypass grafts ♦Runs a research team studying baroreceptor function in the setting of aortic stenosis, the technical and physiological function of both stentless and stented valves (pioneered the technique of stentless valve implantation), evaluation of vector-delivered proteins capable of stimulating angiogenesis in the myocardium *in vivo.*

Pillay, Thaseegaran M 1989

Pollock, James C S 1972

Pozzi, Marco 1981 ■Paediatric cardiac surgery, adult cardiothoracic surgery, aortic valve surgery ●Aortic root surgery ♦Myocardial protection during cardiopulmonary bypass

Prakash, Dhruva 1967 ■Thoracic surgery

Prendergast, Brian 1987 ■Cardiac surgery

Pugsley, Wilfred B 1978

Pullan, David M 1988 ■Adult cardiothoracic surgery ●Off-pump coronary artery bypass, arterial coronary artery bypass grafts, mitral valve surgery, aortic root surgery ♦Off-pump coronary surgery and arterial revascularisation

Punjabi, Prakash 1986 ■Adult cardiothoracic surgery, coronary artery bypass grafting, mitral valve surgery ●Arterial coronary artery bypass grafts, off-pump coronary artery bypass, valvular surgery, heart failure surgery

Rahman, Ali *No further information available*

Rahamim, Yousif 1973 ■Thoracic surgery, oesophageal surgery, adult thoracic surgery, pleural surgery ●Adult thoracic surgery, oesophageal surgery, lung cancer surgery, chest wall deformity ◆Currently engaged in research projects in oesophageal carcinoma

Rajesh, Pala B 1974 ●Video-assisted thoracoscopic surgery

Rashid-Farrokhi-Fathabadi, Abbas 1968 ■Adult cardiac surgery ●Coronary artery bypass grafting, valvular surgery, aortic root surgery, aortic surgery (thoracic)

Ratnatunga, Chandana P 1980

Rees, Gareth M *No further information available*

Richens, David 1981 ●Adult cardiac surgery

Ridley, Paul D *No further information available*

Ritchie, Andrew J 1984 ■Oesophageal surgery

Rocco, Gaetano 1991 ■Thoracic surgery ●Thoracic surgical oncology

Rooney, Stephen J 1986

Rosin, Michael D 1973

Roxburgh, James C 1981 ■Adult cardiothoracic surgery ●Redo cardiac surgery, aortic surgery (thoracic) ◆Prosthetic cardiac valve performance, PET analysis and cardiac surgery outcome in poor left ventricular function, risk analysis and performance monitoring, data validation

Sarsam, Mazin 1974

Satur, Christopher M R *No further information available*

Sayer, Richard 1969 ■Thoracic surgery ●Thoracic surgical oncology

Sethia, Babulal 1975 ■Congenital cardiothoracic surgery, paediatric cardiac surgery, adult cardiac surgery

Shabbo, Fikrat P 1977

Sharpe, David A C 1984 ●Adult cardiac surgery, adult thoracic surgery

Shipolini, Alex R 1985

Shore, Darryl F 1971

Smallpeice, Christopher J *No further information available*

Smith, Edward J 1974 ●Coronary artery bypass grafting, valvular surgery

Smith, Peter L C 1975

Sogliani, F *No further information available*

Soorae, Ajaib S 1966 ■Thoracic surgery ●Lung cancer surgery

Sosnowski, Andrzej 1968 ●Aortic root surgery, mitral valve surgery

Spyt, Tomasz J 1977 ■Adult cardiac surgery ●Mitral valve surgery

Stanbridge, Rex de Lisle 1971 ●Coronary artery bypass grafting, mitral valve surgery

Steyn, Richard S 1984 ■Thoracic surgery, oesophageal surgery ◆Heathcare process design and modernisation with particular emphasis on demand and capacity whilst ensuring both quality and patient focus

Taggart, David P 1981 ■General cardiothoracic surgery ●Arterial coronary artery bypass grafts, off-pump surgery

Taylor, Kenneth M 1970 ■Adult cardiac surgery ◆Heart-lung machine use in cardiac surgery, national and international registries for cardiac surgery

Thorpe, J Andrew 1972 ■Thoracic surgery, oesophageal surgery, pleural surgery ●Oesophageal surgery, endoscopic laser surgery, chest wall deformity, video-assisted thoracoscopic surgery ◆Oesophageal pathophysiology

Tocewicz, Krys *No further information available*

Townsend, Edward R *No further information available*

Treasure, Thomas 1970 ■Thoracic surgery

Trivedi, Uday H 1986 ■Adult cardiothoracic surgery, mitral valve surgery ●Mitral valve surgery, off-pump coronary artery bypass ◆Neurological problems following cardiac surgery, cardiac surgery in the elderly

Tsang, G M K *No further information available*

Tsang, Victor 1981 ■Congenital cardiothoracic surgery

Tsui, Steven S L 1987

Underwood, Malcolm J 1987

Unsworth-White, Michael J 1988 ■General cardiothoracic surgery ●Coronary artery bypass grafting, valvular surgery, aortic surgery (thoracic), adult thoracic surgery ◆Mechanical and xenograft prosthetic heart valve trials, wound healing after cardiac surgery, immune response to cardio-pulmonary bypass and baroreceptor responses following aortic valve replacement

Uppal, Rakesh 1981 ■Adult cardiothoracic surgery, mitral valve surgery, aortic valve surgery, coronary artery bypass grafting

Vaughan, Roger 1974 ●Lung cancer surgery

Venn, Graham E 1977 ■Adult cardiac surgery, thoracic surgery ●Mitral valve surgery, coronary artery bypass grafting, arterial coronary artery bypass grafts

Walesby, Robin K 1970

Walker, William S 1977 ■Thoracic surgery, general cardiothoracic surgery, oesophageal surgery, aortic valve surgery ●Video-assisted thoracoscopic surgery, lung cancer surgery, aortic root surgery, aortic surgery (thoracic) ◆Video-assisted thoracic surgery, lung volume reduction, oesophageal surgery

Waller, David A 1985 ■Thoracic surgery ●Video-assisted thoracoscopic surgery

Wallis, John 1973

Wallwork, John 1970 ■Transplant surgery

Waterworth, Paul D 1988 ■Adult cardiac surgery, coronary artery bypass grafting, aortic valve surgery, mitral valve surgery ●Valvular surgery, off-pump coronary artery bypass, cardiac transplantation

Watterson, Kevin G 1978 ■Paediatric cardiac surgery

Weeden, David F N 1972 ■Thoracic surgery

Weerasema, Nihal *No further information available*

Weir, Ian 1974 ■Adult thoracic surgery

Wells, Francis C 1975 ■Mitral valve surgery, aortic valve surgery, thoracic surgery, thoracic organ transplantation ●Mitral valve surgery, chest wall deformity, lung cancer surgery, adult thoracic surgery ◆Aspects of mitral valve dysfunction, lung volume reduction surgery for emphysema, aspects of lung cancer

Westaby, Stephen 1972

Wheatley, David J 1964 ∎Adult cardiac surgery ●Coronary artery bypass grafting, arterial coronary artery bypass grafts, valvular surgery ◆Design, development and testing of novel artificial heart valves, left heart assist devices, and bioengineering related to cardiac surgery

Wilkinson, Glen A L 1973 ●Adult cardiothoracic surgery, mitral valve surgery

Williams, Bryn T *No further information available*

Wilson, Ian C 1982 ∎Adult cardiothoracic surgery, thoracic organ transplantation ●Coronary artery bypass grafting, valvular surgery

Wong, Kit 1986

Wood, Alan J 1975

Yacoub, Magdi 1958

Yates, Robert *No further information available*

Yonan, Nizar A A 1974 ∎Adult cardiac surgery, thoracic organ transplantation ◆Research in cardiopulmonary transplantation

Youhana, Aprim Y 1977 ∎Aortic surgery (thoracic), valve repair surgery

Young, Christopher P 1980 ●Aortic surgery (thoracic)

Zamvar, Vipin Y 1988 ∎Adult cardiothoracic surgery ●Off-pump coronary artery bypass ◆Neurological injury after cardiac surgery

Private hospital surgeons

BMI THE ALEXANDRA HOSPITAL
Bridgewater, Benjamin J M

Campbell, Colin S

Carey, John A

Deiraniya, Abdulilah H K

Dihmis, Walid C

Duncan, Andrew J

Fabri, Brian

Griffiths, Elaine M

Grotte, Geir J

Hasan, Ragheb I R

Hooper, Timothy L

Jones, Mark T

Keenan, Daniel J M

Lawson, Robert A M

Levine, Adrian J

Millner, Russell W J

Odom, Nicholas J

Pozzi, Marco

Prendergast, Brian

Rahman, Ali

Rashid-Farrokhi-Fathabadi, Ali

Ridley, Paul D

Satur, Christopher M R

Sharpe, David A C

Smallpeice, Christopher J

Waterworth, Paul D

Yonan, Nizar A A

BMI LONDON INDEPENDENT HOSPITAL
Cohen, Andrew S

Edmondson, Stephen J

Magee, Patrick G

Shipolini, Alex R

Uppal, Rakesh

Weir, Ian

Wong, Kit

Wood, Alan J

BMI THE PARK HOSPITAL
Mitchell, Ian M

Richens, David

BMI THE PRIORY HOSPITAL
Bonser, Robert S

Dimitri, Wadih R

Graham, Timothy R

Keogh, Bruce E

Pagano, Domenico

Parmar, Jitendra M

Patel, Ramesh

Rooney, Stephen J

Wilson, Ian C

BMI ROSS HALL HOSPITAL

Berg, Geoffrey A
Brackenbury, Edward T
Butler, John G
Colquhoun, Ian W
Craig, Stewart R

Faichney, Alan
MacArthur, Kenneth J D
Naik, Surendra K
Pollock, James C S

BMI THORNBURY HOSPITAL

Braidley, Peter C
Cooper, Graham J
Hopkinson, David N
Locke, Timothy J

Rocco, Gaetano
Vaughan, Roger
Wilkinson, Glen A L

BUPA HOSPITAL BRISTOL

Angelini, Gianni
Ascione, Raimondo
Bryan, Alan J
Ciulli, Franco

Forrester-Wood, Christopher P
Hutter, Jonathan A
Morgan, John A

BUPA CAMBRIDGE LEA

Dunning, John J
Jenkins, David P
Large, Stephen R
Nashef, Samer A M

Ritchie, Andrew John
Tsui, Steven S L
Wallwork, John
Wells, Francis C

BUPA HOSPITAL LEEDS

Kaul, Pankaj
Kay, Philip H
McGoldrick, P Joseph
Munsch, Christopher M
Nair, R Unni

O'Regan, David J
Papagiannopoulos, Kostas
Thorpe, J Andrew
Watterson, Kevin G

BUPA HOSPITAL LEICESTER

Firmin, Richard K
Galinanes, Manuel
Hadjinikolaou, Leon
Hickey, Mark St John

Leverment, Joseph N
Sosnowski, Andrzej
Spyt, Tomasz J

BUPA HOSPITAL SOUTHAMPTON

Barlow, Clifford W

Haw, Marcus P

Langley, Stephen M

Livesey, Steven A

Monro, James L

Ohri, Sunil K

Tsang, G M K

Weeden, David F N

BUPA HOSPITAL WASHINGTON

Clark, Stephen C

Dark, John H

Hamilton, J R Leslie

Hilton, Colin J

Hunter, Steven

Kendall, Simon W H

Morritt, Graham N

Owens, Andrew W

Wallis, John

CROMWELL HOSPITAL

Amrani, Mohamed

Dreyfus, Gilles

Gaer, Jullien A R

Marrinan, Michael T

Moat, Neil E

Sethia, Babulal

Smith, Peter L C

de Souza, Anthony Charles

HARLEY STREET CLINIC

Anderson, Jonathan R

Casula, Roberto P

van Doorn, Carin

Dreyfus, Gilles

Glenville, Brian E

Hayward, Martin

Jahangiri, Marjan

Kallis, Panayiotis

Kolvikar, Shyamsunder K

de Leval, Marc

Petros, Andy

Punjabi, Prakash

Rees, Gareth M

Smith, Peter L C

Tsang, Victor

Uppal, Rakesh

Venn, Graham E

Walesby, Robin K

Weir, Ian

Wong, Kit

Yacoub, Magdi

Yates, Robert

LEICESTER NUFFIELD HOSPITAL

Firmin, Richard K

Hadjinikolaou, Leon

LONDON BRIDGE HOSPITAL

Anderson, David R
Austin, Conal
Blauth, Christopher I
Desai, Jatin B
El-Gamel, Ahmed M H M
O'Riordan, John

Roxburgh, James C
Shabbo, Fikrat P
Venn, Graham E
Williams, Bryn T
Young, Christopher P

NUFFIELD HOSPITAL LEEDS

Kaul, Pankaj
Kay, Philip H
McGoldrick, P Joseph
Munsch, Christopher M

Nair, R Unni
O'Regan, David J
Watterson, Kevin G

ST ANTHONY'S HOSPITAL

Bhatnagar, Narendra K
Chandrasekaran, Venkatchalam
Jahangiri, Marjan
Kanagasabay, Robin

Sarsam, Mazin
Shabbo, Fikrat P
Smith, E E John

WELLINGTON HOSPITAL

Khaghani, Asghar
Peters, Paul
Walesby, Robin K

Wong, Kit
Wood, Alan J
Yacoub, Magdi

THE YORKSHIRE CLINIC

Kaul, Pankaj
Kay, Philip
Munsch, Christopher M

Nair, R Unni
Watterson, Kevin G

Useful addresses

Association for Children with Heart Disorders
Support group run by families and friends of cardiac children.
Helpline 01706 213632
www.tachd.org.uk
Email: information@tachd.org.uk

British Cardiac Patients Association
Unit 5D, 2 Station Road
Swavesey, Cambridge CB4 5QJ
National helpline 01223 846845
Heart Information Centre
020 8289 5591
www.cardiac-bcpa.co.uk
Email: bcpa@easynet.co.uk

British Heart Foundation
14 Fitzhardinge Street
London W1H 6DH
Tel 020 7935 0185
www.bhf.org.uk
Email: internet@bhf.org.uk

British Vascular Foundation
Fides House, 10 Chertsey Road
Woking, Surrey GU21 5AB
Tel 01483 726522
www.bvf.org.uk
Email: bvf@care4free.net

Cardiac Risk in the Young (CRY)
Unit 7, Epsom Downs Metro Centre
Waterfield, Tadworth
Surrey KT20 5LR
Tel 01737 363 222
www.c-r-y.org.uk
Email: mailto:cry@c-r-y.org.uk

Cardiomyopathy Association
40 The Metro Centre
Tolpits Lane, Watford
Hertfordshire WD1 8SB
Tel 01923 249 977
Freephone 0800 018 1024
www.cardiomyopathy.org
Email: cmaassoc@aol.com

Chest Heart & Stroke Scotland
65 North Castle Street
Edinburgh EH2 3LT
Tel 0131 225 6963
Advice Line 0845 077 6000
(Staffed by specialist nurses, from
9.30am–12.30pm and 1.30pm–
4.00pm Monday to Friday)
www.chss.org.uk

Children's Heart Federation (CHF)
52 Kennington Oval
London SE11 5SW
Freephone 0808 808 5000
(9.30am – 9.30pm
Monday to Friday)
www.childrens-heart-fed.org.uk
Email: chf@dircon.co.uk

Coronary Prevention Group
2 Taviton Street
London WC1H 0BT
Tel 020 7927 2125
www.healthnet.org.uk
Email: cpg@lshtm.ac.uk

The Family Heart Association
National charity for patients with
inherited high cholesterol.
7 North Road, Maidenhead
Berkshire SL6 1PE
Tel 01628 628 638
www.familyheart.org
Email: fha@familyheart.org

The Grown Up Congenital Heart Patients Association (GUCH)
12 Rectory Road
Stanford-le-Hope
Essex SS17 0DL
Freephone helpline 0800 854759
www.guch.demon.co.uk
Email: info@guch.org

HeartLine
Voluntary organisation for children with heart problems and their families.
HeartLine Association
Community Link
Surrey Heath House
Knoll Road, Camberley
Surrey GU15 3HH
Tel 01276 707636
www.heartline.org.uk
Email: heartline@easynet.co.uk

Hearts for Life
www.heartsforlife.co.uk

Medic Alert Foundation
1 Bridge Wharf
Caledonian Road
London N1 9UU
Tel 020 7833 3034
www.medicalert.org.uk
Email: info@medicalert.org.uk

National Heart Research Fund
Suite 12D
Joseph's Well
Leeds LS3 1AB
Tel 0113 234 7474
www.heartresearch.org.uk
Email: mail@heartresearch.org.uk

NHS Smoking Helpline
Freephone helpline 0800 169 0 169
(Line open 7.00am–11.00pm
Monday to Sunday. Counsellors
available 10.00am–11.00pm)

Northern Ireland Chest, Heart and Stroke Association
21 Dublin Road
Belfast BT2 7HB
Tel 028 9032 0184
Advice helpline 084 5769 7299
www.nichsa.com

UK & Overseas Heart Society – Heartlink
Independent support group offering help, advice and comfort for heart patients, their families and carers.
60 Heatherley Drive
Forest Town, Mansfield
Nottinghamshire NG19 0PY
Tel 01623 635798
Freephone 0500 676 670
www.heartlink.org.uk
Email: Support@heartlink.org.uk

Dr Foster Help at Hand Service
Tel 0906 190 0212
www.drfoster.co.uk

Methodology

The *Dr Foster Heart Disease Guide* has been produced in consultation with the Society of Cardiothoracic Surgeons of Great Britain and Ireland (SCTS). The Society was set up by the profession and represents the views of cardiothoracic surgeons on all major topics of interest in the specialty, as well as developing guidelines on clinical management and working practice. Together with the Royal College of Surgeons the Society also helps monitor standards and investigate problems.

Data in this guide comes from a number of sources. The outpatient waiting time information is taken from figures published by the Department of Health, Scottish Executive and the Welsh Assembly. The volumes and waiting times for individual procedures are calculated from inpatient data by Imperial College (for England) and by the Information and Statistics Division of the Scottish Executive for Scotland.

Information on NHS services and on private hospitals is as reported by the hospitals in response to questionnaires. The questionnaires were developed in association with the SCTS and the Independent Healthcare Association. All major cardiac units within the NHS and the private sector were surveyed in October 2002.

Information on the special interests of consultants are as reported by the consultants. Note that the fact that a consultant has a particular interest or specialism does not necessarily imply that they are more clinically skilful in that area than other doctors.

Standardised mortality ratios are derived from Hospital Episode Statistics for England by Imperial College of Science Technology and medicine. For a full description of the methodology used please go to www.drfoster.co.uk.

Glossary

Ablation A procedure used to correct certain types of heart rhythm disorders. The origin of the arrhythmia is located and radio frequency energy is used to destroy the affected areas.

ACE (angiotensin-converting enzyme) inhibitors Drugs used to slow the progression of heart failure. They expand the blood vessels, decreasing the pressure the blood needs to be pumped at to travel around the body, thereby reducing the heart's workload.

Adrenaline A hormone secreted in response to low blood glucose, exercise or stress. It makes the heart beat faster and can raise blood pressure.

Alpha-blocker A drug that decreases muscle contraction of blood vessel walls, reducing blood pressure.

Ambulatory ECG monitor See Holter monitor.

Aneurysm Dilation or 'ballooning' of a blood vessel, usually caused by atherosclerosis.

Angina Chest pain or other discomfort in the chest, shoulders, arms, or abdomen caused by narrow arteries preventing oxygen-containing blood reaching the heart muscle. Also referred to as angina pectoris.

Angiogram An invasive diagnostic procedure in which dye is injected into the blood vessels, allowing an X-ray to be taken showing where the arteries are narrowed and how narrow they have become.

Angioplasty A surgical procedure to improve the blood supply through an artery. A catheter with a small inflatable balloon at its tip is inserted into a vein in the groin and passed through to the narrowed artery. The balloon is then gently inflated so that it squashes the fatty tissue causing the narrowing.

Angiotensin A substance in the blood that causes vessels to tighten and raises blood pressure.

Angiotensin-2-antagonists drugs similar to ACE inhibitors but which can be used for those patients who suffer side-effects from ACE inhibitors. Also called Angiotensin II antagonists.

Anti-arrhythmic drugs These drugs control the rhythm of the heart. Examples are amiodarone, lidocaine and propranolol.

Anticoagulant Drug that reduces the risk of blood clots forming. Examples are aspirin, heparin, warfarin, clopidogrel.

Antihypertensive medication Used to treat hypertension. See ACE Inhibitors, Angiotensin-2-receptor blockers.

Anti-platelet drug Medications that, like aspirin, reduce the tendency of platelets in the blood to clump and clot.

Aorta The large artery leading out of the left side of the heart which supplies the whole body with blood.

Aortic aneurysm A swelling of the aorta. These swellings can occur in the chest (thoracic aortic aneurysm) or in the abdomen (abdominal aortic aneurysm).

Aortic stenosis A narrowing of the aortic valve.

Arrhythmia A disorder of the heart's electrical system, causing a heart rate that is either too slow, or too fast.

Arrhythmogenic right ventricular cardiomyopathy A rare form of cardiomyopathy which causes the heart muscle to be replaced by fibrous scar and fatty tissue.

Arteriosclerosis A thickening of the walls of the arteries caused by the build-up of calcium. This results in the loss of elasticity of the blood vessels and narrowing of the smaller arteries, which interferes with blood circulation.

Artery A main blood vessel carrying blood from the heart to the rest of the body.

Artificial heart A mechanical pump used to replace the function of a damaged heart.

Atherectomy A procedure for opening blocked coronary arteries using a laser catheter, or a rotating shaver.

Atheroma Fatty material that can build up within the walls of the arteries. When atheroma affects the coronary arteries, it can cause angina, heart attack or sudden death.

Atherosclerosis The build-up of fatty materials within the walls of the arteries.

Atria The two upper chambers of the heart which act as collecting chambers to fill the ventricles.

Atrial fibrillation A rapid, highly irregular heart rhythm.

Atrial tachycardia Any rapid heart rhythm originating in the atria. Atrial fibrillation and atrial flutter are types of atrial tachycardia.

Atrio-ventricular node The part of the heart through which electrical impulses pass from the atria to the ventricles, to stimulate a heartbeat.

Balloon angioplasty See Angioplasty.

Balloon valvuloplasty A catheter is inserted into the opening of a narrowed heart valve and a balloon is opened to stretch the valve.

Beating heart bypass surgery See MIDCAB.

Beta-blockers Drugs that block the actions of the hormone adrenaline, which makes the heart beat faster and more strongly. They are used to help prevent angina attacks, to lower blood pressure, to help control abnormal heart rhythms and to reduce the risk of further heart attacks. They are occasionally used in heart failure. Examples are atenolol and metoprolol.

Bifurcation Where the aorta or pulmonary trunk divides into two parts, forming arteries.

Bile acid-binding drugs Drugs used to lower cholesterol levels.

Blood vessel Any of the elastic tubular channels through which blood circulates in the body, such as the arteries, veins and capillaries.

Body mass index (BMI) A formula to work out whether a person is overweight, calculated by dividing weight (in kilograms) by height (in metres) squared.

Bradycardia An abnormally slow heart rate.

Bundle branch block A condition in which the speed of the electrical impulse producing the heartbeat is unequal as it travels to the ventricles via the two branches of a pathway called the bundle of His, causing one of the ventricles to contract just before the other.

Bundle of His (pronounced 'hiss') rapidly conducts electrical impulses from the atrio-ventricular node to the ventricles.

CABG coronary artery bypass graft. See Coronary artery bypass surgery.

Calcium channel blockers Drugs that decrease the amount of calcium that enters the muscle cells of the arteries. This improves blood supply to the heart, relieving angina and high blood pressure. Examples are nifedipine and verapamil.

Cannula A small tube inserted into a body cavity for draining fluid or introducing medication.

Capillaries The smallest blood vessels, which join the small arteries to the small veins.

Cardiac arrest A disturbance of the heart's rhythm causing it to stop pumping altogether.

Cardiac catheterisation An invasive procedure to obtain information about the blood pressure within the heart, the function of the pumping chambers and valves, and the severity and position of any narrowings in the coronary arteries. A catheter is inserted into a vein or artery in either the groin or the arm and is directed through the blood vessels and into the correct position within the heart. X-ray films are then taken by injecting a fluid down the catheter and running a camera.

Cardiomyopathy A weakness of the heart muscle, often leading to heart failure.

Catheter A tube for withdrawing or introducing fluids into the body. Often used to withdraw urine from the bladder.

Cholesterol An important fat made in the liver, necessary for building cell membranes and making several important hormones. However, an excess can increase the risk of coronary artery disease.

Circumflex One of the two major branches of the left coronary artery (left main stem).

Computerised tomography (CT or CAT) scan An X-ray that takes pictures from different angles, allowing the heart and blood vessels to be seen.

Congenital heart disease Heart disease present at birth caused by abnormalities of the heart or major blood vessels due to abnormal fetal development.

Congestive heart failure A condition where there is ineffective pumping of the heart leading to an accumulation of fluid in the lungs.

Coronary artery bypass surgery a type of open-heart surgery performed to re-route blood around blocked coronary arteries.

Coronary artery disease (CAD) A condition caused by thickening of the walls of the arteries that supply blood to the heart muscle.

Coronary thrombosis The term for when a blood clot forms in a coronary artery and causes a heart attack.

Cyanosis When the skin appears bluish due to inadequate oxygenation of the blood caused by circulation problems.

Defibrillator A device that delivers a controlled electric shock through the chest wall to the heart in order to restore a normal heartbeat.

Diastole The phase of a heartbeat that occurs between two contractions of the heart, during which the heart muscles relax and the ventricles fill with blood.

Diastolic blood pressure The pressure of blood inside the arteries between heartbeats (the bottom number in a blood pressure reading).

Diuretic Drugs that increase the output of water and salt in the urine. They are used to treat heart failure and to lower high blood pressure. Also known as 'water tablets'.

Doppler echocardiography A technique used to measure the speed of blood flow in different parts of the heart.

Drug-eluting stent A mesh tube that props open the arteries and releases a drug to prevent re-narrowing of the arteries after angioplasty.

Echocardiogram An ultrasound examination of the heart which shows its structure and how it is working.

Electrocardiogram (EKG or ECG) A test to record the rhythm and activity of the heart. Sensors are put on the arms, legs and chest and are connected to a recording machine, which records the electrical signals produced by each heartbeat, detecting abnormalities of heart rhythm and giving information on whether the heart has become enlarged or is working under strain.

Electrode catheter Small tubes with electrodes attached which record electrical signals and allow doctors to 'map' the spread of electrical impulses during each heartbeat.

Electron beam computed tomography (EBCT) A very fast imaging technique used to measure calcium deposits in the coronary arteries.

Electrophysiological testing A technique for detecting and giving information about abnormal heart rhythms. Fine tubes called electrode catheters are introduced through a vein, usually in the groin. They are then gently moved into position in the heart where they stimulate the heart and record the electrical impulses. The test is done under local anaesthetic.

Endocarditis An infection of the heart lining and valves.

Endotracheal tube A tube inserted into the lungs attached to a ventilator that aids breathing after surgery.

Exercise ECG A test in which heart rhythm and activity are recorded while the patient is active, usually pedalling an exercise bicycle or walking on a treadmill.

Extracorporeal membrane oxygenation (ECMO) A machine used to provide a temporary heart and lung function for children and babies who have conditions preventing their lungs functioning properly. It is similar to a heat-lung machine used for open-heart surgery.

Familial hypercholesterolaemia/hyperlipidaemia An inherited condition in which the body is unable to process cholesterol effectively.

Fasting lipid profile A test to measure cholesterol level.

Fibrates (fibric acid derivatives) A class of cholesterol-lowering drug most effective at lowering triglycerides and elevating HDL levels.

Flavenoids Antioxidants that reduce the effect in the body of molecules called free radicals that cause chemical reactions that damage cells.

Folic acid A B vitamin that can be found in some foods (green leafy vegetables and dried beans) which might reduce damage to artery walls.

Gamma camera A piece of scanning equipment used during radionuclide scans. When a radioactive substance is injected into the body, the gamma camera can detect the radioactivity given off. The pictures can then be analysed to look at the heart's function.

Ginkgo biloba Herbal supplement sometimes used to aid stroke recovery and enhance poor blood flow in the legs.

Ginseng Herbal supplement used to reduce stress and fight fatigue, improve stamina and healing.

Glyceryl trinitrate (GTN) A drug used to help prevent and relieve angina attacks.

Heart attack (myocardial infarction) This occurs when a blood clot blocks one of the coronary arteries causing part of the heart to be starved of oxygen.

Heart block When the heart's electrical signals are slowed down or delayed by an interruption in the heart's normal electrical activity.

Heart bypass See Coronary artery bypass surgery.

Heart failure A degenerative disease causing the pumping action of the heart to become inadequate because of progressive muscle weakness.

Heart-lung machine A machine to take over the work of the heart and provide oxygenated blood to the body's organs during surgery.

Heart transplant Surgery that replaces a damaged heart with a healthy heart taken from a donor who has been declared dead.

Heart Valve Registry National register of all artificial heart valves implanted through NHS hospitals in the UK.

High blood pressure See Hypertension.

High-density lipoprotein (HDL) 'Good' cholesterol which returns excess cholesterol to the liver, so high levels in the blood reduce the risk of coronary artery disease.

High resolution ECG See Signal-averaged electrocardiogram.

Holter monitor (or ambulatory ECG monitor) A 24-hour recording of an electrocardiogram (ECG).

Homograft Replacement valve(s) from another human heart used in transplant surgery.

Hyperlipidaemia An elevation of lipids (fats) in the blood, including cholesterol, cholesterol compounds, phospholipids and triglycerides. Also known as hypercholesterolaemia.

Hypertension High blood pressure.

Hypertrophic obstructive cardiomyopathy Another term for hypertrophic cardiomyopathy.

Hypertrophy An abnormal thickening of the heart muscle, usually caused by high cardiac pressures.

Hypotension Abnormally low blood pressure.

Immunosuppressant drugs Drugs used to decrease or suppress the body's immune function, used after any transplant surgery.

Implantable defibrillator A device, implanted within the chest wall to monitor the heart rhythm, which is able to sense severe disturbance in heart rhythm and deliver an electrical impulse to allow the normal rhythm to resume.

Inferior vena cava The main vein taking blood from the abdomen and lower limbs back to the heart.

Internal mammary artery An artery from the inside of the chest wall that is most often used as an alternative channel for blood during CABG.

Ischaemic heart disease Inadequate blood flow through the coronary arteries causing decreased blood flow to the heart muscle.

Ischaemia Inadequate blood supply to a portion of the heart muscle.

Left anterior descending One of the two major branches of the left coronary artery (left main stem).

Left main stem (the name given to the left coronary artery)
It is short and divides into two major branches, the circumflex and the left anterior descending.

Left ventricular hypertrophy Abnormal thickening of the muscle of the left ventricle.

Long Q-T syndrome An inherited disorder in which there is a longer interval than usual between activation and inactivation of the ventricles during the heartbeat. This can cause fainting and an abnormal heart rate or rhythm.

Low-density lipoproteins (LDL) 'Bad' cholesterol, associated with coronary heart disease as it carries cholesterol from the liver to the cells of the body.

Magnetic resonance angiography (MRA) 3-D pictures of the coronary arteries made using directed magnetic pulses.

Magnetic resonance imaging (MRI scan) An imaging technique which produces detailed pictures of internal organs using a strong magnetic field. Also called nuclear magnetic resonance (NMR).

Minimally invasive coronary artery bypass (MIDCAB)
A procedure performed while the heart is still beating, used when only one or two arteries are to be bypassed.

Mitral stenosis Obstruction in the mitral valve.

Mitral valve The heart valve regulating the flow of blood from the left atrium to the left ventricle.

Mitral valve prolapse When a mitral valve is abnormally shaped.

Mitral valvuloplasty A procedure to stretch a narrowed mitral valve.

MmHg (millimetres of mercury) Unit used for measuring blood pressure.

Mmol/l millimoles per litre A unit of measurement used to show the level of cholesterol and other fats in the blood.

Monounsaturated fat 'Good' fat that can help lower the blood level of LDL cholesterol but does not lower the 'protective' HDL cholesterol level. It can be found in foods such as olive oil, avocado and nuts.

MUGA test or scan (multi-gated acquisition) A test/scan using a radioactive tracer which is performed to assess the heart's ability to pump blood.

Murmur An extra noise in the heart which can be heard with a stethoscope.

Myocardial infarction see Heart attack.

Myocardial perfusion scan See Thallium stress test.

Myocarditis Inflammation of the heart muscle.

Myocardium The heart muscle.

Nasogastric tube A tube inserted into the stomach to drain it, to prevent feelings of sickness after surgery.

National Service Framework (NSF) Government guidelines for treatment which aim to address variations in standards of care and to achieve greater consistency in the availability and quality of services throughout the NHS.

Nitrates Drugs that relax the muscles in the walls of the veins and arteries (including the coronary arteries) and make them wider, lowering blood pressure and improving the blood flow. Used to relieve angina pain and to prevent angina attacks.

Nitroglycerine Prescribed for acute angina attacks. Widens the arteries, increasing blood flow to the tissue.

Non-invasive test A test that is done without inserting a needle, instrument or fluid into the body.

Nuclear magnetic resonance (NMR) See MRI scan.

Oedema Fluid accumulation in the body's soft tissue which causes swelling, particularly in the legs and abdominal organs.

Omega-3 A type of fatty acid found in oily fish which can help prevent blood clotting and help reduce triglyceride levels.

Open-heart surgery Surgery in which the thoracic cavity is opened to expose the heart and the blood is re-circulated and oxygenated by a heart-lung machine.

Pacemaker An electronic device implanted in the body that sends tiny electrical signals to stimulate contractions of the heart each time the heart fails to generate its own signal.

Pacemaker cells Specialised heart tissue that control the heartbeat.

Partial lipodystrophy A condition that prevents the body from storing fat under the skin. It also causes raised blood fat levels and insulin resistance, increasing the risk of heart disease.

Percutaneous transluminal coronary angioplasty (PCTA) See Coronary angioplasty.

Perfusionist A doctor who specialises in looking after the blood flow of patients when heart-lung machines are used.

Pericardium A membrane sac surrounding the heart.

Plaque A build-up of fatty material on the inner lining of an arterial wall.

Platelet A tiny blood vessel which is essential for blood clotting.

Polyunsaturated fat Fats associated with lowering cholesterol levels. Found in soya beans, corn and sunflower oil and oily fish and provide essential fatty acids.

Positron emission tomography (PET) A test to examine heart function and blood supply using a radioactive isotope injected into the bloodstream.

Pre-eclampsia A potentially life-threatening complication that can occur during pregnancy and that causes circulatory problems, hypertension in particular.

Pulmonary artery The artery that carries blood from the heart to the lungs.

Pulmonary embolism A blockage of an artery in the lungs, usually by a blood clot.

Pulmonary valve The valve regulating the flow of blood from the right ventricle to the pulmonary artery.

Purkinje fibres Fibres which transmit electrical impulses through the heart.

Radial artery An artery from the forearm that is often used in CABG.

Radioisotope scan An imaging test using gamma cameras to take very clear pictures of the heart.

Radionuclide test Tests such as the thallium test, myocardial perfusion scanning and the MUGA scan which provide information about the blood flow to the heart and heart muscle using injections of radioactive isotopes.

Rapid access chest pain (RACP) clinic A clinic that will fast-track diagnosis and treatment of people with chest pains.

Regurgitation The leakage of blood caused by a cardiac valve failing to close properly.

Resins (bile acid-binding drugs) Cholesterol-lowering drugs that attach to bile acids and salts in the intestinal tract forming complexes that cannot be reabsorbed into the blood, and are excreted.

Restenosis A re-narrowing of the coronary arteries after a previous blockage has been treated.

Revascularisation A procedure that either widens existing blood vessels or encourages new ones to form through grafting. See also Angioplasty and Coronary artery bypass surgery.

Rheumatic fever (and connection to heart disease) A rare inflammatory disease that can affect many of the body's connective tissues and that sometimes causes valve disease.

Rotablation A type of angioplasty in which a rotating shaver is used to cut away plaques from the inside of the arteries.

Saphenous vein A vein from the leg often used in CABG.

Saturated fat A type of fat found mainly in food from animal sources and which is the biggest dietary cause of high LDL levels ('bad cholesterol').

Septum The muscle wall between the left and right sides of the heart.

Signal-averaged ECG A type of ECG that uses a computer to filter signals called 'late potentials' for a more detailed analysis of the heart's electrical function.

Silent heart attack A heart attack in which the patient feels no pain or typical symptoms.

Silent ischaemia When blood and oxygen flow to the heart muscle is restricted but with no obvious symptoms.

Single photon emission computed tomography (SPECT) A non-invasive technique for creating clear, three-dimensional pictures of a major organ (eg the heart).

Sinus node The structure located high in the right atrium that generates the cardiac electrical impulse. The sinus node is sometimes called the 'pacemaker of the heart'.

Stable angina Angina that can be controlled with tablets or spray and has not increased in severity, duration or frequency of attacks.

Statin Drugs for lowering cholesterol that work in the liver to prevent the formation of cholesterol. Also known as reductase inhibitors.

Stenosis An area of narrowing or blockage in a coronary artery caused by atherosclerosis or a cardiac valve that is no longer able to open properly.

Stent A collapsible wire mesh tube used to prop open an artery that has recently been cleared using angioplasty.

Sternum (breastbone) This is the part of you chest cut through during CABG.

Stokes-Adams disease A condition in which the electrical signal between the atria and the ventricles is interrupted, causing an arrhythmia. This usually leads to a slowed heart rate and heart block and may also cause fainting due to lack of oxygenated blood in the brain.

Stress echocardiography An echocardiogram taken after the heart has been put under stress, either with exercise or with a drug. If parts of the heart are damaged, they will contract less effectively and this shows up on the echocardiogram.

Superior vena cava Returns blood to the heart from the upper part of the body and is smaller than the inferior vena cava.

Supraventricular tachycardia (SVT) A rapid heart arrhythmia starting in the upper chambers of the heart.

Syncope The medical term for fainting.

Systole The contraction period of the heartbeat.

Systolic pressure The pressure of blood inside arteries when the heart contracts. This is the top number in a blood pressure reading.

Tachycardia An abnormally rapid heart rate.

Thallium test A radionuclide test using the radioactive substance thallium. Also called a myocardial perfusion scan.

Thrombo-embolitic disease When a blood clot forms in a blood vessel and blocks the blood flow. In some cases, the clot then travels to other sites in the body. This is called an embolism.

Thrombolysis Treatment to help dissolve a blood clot blocking an artery.

Thrombolytic drugs Drugs used to dissolve blood clots blocking an artery during a heart attack.

Thrombosis The formation of a blood clot inside a blood vessel or the heart.

Thrombus A blood clot.

Thyroid disease Imbalances in hyperthyroid arrhythmias such as tachycardia and multifocal premature ventricular contractions may contribute to angina. Hypothyroid may increase the risk of atherosclerosis.

Tilt table study Used to find out why patients have fainting spells. The patient's heart rate and blood pressure are measured while the table is tipped at different angles.

Transoesophageal echocardiography (TOE) An echocardiogram of the heart taken from the back of the gullet (across the oesophagus). Used to diagnose heart problems.

Triglycerides A form of lipid, essentially chains of fatty acids, that provides much of the energy that the body's cells need in order to function. However, a high level of triglycerides increases the risk of coronary heart disease.

Type 2 diabetes Diabetes caused either by a shortage of insulin or by the body developing an inability to utilise insulin (insulin resistance). Sometimes called non-insulin dependent diabetes, although it is a progressive condition and some patients will need to inject insulin. Usually occurs in people over 40.

Unsaturated fats A type of fat found mainly in plants and fish. These fats can help to lower blood cholesterol if used in place of saturated fats.

Unstable angina The most serious form of angina where severe attacks occur, sometimes frequently, and even when the patient is at rest.

Valve replacement Surgery to replace a defective or diseased heart valve.

Valvular heart disease When one or more of the heart valves are damaged or diseased.

Vasodilator A medicine that causes widening or relaxation of blood vessel walls. Examples include nitrates such as nitroglycerin.

Ventricular arrhythmia An irregular heartbeat originating in the ventricle.

Ventricular fibrillation An extremely rapid, highly irregular heart arrhythmia originating in the ventricles that is potentially life-threatening.

Ventricular tachycardia An abnormally fast heartbeat occurring in the ventricles.

Viral heart infection A virus affecting any part of the heart which may leave it susceptible to weakness or malfunction.

Wolff-Parkinson-White syndrome Occurs when there is an extra electrical pathway in the heart, causing the signal to arrive at the ventricles too soon. Can cause palpitations, dizziness and fainting.

Xenograft The use of animal tissue to replace defective heart tissue.

Index

abnormal cells 6
Accident and Emergency (A&E) department 28, 31, 35
ACE (angiotensin-converting enzyme) inhibitors 61, 62-3, 84, 123, 129
acupuncture 114, 115
adrenaline 112, 113
aerobic exercise 112
Afro-Caribbean people 110, 111
age
    and heart rate 5
    and ischaemic heart disease/high blood pressure 110
ageing 19
alcohol 15, 19, 87, 110, 112, 113, 137, 138
allergy 99, 104
alpha-blockers 130
alternative treatments 114-17
ambulances 35
anaemia 104
anaesthesia 108, 120
anaesthetist 104, 105
aneurysm 77
anger 124
angina 6, 12, 18, 112, 115, 124, 125, 133
    and exercise 139
    symptoms 7, 24
    what is it? 10
angiogram 24, 50, 132
angioplasty 73-82, 106, 109, 125, 130
angiotensin-2-receptor antagonists 63

anti-arrhythmic drugs 69-70, 99, 130
antibiotics 13, 84, 87, 90
anticoagulants 19, 129
antidepressants 19
antioxidants 114-15, 140
antiplatelet drugs 63, 68, 76, 129
anxiety 120, 121, 135
aorta 3, 5
aortic regurgitation 14
aortic valve 3, 4, 13, 14, 83
appetite 120
appointments
    cancelled or changed by the hospital 31
    changing 31
    length of 32
    a missed 32
arc-welding equipment 99
arnica 116
arrhythmias 7, 17, 18-20, 46, 90, 95-102
    causes 19
    conditions associated with 19-20
    how do they develop? 19
artherosclerosis 6
artificial hearts 94
aspirin 19, 35, 76, 129
atherectomy 75
atheroma 6, 10
atherosclerosis 6, 7, 11, 13, 111, 116, 117
atria 2, 3, 4, 18, 19
atrial fibrillation 19
atrio-ventricular node 4, 18

diet
good 73, 137
improving 117
poor 11, 113
dieticians 127
digoxin 84, 123
district nurse 120
diuretics 58-9, 60, 84, 129
dizziness 18, 20, 101, 122
Doppler echocardiography 44, 48
Dr Foster Q&A 274
driving 134
drugs 121, 129-30

eating sensibly 11
ECHO (echocardiogram) 44, 47-8, 51, 83, 95
EDTA 116
electrocardiogram, electro-cardiography (ECG, EKG) 20, 35, 44, 45-7, 50, 83, 95, 104, 152
24 hour Holter monitoring 44, 46-7
event recording 44, 47
exercise (stress) 44, 45, 46
electrode catheters 53
electrodes 46
electron beam computer tomography (EBCT) 44
electrophysiological tests (EPS) 44, 52-3, 95
endocarditis 83
endotracheal tube 106
energy 2, 5
epicardial implantation 98
exercise 2, 7, 11, 16, 46, 47-8, 73, 110, 112, 114, 121, 126, 129, 136-7, 139

fainting 18, 19, 20, 53, 101

familial hypercholestero-laemia/hyperlipidaemia (FH) 11
effects of 12
and pregnancy 12
signs of 11
familial hyperlipidaemia 22, 112
family history 11, 110
fasting lipid profile 131
fatty deposits (plaques) 6, 10, 111
fetus, heart defects in 47
fibrates 57
flavenoids 140, 142
folic acid 114
free radicals 22, 115
fruit 114
frustration 124

'gamma camera' 52
garlic 116
gender
heart disease in older women 110
and heart rate 5
General Medical Council 27
general medical wards 35
genetic counselling 12
ginkgo biloba 114, 115
ginseng 114
glossary 249-61
GPs (general practitioners)
monitoring care 34
questions for 131
referral by 29-30
returning to the care of 109, 113, 127
grape seed extracts 115
GUCH (Grown Up Congenital Heart patients) 103
guilt 124
gum disease 13

stokes 6
Stokes-Adams disease 19
stomach, swollen 15, 16
stomach ulcers 13
stress 2, 11, 110, 113, 114, 126, 138, 141-2
stress echocardiography 44, 47-8
strokes 6, 7, 8, 19, 70, 95, 111
superior vena cava 3
support stockings 120, 122
surgeon 104, 105
sutures 106, 108
sweating 10, 34, 120, 122
swollen feet/ankles/legs 15, 16, 120
syncope 53
systole 4, 6
systolic pressure 6

tachycardia 18, 20, 96
tea 142
technicians 105
tests at the hospital
    advice following 54
    invasive 44, 45
    non-invasive 44, 45-9, 49-53
thallium test 44, 51-2, 52
thoracic cage 2
thrombolysis 36, 152
thrombolytic drugs (clot-busters) 69
thrombosis 8
thyroid disease 19, 112
tilt tests 53, 95
tiredness 7, 16, 18, 50, 120, 136
transcendental meditation 116
transoesphageal echocardio-graphy (TOE) 44, 51
transvenous implantation 98, 99

tri-nitrate 24, 25
tricuspid valve 3, 13, 14, 17
triglycerides 113

University of Leicester 12
unsaturated fats 111
urinary catheter 106
useful addresses 248-9

valve disease 13-15, 47
valve incompetence or regurgitation 13-14, 17
valve repair 85
valve replacement 85-7, 90, 125
    artificial 85, 86
    biological 85
valve stenosis 13-14
varicose veins 8
vegetables 114
vena cava 4
ventilator 106, 107
ventricles 2, 3, 4, 18, 19
ventricular fibrillation 19, 97
ventricular tachycardia 95, 97
viagra 140-1
viral heart infection 15
visual disturbances 120
visual problems 7
vitamin supplements 114-15, 116
vomiting 10, 34, 130

waiting lists 29, 37, 38, 77-8, 84, 92, 98, 153, 156
warfarin 19, 87, 104, 134-5
water tablets 123
weight
    apple-shape fat 21, 111
    losing 126
    obesity 23
    overweight 12, 61, 110, 112, 126
    watching 11, 82, 110

Dr Foster Q&A

Vermilion
LONDON

What is Dr Foster?

Dr Foster is an independent organisation which measures healthcare standards through ongoing assessments of every major hospital, maternity unit, care home, consultant, dentist and complementary therapist in the UK. Information from Government, hospitals and medical professionals is analysed with the help of leading universities such as Imperial College of Science, Technology and Medicine, Exeter University and City University. An Ethics committee, made up of some of the most distinguished figures in healthcare, ensures accuracy and impartiality. Supported by the Government and leading professional healthcare organisations, Dr Foster brings together world-renowned academics, healthcare experts and media professionals. For updated information go to www.drfoster.co.uk.

What makes Dr Foster unique?

For the first time ever, an independent body of experts has assessed the UK's health services ranging from hospitals to maternity services, dentists and complementary therapists. Their unique content derives from questionnaires, statistical research and analysis, contributions from industry experts, individual hospitals, the Department of Health and individual GPs and consultants. These outstanding guides give you the public an unprecedented opportunity to find out how and where to get the best possible care and service.

Dr Foster Guides
Available now:

0091883792	Dr Foster Good Birth Guide
0091883776	Dr Foster Good Hospital Guide
0091883784	Dr Foster Good Complementary Therapist Guide
0091883814	Dr Foster Fertility Guide
0091883822	Dr Foster Breast Cancer Guide
0091883849	Dr Foster Good Consultant Guide
0091883806	Dr Foster Heart Disease Guide

Forthcoming titles:

0091883857	Dr Foster Good Care Home Guide
0091883830	Dr Foster Good Dentist Guide

How can I order more Dr Foster titles?

To order copies of any of these books direct from Vermilion, an imprint of the Random House Group Ltd, call The Book Service credit card hotline on 01206 255800.

The Dr Foster guides are also available from all good booksellers.